Gardening
on
Long Island
with
Irene Virag

Dedication

To Harvey Aronson,
who turned my life
into a garden

Printed in Brentwood, N.Y.
ISBN 1-885134-19-3

Newsday books are available at a special discount for sales promotions, premiums, fund-raising or educational use. For information on bulk purchases, contact:

New Content Development
Newsday Inc.
235 Pinelawn Road
Melville, N.Y. 11747-4250

Contents

A Personal Note   *Page 1*
How Our Gardens Grew   *Page 2*

Acknowledgments

Good editors are a treasure. I was blessed. I want to thank my editor Phyllis Singer for her skill, her patience, her friendship and her compassion.

Other colleagues deserve thank-yous. Tony Jerome for being such a sensitive photo editor, Ken Spencer for so many lovely photographs, Bob Eisner for his design genius, Joe Baron for his artful layouts, Linda McKenney for her helpful graphics and Tim Drachlis for making it all come together. Also, Gina Martorella and Laura Mann for their exhaustive research, Sandy Miller for her copy editing, Barbara Marlin for keeping us all sane and the very talented Bob Newman for his beautiful illustrations. And last but never least, Howard Schneider for being himself and believing in the impossible.

My heartfelt thanks go to the special people in the plant world who have helped me along the garden path. Bob Bon Giorno, Vinnie Simeone, Richard Weir, Donna Moramarco, Nelson Sterner, Fred Soviero, Richard Iversen, Debbie Van Bourgondien, Sally Ferguson and the inimitable Conni Cross.

And finally, my deepest appreciation to all the people who let me into their gardens and share their dreams with me.

A Personal Note

It is winter as I write this. Flocks of gulls walk on the frozen pond behind my house and cold rain falls on the silver stalks of Russian sage and the brown heads of *Sedum* Autumn Joy. I see the rain but I think instead of a sunny morning in the midst of spring — the lilacs scenting the driveway and the azaleas white as snowbanks around the patio, and the dogwoods and the Japanese cherry trees putting on the sort of show painters die for. I can't wait to tie back my hair and pull on my Wellies and an old denim shirt and burrow in the dirt.

I long for weeds to pull, hostas to divide, lantana to plant. I want to make a bean teepee, put in early peas, sow lettuce. I dream of dirt-encrusted gardening gloves and pruners and trowels. I look for warmth in the stark white plastic stakes that mark the underground wombs where the daffodils grow. I stare at the bare and lonely branches of the birch trees and envision them in leaf.

I think often about how the garden of my own earth has nurtured the garden of my life. Especially over the last few years when I've had to deal with a wild seed in my own body. A wild seed called breast cancer. Breast cancer survivors wonder a lot about life and death. About rebirth and survival. About beauty. About hope. So do gardeners.

The way I see it, we're going to share the pages that follow and so it's important that I let you in on my musings. You should know what you're getting.

What you're getting is a work of love by a late bloomer. I didn't always know about the heartbreaking beauty of lacecap hydrangeas or the lustrous magic of Swiss chard. Or the pure joy of letting the earth run through my fingers. If anyone had told me not quite eight years ago that I would become a gardener, I would have howled. Gardening simply wasn't in my vision of who I was.

I always thought gardening was genetic — like long legs. Like cooking. You inherited it from your mother. Well, my mother is no panty-hose model and she views the kitchen as a torture chamber and the garden as a place for extra-terrestrials. I grew up calling hostas green-and-white leaves and hydrangeas snowball bushes. My childhood without a garden turned me into someone who approached nature like Morticia Addams. I was apt to cut off the roses and keep the stems. I wore black a lot — navy blue was a wild day for me.

Things I never thought would be part of my life have changed me — love and marriage and my own home. A house by a golden pond on the North Shore of Long Island. A place where a prickly pear cactus blooms by the mailbox and morning glories greet the day along the picket fence of a garden where vegetables and flowers grow in the middle of the front lawn. A place where I could cherish the miracle of bulbs and savor the taste of summer-fresh tomatoes and find solace and hope through the long months that stretched from a lumpectomy to chemotherapy and radiation.

I wear bold Crayola colors nowadays — red and yellow and purple. I love my prematurely gray hair. I get my nails done. I even use perfume. And I became a master gardener. That's a big change for someone who once thought a flat was just a place to rent. And like all gardeners, I'm still learning.

For the past four years, I've been Newsday's garden columnist. This book chronicles some of my adventures along the garden path. It's about gardeners and gardens across Long Island, where nurseries proliferate and home-grown tomatoes are as popular as impatiens. It's also about the gardens that grow in my own heart. I've organized it by what I think of as the gardener's calendar — from spring to winter. And I've included a lot of practical information to grow by. It's tailored to our Zone 7a island, which has naturally acidic soil and enjoys a temperate climate and a long growing season. From the flat sandy lands of the South Shore to the hilly clay terrain of the North Shore, Long Island is a near paradise for those of us who like to get our hands dirty.

One other thing. If my genetics are barely garden-variety, at least I was born with a good name for a gardener. My family's roots go back to Hungary, and my name blooms in storefronts all over Budapest.

Virág is the Hungarian word for flower.

Irene Virag
February, 1999

How Our Gardens Grew

The garden springs eternal. So does history. In Roslyn, the garden of poet-editor William Cullen Bryant is being restored to the glory it once was. At Old Bethpage Village Restoration, a colonial vegetable patch comes to life. On Shelter Island in a place called Sylvester Manor, friendly ghosts of gardeners past wander among the wisteria and a woman named Alice Fiske, who in her 70s is younger than springtime, cares for boxwoods that are considered to be the oldest in the country. In Westbury, a man named Fred Hicks tends a nursery his great-great-

grandfather started more than a century ago.

And in a Levitt house in Wantagh, a homeowner named Vivian Montgomery looks at the 70-by-100 foot plot she has cultivated for the last 47 years and speaks to the ages and to all of us who love the feel of the good earth. "I really could have used an acre."

From the vegetable fields of long ago to the flower gardens of here and now, Long Islanders have defined themselves by their landscapes. Blessed with a temperate climate and a long growing season, the island is a gardener's eden with its beginnings firmly rooted in the past.

When the first Europeans arrived on this fish-shaped island a poet would call Paumanok, the Indians were fertilizing their fields of corn and squash with mossbunker they scooped from the bays and hunting game in the virgin woods. The island was, for the most part, an untamed paradise tended by time and tide and sun and wind.

The settlers couldn't help but wonder at the richness of the earth. In 1670, a minister's son named Daniel Denton traveled across Long Island and wrote of his enchantment with the land — thickets of elder and sumac and "groves gleaming in spring with the white bloom of the dogwood, glowing in fall with liquid amber and pepperidge, with sassafras, and the yellow light of the smooth shafted tulip tree." He cataloged mulberries, persimmons, "plums of all sorts," "grapes great and small" and "strawberries of which is such abundance in June, that the Fields and Woods are died red."

"The Island is most of it of a very good soyle," Denton wrote. He rhapsodized about "an innumerable multitude of delightful Flowers not only pleasing to the eye, but smell, that you may behold Nature contending with Art, and striving to equal, if not excel many Gardens in England."

Centuries later, estate and public gardens would indeed challenge the great gardens of Britain, but the first English and Dutch settlers were more interested in food than flowers. "Ordinary people didn't have time to indulge in flower gardens back then," says Muriel Tatem, who tends the gardens at Old Bethpage, where the colonial vegetable patch contains such settlers' staples as white scallop squash, dwarf gray sugar peas, black Spanish radishes and New Zealand spinach.

Long Island's colonial kitchen gardens were the goodwife's responsibility. She worked the soil by hand, and naturally she was an organic gardener — mossbunker was the prime fertilizer. Crops consisted of vegetables that could be eaten fresh, such as greens and peas, and those that were dried or stored, such as

parsnips and navy beans. Even flowers weren't frivolous — hollyhocks were grown to cure sore throats, irises came in handy to soothe bruises and larkspur repelled lice.

There were, of course, exceptions — places such as Sylvester Manor, where Grissel Sylvester, a royalist escapee from the regime of Oliver Cromwell, made horticultural history by planting the first European boxwoods in the New World. Grissel was the young bride of Nathaniel Sylvester, one of four sugar merchants from Barbados who purchased Shelter Island from the Manhasset Indians in 1652.

Quaker founder George Fox once wrote of preaching to the Indians in "Madame Sylvester's yard." Today, it is tended by a sprightly woman named Alice Fiske, whose late husband was the 13th lord of the manor. "My father had a love of gardens and horticulture," she says. "I think gardening is in your blood. Once I came here to live, well it's like the garden was my destiny."

As she walks by the rose pergola and the 80-year-old climbing hydrangea and the lilies and lupines and

At left, Anna Gilman Hill at Grey Gardens in East Hampton. Above, Alice Fiske tending her garden at Sylvester Manor. Her late husband was the 13th lord of the manor at this Shelter Island estate.

3

Preface

the 19th-Century water garden and a beech tree that botanist Asa Gray planted in the 1880s, Alice thinks about Cornelia Horsford, her husband's great-aunt who cared for the garden before her. "Miss Cornelia and I are the only mothers the garden has had in close to 100 years. I talk to her when I'm in the garden. I believe in friendly ghosts."

As colonists found sustenance in the land, a harbinger of things to come took root in western Flushing, where horticulturist Robert Prince planted fruit trees on an 8-acre parcel in 1737 and created America's first commercial nursery. Prince Nursery blossomed with rare specimens from every corner of the world and eventually covered 113 acres. President George Washington didn't sleep in the nursery but he sailed by barge from New York to visit "Mr. Princes fruit gardens and shrubberies." And by the early 1800s, the trail of two of America's greatest explorers led to Flushing. Many of Lewis and Clark's botanical discoveries — such as *Mahonia* — found a home at Prince's.

Other nurseries sprang up in Queens — Bloodgood Nursery and Garretson Seed Farm and Parsons, which introduced the pink flowering dogwood and the weeping European beech. John Lewis Childs of Floral Park boasted a four-story fireproof seed house and an 80-page catalog that offered "Grand Specialties and Novelties" like 75-cent giant moonflowers that grew 100 feet in a month.

Still, working the earth was serious business. By the 1800s, farming was a way of life for about one out of every five Long Islanders. The largest cultivated crop was Indian corn, and manure was so profitable that in one estate inventory, it was appraised for almost as much as a 2-year-old horse. In the 1900s, potatoes would come into their own as money crops and cauliflower and strawberries would become staples.

But in 1850, a 35-year-old Westbury farmer and Quaker preacher named Isaac Hicks saw a new market. He drove his wagon to either Prince or Parsons Nursery and purchased a load of trees. Three years later, Hicks made his first sale — and launched a nursery that helped shape the Long Island countryside and still thrives today.

"Hicks brought in mature trees and worked out a way to move them," says Barbara Kelly, curator of the Long Island Studies Institute at Hofstra University. "This was important to the landscaping of the great estates."

Isaac's son, Edward, devised a horse-drawn "apparatus" capable of transporting large trees "in full leaf." By 1875, the company was selling fruit trees for 25 to 50 cents each and hauling them within a 10-mile radius for as little as a penny. By 1919, Hicks was offering 16-foot-high American elms for $10. "Have you provided plenty of shade for the children?" the catalog asked beneath a photo of a Norway maple on an imposing lawn. "Shade means outdoor play. Outdoor play means fresh air, rosy cheeks, big appetites. That's the advantage of living in the country."

In the late 1800s, Hicks trees shaded the streets of Great Neck and the subdivisions of A.T. Stewart's planned community of Garden City. But in most instances, the country meant estate living. "Up to the 1930s, the Gold Coast estates drove horticulture on Long Island," says Fred Hicks, Isaac's great-great-grandson, who now runs the nursery in Westbury.

The very rich are different from you and me, but their great lawns and formal gardens and hedged terraces would, in Barbara Kelly's words, "set the stage for American landscape gardening." The idea was to control nature or at least to make it look that way, and the pattern would leave its marks on the land for decades to come.

The North Shore of Nassau was increasingly accessible with the extension of the Long Island Railroad to Oyster Bay in 1854 and the opening of the East River tunnels in 1910. Between 1865 and 1940, about 900 estates — many of them covering more than 150 acres each — were constructed on Long Island.

In Roslyn in the 1840s, William Cullen Bryant led the way with the retreat he would name Cedarmere. About a half-century later, William Robertson Coe bought an Oyster Bay estate he called Planting Fields and undertook a labor of love. He transported two 29 ton copper beeches from the childhood home of his first wife, Mai Rogers Coe, in Fairhaven, Mass. One survived and still holds court today at Planting Fields Arboretum, with leafy arms that reach out 100 feet.

History is also alive at Old Westbury Gardens, where the English walled garden that John Phipps established in 1906 for his young bride, Margarita, blooms through the season with irises and peonies and roses and delphiniums and lilies and dahlias. It was a wedding gift for Margarita, who missed the flower gardens of her native England. When a writer for House Beautiful came to call at Westbury House in August of 1925, she was impressed by the allée of linden trees and the path to the lotus pool bordered by pink lilies and fragrant heliotrope. "The Pleasure Grounds of Westbury House," the headline read, and the pictures by Mattie Edwards Hewitt, the premier garden photographer of the early 20th Century, illustrated the point.

Her photos also record Otto Kahn's castle in Cold Spring Hills, George D. Pratt's Killenworth in

Glen Cove and Grey Gardens, where Anna Gilman Hill cradled her walled garden in the East Hampton dunes. The names of estate owners were a social register of wealth and privilege — Tiffany, Morgan, Woolworth.

But by the 1920s change was upon the land. "Gardening as we know it is a 20th-Century phenomenon," says Kelly. Or as a newspaper report of the 1925 census, put it: "Nassau's Decline As Farming Community — Entire County Boasts Population of Only 219 Hogs on 766 Farms." Just 15 years earlier, there had been 1,017 farms.

The influence of the great estates had trickled down — carried forward by the European gardeners who came to Long Island to work. And propagated by the middle-class homeowners moving into Queens and Nassau. By the 1920s, says Kelly, "gardening takes hold as a competitive sport among the middle class. To create a garden was to emulate the rich. To make a statement that I have arrived — wherever that was."

Long Island was where it was. Especially after World War II. After the war, says Fred Hicks, "the estate era didn't come back. Suddenly, it was the growth of small homes. Nursery lots were opening up all over the place. They'd bring loads of plants up

At left a view of the gardens at Cedarmere, the estate of William Cullen Bryant. Above, the copper beech that holds court at Planting Fields.

Preface

Roses in their glory at Old Westbury Gardens.

stemmed from the green expanses of the big estates and became a culture in themselves. "In Levittown, no fencing — natural or otherwise — was allowed on any plot," says Kelly. "Once you have a contiguous lawn, it becomes more obvious when mine is clipped to a fare-thee-well and yours isn't."

If you didn't clip it, Bill Levitt's gardening enthusiast father, Abraham, might have it done for you. In the column he wrote for the Levittown Tribune, Abe Levitt cut right to the soil line. "Grass is the very foundation of life. Without it, the earth would be a dust bowl, blown into the sea."

Abe drove around in his limousine to check out lawns. Bill and Vivian Montgomery, who rented a Cape Cod in Levittown in 1947 before moving into a $9,000 Levitt ranch in Wantagh four year later, remember the visit. "I was working days and going to school nights on the GI bill," Bill recalls, "and I was too tired to mow the lawn one week. That Saturday, we woke up to the sound of Levitt's crew cutting our lawn. We got a bill in the mail. I don't remember what it cost, but I was so embarrassed I never missed mowing the lawn again."

As the developments moved east, so did the lawns and the foundation plantings. New settlers learned about turf builders and perennial rye and red salvias and Big Boy tomatoes. Greenery grew along with children. Once-young evergreens walled off picture windows, and trees that were planted as saplings arched over streets of remodeled and expanded homes. Nursery owners like Fred Hicks in Westbury and the late Jim Cross in Cutchogue pioneered the use of container-grown plants, and perennials became the rage. Water gardens flowed into fashion; mauve rhododendrons fell out.

Now some of the old ways are coming back. Heirloom flowers and vegetables are in vogue, and organic gardening and native plants are popular again. And, heresy of heresies, an anti-lawn movement is abroad in the land. Instead of turf, some visionaries are planting everything from backyard bird sanctuaries to moss gardens to drought-resistant xeriscapes and all-American meadows.

And as planting for beauty becomes universally accepted, Long Island may be just entering the golden age of gardening. History murmurs in the rustle of the rhododendrons that William Coe brought to Planting Fields and lingers in the scent of the roses that Margarita Phipps nurtured at Old Westbury Gardens. It is written in the boxwoods and the wisteria that Alice Fiske tends so lovingly at Sylvester Manor and across the restored parterre that William Cullen Bryant designed at Cedarmere.

But history also goes forward in all our landscapes. On Long Island the garden springs eternal.

from Tennessee and sell from the back of their trucks. People came out from the city to a new life on Long Island, and they were thrilled at the thought of small evergreens and azaleas and rhododendrons and seeding their own lawn."

Suddenly, there was Levittown — a promised land of cellarless Cape Cods and ranch-style homes with fruit trees and shrubbery and lawns that

SPRING

March

I can't wait to crumble the earth in my hands. March is the month when rakes and hoes come off their hooks and into the light and gardeners can get their hands dirty. There is an epiphany in that moment when a gardener comes back to earth after a long winter. Forsythia stirs and winter aconite glows. By St. Patrick's Day, the garden, too, is ready for the wearing of the green. It's time to plant peas. By mid-March, the first ospreys are taking up residence in their high rises. Spotted salamanders mate and mourning doves call. Whether lions or lambs dictate the weather, there is the sure sense that the ground is warming. It is as if flora and fauna are moving to the instant when the sun crosses the equator and night and day are equal all around the Earth. It is the vernal equinox — the first day of spring.

Savvy About Soil

Enriched by earthworms, good compost like the handful above, is brown gold for the garden.

I t's time, fellow gardeners, to get down and dirty. To stop dreaming about what could be in the garden and get out there and make it happen. To ask not what your garden can do for you but rather what you can do for your garden. Especially if it's a vegetable patch and you're growing your greens organically.

To find out what's cooking — and not just in the compost heap — I went out into the field. More specifically, I visited Scott Chaskey at Quail Hill Farm in Amagansett, where the fields are fertile and vegetables rule. When it comes to veggies, I've always tried to be organic, and the motivation became even stronger a few years ago when I had to deal with breast cancer. I figured I could pick up tips at Quail Hill, which is part of the Peconic Land Trust and where all 25 acres under cultivation are organically certified by the Northeast Organic Farming Association.

Quail Hill is a people's enterprise — one of the country's first community-supported agriculture pro-

jects. The basic concept is that people in the community buy shares of the season's crops in advance — or, as Scott, the man in charge puts it, "members share the risks with the farmer. If there's a late spring, you might get lettuce two weeks late. Or if there's a problem with potatoes, you might get fewer potatoes."

It's more likely, though, that you'll get scrumptious organic produce through the year. So I knew it made sense to put my ear to the ground and listen to Scott, who has a healthy gray-red beard and the ruddy complexion of a man who works in sun and wind and morning cold. He wore a navy blue Johnny's Seeds cap and boots and overalls that looked comfortable and worked-in. And I liked the fact that he has a master's degree in English and a poet's sense of miracles when it comes to things like compost and cover crops.

It was a chilly March day — rain had fallen the day before and would fall the following day — and the fields of Quail Hill Farm lay waiting for warmth and for the early spring crops of onions and lettuce that were being nurtured in one of the farm's greenhouses. From Quail Hill to our own yards, the miraculous process of planting and reaping starts with the soil. And what we put into the earth is what we get. "We forget that the food we eat supplies our bodies with nutrients," Scott said. "If you want to do your best to have a healthy body, you'll eat healthy food, which comes from the healthiest soil."

So before you even sow, get savvy about your soil. The first thing you should know about your dirt at this time of year is whether it's ready for shovels and trowels and tillers. Because of snow melt and early spring rain, it may be too wet. If you work wet soil, you're likely to damage its structure. So size up your soil by giving it a simple squeeze test. Grab a handful and squeeze. If it forms a solid sticky lump or if water trickles out, forget about it, the soil's too wet. If it forms a moist clump that crumbles easily, you're in business.

Good soil is rich and healthy as well as crumbly — chock full of nutrients and organic matter and earthworms, those industrious aerators that can wriggle down as deep as 6 feet. The right stuff also has plenty of air pockets and water pores so that plants can eat and drink and breathe and be happy.

Soil is a living entity composed mostly of tiny bits of pulverized rock. The size of these particles determines the soil texture. Clay particles are so fine they can only be seen with an electron microscope. Silt particles are somewhat bigger — you can see them with a regular microscope. Pure clay or silt feels smooth to the touch. But sand particles — which can be as big as a grain of, well, sand — are visible to the naked eye and feel gritty.

The larger the particles, the bigger the pores

between them. That's why water runs so quickly through light, sandy soil — washing away nutrients along with it. And why heavy clay soil holds moisture so tightly that drainage problems can develop and drown plants. Long Island's North Shore tends to have clay soil, while the South Shore is sandy. The ideal loamy soil that all gardeners should lust after is a balance of sand, silt and clay. It is porous and spongy. It's easy to dig and retains nutrients and just enough water.

If you want to cure most of what may be ailing your soil and improve its texture and structure, add organic matter. Compost is the magic word. It creates humus — the fancy word for the decomposed organic matter that enriches the soil better than anything else. It helps sandy soil retain water and nutrients. It also opens the pores in clay soil, making it more permeable. And you can make your own compost.

Scott Chaskey calls composting "a miraculous process." It really is magic the way all those banana peels and raw vegetable scraps and tea bags and shredded leaves turn into what gardeners call brown gold. You don't need a degree in organic chemistry to compost, you just have to remember that green things equal nitrogen and brown things equal carbon. At my house, we break up the layers of vegetable scraps with brown material such as leaves or dirt or manure. The layers provide air circulation, and we water the pile occasionally and mix it up with a handy tool called an aerator. For big jobs, we truck in composted horse manure.

Scott gets horse manure from a local stable and composts it himself. It was a good time for me to talk to him, because I had dug myself in deep a few days before trying to explain to a friend why I prefer amending the soil with compost rather than pouring on fertilizer. "Compost is a long-term approach while fertilizers are a quick fix," Scott explained. "If you compost well, in most cases you don't have to fertilize."

This is especially true if you pay attention to your soil's pH. When I started gardening, I didn't know a pH from a PhD. A lot of people's eyes glaze over the minute they hear the word, which, by the way, stands for the French pouvoir and hydrogene — literally, hydrogen power. Basically, pH — which is based on a scale of 1 to 14 — is a measurement of the soil's acidity and alkalinity as determined by the concentration of hydrogen ions in a water or salt solution. Soil below 7 is acid, and soil above it is alkaline. If you know your soil's pH, you know what nutrients are available. Different plants require different amounts of nutrients. Most plants and vegetables will find most of what they need in a near neutral pH of 6.5 to 7. There are exceptions, however. For example, rhododendrons, blueberries and heathers crave

iron, which is more available in acid soil between 5 and 5.5. Hellebores, irises and hollyhocks like a sweeter soil and can go as high as 8.

Adding sulfur lowers the pH, while applying lime raises it. But compost is the answer for the masses. It keeps the soil slightly acidic in the pH range that offers the best diet for most plants.

The best time of all to compost is in the fall before you plant a cover crop in your vegetable beds. Cover crops like hairy vetch and winter rye and various clovers are among Scott Chaskey's favorite things. They stimulate microbes in the soil. As Scott said, "There's more life in a square foot of healthy soil than anywhere else in the world."

If you didn't add compost last fall, do it as soon as your soil is workable. It's a matter of respect. "Good farmers and gardeners always leave the soil in better condition than they found it," Scott said "It's that simple." Take care of the soil in your field of dreams and the greens will come.

The Real Dirt on Soil

Test soil's texture by measuring its sand, silt and clay content. Here are two simple methods:

 The Touch Test. Roll a handful of moist soil into a ball. Squeeze it upward with your thumb to make a ribbon. Light-textured sandy and silt loams form shorter ribbons than heavy-textured clay and silty clay. If your soil doesn't form a ribbon, it's loamy sand.

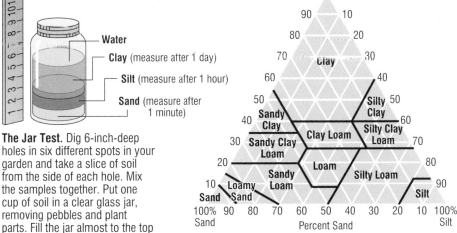

The Jar Test. Dig 6-inch-deep holes in six different spots in your garden and take a slice of soil from the side of each hole. Mix the samples together. Put one cup of soil in a clear glass jar, removing pebbles and plant parts. Fill the jar almost to the top with water. Cover and shake, then place the jar where it won't be jostled for the next 24 hours. Let the solids settle and measure each layer. Sand will settle after about a minute — silt after about an hour and clay after a day.

- To calculate the percentages of sand, silt and clay, divide the depth of each layer by the total depth of settled soil in the jar, then multiply by 100.
- Locate your percentages on the sides of the USDA Textural Triangle. The area where the three lines intersect is your textural class.

Ode to the Handiest Helpers

I love my trusty Felco pruner. I like the grip, the way it closes, the smooth noiseless snip as the blades cut away dead wood and trim unwanted shoots. I even like the fabric holster that fits onto my belt. My husband is equally hooked on his pruner and the reasons go beyond gardening. He has a leather holster. I've caught him practicing quick draws in the garage.

We're part of a horticultural tradition. Gardeners have been caring about their tools ever since the first humans grabbed a tree branch or an animal bone and used it to turn the earth. A wooden digging stick unearthed in Rhodesia goes back about 60,000 years. And cave paintings from the Paleocene show dibbers — pointed tools to make holes in the soil — fashioned from the ribs of mammoths.

As is the case with art and music, each succeeding civilization made its own contribution. The ancient Egyptians created hoes out of V-shaped branches tied to stout pieces of wood. The Greeks developed rakes, shovels and toothed hoes made of wood, and the Romans improved them with metal. By the 18th

Century, professional gardeners were traveling around France lugging everything from shears to water barrels.

People who cultivated the earth developed strong feelings about their gardening implements. Such pride was no tom-toolery. The British had already perfected the spade when the upstart colonists of the New World took a shine to the shovel. There was a time when I didn't know a spade from a shovel, but reporters as well as gardeners have to keep digging. Basically, a spade cuts into the soil and is designed to dig. The primary purpose of a shovel is to loosen and lift earth or gravel and toss it aside. You can dig with a shovel, but not as easily. A spade has a nearly flat straight-edged blade whereas a shovel usually has a cupped blade that is set at an angle to the handle. The short-handled spade is a European standby, while the long-handled, round-pointed shovel is an American classic.

Or consider the watering can. The first watering cans weren't cans at all. They were pouches made of goatskin or leather. When metal cans flooded the scene, national rivalries developed once again. The competitors were England and France. The English watering can was a burly model with two handles — one at the top and one at the back. The French style was single-handled and more graceful. In the late 1800s, a colonial vanilla-bean planter named John Haws came up with a compromise that combined the best of both.

I have several watering cans and they're all plastic. But I've decided to give up my miserly ways. As a result of my research, I just bought a galvanized Haws model with a brass seal of authenticity that contains the company's emblem — a hawthorn berry and a tag that says it was made in Smethwick, West Midlands, England. Whoever thought a Hungarian girl from Bridgeport, Conn., would grow up to own a watering can from Smethwick, West Midlands, England? Wow!

The tag says it all: "Designed with two handles for perfect balance so watering requires less effort and becomes an enjoyable experience." It also says the extra-long spout is good for watering "difficult-to-reach areas of the garden, greenhouse or conservatory." I don't have a greenhouse or a conservatory but now that I own an $89 watering can, who knows? And I love the name for the brass thingama-jig that fits onto the end of the spout. We watering-can buffs call it a "rose."

Gardeners become attuned to their tools — there is a visceral satisfaction to the heft and feel of a trowel or a pair of shears or a good lopper. The more we use our tools, the more we care about them. "It's the same with tools as with clothes," Gertrude Jeykll once wrote. "The familiar ease can only come of use and better acquaintance."

Garden tools are new acquaintances that become old friends. And like old friends, they evoke memories.

I look at my pruner and think of the first time a novice gardener cut back her *Buddleia* and anguished over whether it would return. It grew back beautifully, of course. My husband — a known softie — is sentimental about the sky-blue wheelbarrow I gave him seven years ago as a birthday present. It was the first spring of our marriage. Our first spring in our house. Our first spring together in the garden.

Just as we nurture friendships, we have to take care of our tools. I talked to my friend Nelson Sterner, the director of horticulture at Old Westbury Gardens, about this the other day, and we agreed that tool maintenance is really a fall chore. But better late than never. You should take stock of what's in your toolshed now, before things really heat up in the garden. Check what needs to be repaired or replaced. Sharpen your pruners with a folding hand file, and a little WD-40 won't hurt either. And don't leave your tools out in the rain — wooden handles can warp and blades can rust.

Also, Nelson made a point that I've come to appreciate: Garden tools are an investment and it pays to buy the best you can afford. "A spade, a good pair of pruners, a spading fork with square tines that are cast iron — these are essential tools, and if you buy the best, they'll last a lifetime."

I guess the thing about garden tools is that we don't just want them to fit into our hands. We want them to fit into our lives. And like good friends, we want to be able to rely on them. We want them to be around for a long time.

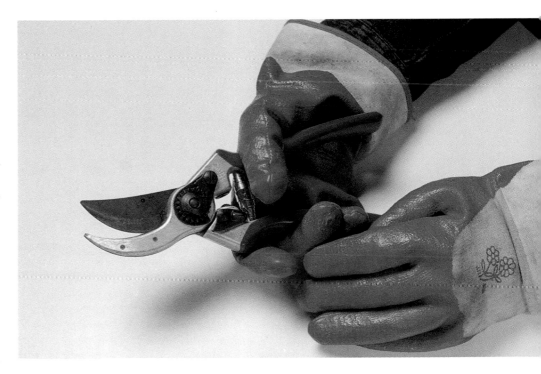

On the Primrose Path

When I think of primroses, I visualize the kind of older and wiser woman I would like to be when I grow up. The kind who has silver hair and a sweet disposition and who knows how to make floppy hats and baggy slacks and knee pads look fashionable. I already have the silver hair — premature of course — but I would so like to have the other attributes as well. And I would love to have lots of primroses. Except I want them now.

Who wouldn't? Primroses have a reputation as gentle flowers —even-tempered and, to a large degree, able to fend for themselves. They are small and light and do not require any deep digging or heavy lifting, which may explain why I associate them with silver-haired gardeners of mature judgment. Like my neighbor and garden savant, Jeanette

Stellmann, who wisely insisted that I come by one afternoon last spring and dig out some of her *Primula*, as the genus is called.

Actually, the primrose is a flower for all ages and has been so for centuries. Elizabethan poets loved the *prima rosa* — the "first rose" of the year, and you can check it out with Shakespeare, who cast the primrose in various lights. In "A Winter's Tale," the bawdy Bard wrote of "... pale primroses that die unmarried ere they can behold Bright Phoebus in his strength — a malady Most incident to maids." Whereas in "Hamlet," he connected *Primula* to libertine behavior, commenting upon "the primrose path of dalliance." He went even further in "Macbeth," writing about "the primrose way to the everlasting bonfire."

With all due respect to Shakespeare, I think the bonfire reference should be extinguished. Primroses were proper enough to become high fashion in the Victorian era, when the flower was favored by Benjamin Disraeli. Queen Victoria herself sent the prime minister bouquets from the royal garden, and when he died she made sure that the floral tributes included a wreath of primroses. Flower fanciers have been delighting over primroses ever since the plants' ancestors grew wild in the English countryside, and the results have been consistently delightful. Louise Beebe Wilder once asked about primroses, "Could anything more delicious be asked for or imagined?" I don't think so.

Primula can be found from the Alps to the Himalayas. There are more than 400 species, including the golden oldies we know as oxslip and cowslip. The genus offers something for everyone — from tiny rock-garden favorites to big-leafed, 2-foot-high plants. Nowadays, one hears mostly about English primroses (*P. vulgaris*) and Japanese primroses (*P. japonica*).

P. vulgaris goes back to Elizabethan times and is a parent of *P. x polyantha*, the early springtime favorites most people think of when they hear the word "primrose." Some show their leaves as early as the beginning of March, when flowers are likely to appear, too. They make their splash in the month of the lamb and the lion as one of the first bursts of spring to hit local nurseries and garden centers. A primrose path is a virtual palette of spring. The flowers all have yellow eyes and come in just about every color except green. It's as if someone scattered dozens of Easter eggs on the ground.

Japanese primroses are a little different. Not what you'd expect if you're used to seeing primroses on sale in the supermarket. They bloom from midspring to early summer — putting on their best display as May turns into June. They show up in

magenta, pink, crimson, purple and almost pure white and are dotted with eyes of different colors. They're giants compared to the *Polyanthus* group with sturdy 2-foot-high flower stalks that rise like candelabras from clumps of pale green foliage.

It's no surprise that the primroses I see in flower shows — I especially love it when they garland English cottages — look far better than the ones I have in my backyard. I started with the *Polyanthus* cultivars I dug out of my friend Jeanette's garden and bought a few at a local nursery. I planted them in the dappled light of my unruly shade garden, but I suspect I didn't put enough compost in the rocky, root-laden ground.

The best time to plant English primroses is in early spring, and *P. japonica* a little later in the season. It's a good idea to buy nursery plants when they're in bloom so you know what color you're getting. English primroses do best in light shade and like well-drained, compost-rich soil with plenty of moisture. Japanese primroses enjoy light shade and acidic, boggy sites near ponds and brooks. English primroses should be planted one foot apart, while their taller Japanese relatives need more room — about 3 feet — because they will form clumps that are at least 18 inches wide.

I'm clearly no expert when it comes to primroses and can't testify to this from experience, but I'm told that primroses offer the promise of adventure to their growers — they reseed themselves and sometimes produce hybrids that surprise and delight.

Soon I'll be putting on my floppy hat and getting out my baggy slacks and knee pads and calling on my friend Jeanette. Before long, it will be time to plant a new primrose path.

Chores Galore

SPRING into action for the queen of flowers. Remove winter protection from roses and prune severely to encourage sturdy new growth.

CUT back faded plants of ornamental grasses before new growth gets too high. Likewise, trim perennials that were left standing for wintertime interest, but be careful not to harm the soil by trampling on wet ground.

SPRUCE UP the lawn — spring seeding is best done between March 20 and April 15.

PLANT potatoes, horseradish and rhubarb as soon as the soil is workable. They thrive in cool soil.

SOW spinach, with repeat sowings till May 1.

PUT in your snap peas in the second half of the month and you should be eating them by late May.

BROCCOLI, kohlrabi, cauliflower, Brussels sprouts and cabbage need about 8 weeks indoors from seed, so start them early this month.

ADD blood meal, cottonseed meal, linseed meal or fish meal to perk up the compost pile. They're natural sources of nitrogen and will jump-start decomposition.

START seeds indoors for fast-growing annuals like marigolds, cosmos, zinnias, calendulas and asters.

GATHER daffodils to bring inside. But be sure to cut stems at an angle and let them sit in a vase filled with lukewarm water for an hour or two. Daffodils release a sappy substance that can harm other flowers in an arrangment. After soaking, add daffodils to the vase and throw away the water. If you recut the stems, repeat the procedure.

GET the dirt on your soil: Testing the pH is the only way to find out if your soil is sweet (alkaline) or sour (acid). Do-it-yourself kits are available at local nurseries or call the Nassau or Suffolk offices of Cornell Cooperative Extension.

TAKE note of blooming bulbs. Jot down what combinations of colors and textures look good. Place stones in empty spots that could use a shot of color — the markers will serve as reminders when it's time to plant in the fall.

A Woman of Many Gardens

When my neighbor Jeanette Stellmann touches plants, it's almost as if she's caressing them. When she talks about them, it's clear she's speaking from the heart. Her face lights up and her voice fills with love.

And best of all for any gardener who meets her, she's always ready to share her feelings and her flowers. "Come by this afternoon," she says in the spring. "I've got some *Primula* for you." Jeanette's garden Latin is impeccable. But she's not condescending — she doesn't mind if I say primrose. She beams when my husband and I show up with trowels in hand and help ourselves to some primroses or some Solomon's seal or foxglove or lilies of the valley. And while we're there, she digs out some forget-me-nots, some *Campanula*, some *Scilla*. Then in the fall, she invites us over for daylilies.

Jeanette has been gardening for more than 40 years. She and her husband, Hank, have moved at least five times, and each time, Jeanette has left a garden behind her and made up for the loss by replanting. Her front yard is a land of enchantment with rock gardens and hostas and tomatoes and lettuce and daphnes

> *You can't call yourself a gardener, you know, unless you compost.*

and rhododendrons and a spring border of masses of daffodils that give way to hosts of *Hemerocallis*.

I think that if I had to leave my own garden, I would mourn for months. But perhaps a true garden is where the heart is. A year and a half ago, Jeanette and Hank considered moving again — this time to a smaller home in our neighborhood that would have been easier for them to take care of.

"But what about your garden?" I asked.

"I can start a new one," Jeanette said. We were sitting on a patio and the breeze rustled her white hair and her eyes were even brighter than usual as she started dreaming out loud about what she would plant. "I can clear out that overgrown area, you know, down by the road."

Jeanette was in her 70s and I was just entering my 40s, but I wondered which one of us was younger.

For the past several years, Jeanette has been my mentor as well as my friend. She helped make me into a gardener — often taking up where my master gardener's course left off. She schooled me on the vagaries of finicky flowers and enlightened me on the finer points of deadheading and dividing. And more important than anything else, she showed me the secret of composting, or how to turn garbage into brown gold.

She did it very nicely the first time she visited the cluttered yard that was once my excuse for a garden. "You're a little overgrown here," she said. And then she smiled sweetly and touched the guilt I felt every time I tossed a carrot peel or a celery stalk or a used tea bag into the trash can.

"Where's the compost pile?" she asked

I shrugged in embarrassment. "I've been thinking about that" was the best I could muster.

Jeanette made it clear I shouldn't think too long. "You can't really call yourself a gardener, you know, unless you compost," she said quietly.

When she and Hank showed me their compost piles — they usually have two going at the same time — you could have knocked me over with a banana peel. And I was stunned by her soil. "You should see her dirt," I told my husband. "Forget about Oriental rugs and a new kitchen. I want dirt like that."

I'm getting it. I'm making it myself. Now I, too, turn raw vegetable scraps and eggshells into my own brown gold. Diamonds may be a girl's best friend but I'm happy with a compost bin. When I told Jeanette I'd gotten a store-bought composter, she was unfailingly polite. "Oh," she said and let it go at that. But I have come to think of my compost bin, which sits decorously behind a stand of forsythia, as an old friend. And I keep a bright blue plastic compost bucket in the kitchen for scraps for the bin.

Despite all she knows about gardening and despite all she's created in her own yard, Jeanette can still look at my garden with a smile of absolute joy and enthuse over what somebody else has accomplished. When my husband and I dug up a 40-by-40-foot section of our front yard and turned it into a vegetable and flower garden, Jeanette was one of the first people to see it in bloom. "It's beautiful," she said. "You could charge admission."

I don't know that I've ever had a finer compliment as a gardener. True gardeners possess a generosity of spirit. They are the most sharing people I know. They share their knowledge and their seeds and their secrets and their cuttings.

"I love three things," Jeanette once told me. "My grandchild, my garden" — she paused as if to think — "oh yes, and my husband Hank." Then she smiled her fey smile. Hank was nearby and he smiled, too.

My friend Jeanette epitomizes what it means to be a steward of the soil. True gardeners are recognizable by how much they love the good earth.

A gardener for more than 40 years, Jeanette Stellmann shares both plants and advice.

Pass the Peas, Please

March signals our return to the warming soil. Growth as well as snow is in the air, and tradition holds that by St. Patrick's Day, the garden is ready for the wearing of the green. Folklore tells us that we should plant onions when the mourning dove calls, broccoli when forsythia turns yellow — and peas on St. Patrick's Day.

And if you really like legends, there's the one that claims the way to perfect peas is to wear a green flannel nightgown and plant them by the light of the moon on the night of March 17.

When I was a kid, I never planted peas on St. Patrick's Day — or any other day for that matter. My family wasn't into gardening. They certainly weren't Irish. They were strictly Hungarian. Their expertise ran to stuffed cabbage, not corned beef and cabbage. And the only peas I ever ate came from a can. Pale, mushy things that were barely green. They were, without a doubt, my least favorite vegetable.

I didn't taste fresh peas until I went to college. That's when I learned that the tasteless stuff from the tin has about as much to do with the real thing as Wonder white bread has to do with a fresh-baked loaf.

And when I took my junior year in London — I'm sorry, I wish it was Dublin but it wasn't — I was absolutely fascinated by the wrinkled green beauties the English called peas, not to mention the manner in which they ate them. The English not only have a way with flower gardens and teapots and tabloid headlines. They also know how to put away peas. They don't jab them with a fork or scoop them up with a spoon as we do in the colonies. Instead, they use a knife to shovel mashed potatoes onto the back of a fork and then balance the peas on top of the heap. The most amazing part is that they look genteel when they do it.

Finally, I graduated — and not just from college. I ate peas straight from the garden — as soon as I picked them. It was taste-bud heaven. At the time, I didn't know there was a scientific reason for this. As is the case with corn, the sugar in peas starts converting to starch the moment they're picked so they lose flavor rapidly. I just knew that I'd stumbled onto a better way of life when it came to *Pisum sativum*, one of the oldest cultivated plants in the known world.

Nor did I realize that I was getting a taste of history. Christopher Columbus is said to have planted the first peas in the New World in 1493, and according to no less an authority than Capt. John Smith, the Indians were growing them when the Pilgrims arrived. Thomas Jefferson grew 30 varieties of his favorite vegetable at Monticello. While he was president he even took time out from affairs of state to write his overseer about planting "Ravenscroft peas, which you will find in a canister in my closet."

For that matter, peas are prehistoric. The oldest peas we know about were found in a cave on the Myanmar-Thailand border and carbon-dated at 9750 BC. Peas have been found at Stone Age sites in Hungary and Switzerland. The ancient Greeks cultivated peas and ate them dried. The Greeks really had a terrific civilization going. By the time of Pericles — about 450 BC — they were selling hot pea soup in the streets of Athens. There is no record as to whether they threw in croutons.

Louis XIV's doctor wrote that his royal patient suffered indigestion from eating petits pois. Still, they were so popular during the Sun King's reign that a member of his court, Mme. de Maintenoy, wrote in a letter in 1695, "The subject of peas is being treated at length: impatience to eat them, the pleasure of having eaten them, and the longing to eat them again are the three points about which our princes have been talking for four days ... It is a fad, a fury." She added that some ladies of the court who were in sufficient favor to dine with the king couldn't wait to get home and devour more peas on their own before calling it a night.

Since I found all this out, I can't wait to get my Sugar Bon and Burpeeana Early in the ground. According to the catalogs, Sugar Bon is a bountiful dwarf form of snap pea, and Burpeeana Early is extremely prolific and freezes well. The catalogs didn't say anything about Louis XIV or Mme. de Maintenoy, but I know I'll eat royally by summer.

All of this is nice to contemplate, but of course

you have to go by the weather. Generally the catalogs advise planting peas in early spring as soon as the soil can be worked. There are usually winter thaws when the ground is workable, but peas will germinate in soil as cold as 40 degrees — although the optimum temperature is 50 degrees. The thing not to do is sow peas in soil that is both cold and wet, because that's the road to rot.

My friend Ed Langlieb, the organic gardener and tomato king of West Hempstead, is also a pea-planter. Ed isn't tied to St. Patrick's Day. He agrees that the soil shouldn't be too wet. If the snow and rain go away, March winds will help dry out the earth. Ed waits till about March 22 to put in his peas. He says that as long as they're in the ground by April 10 — "the absolute latest" — you should have several pickings of great peas before the heat of summer does them in. "I've had people say, 'I have beautiful plants but no peas. What did I do wrong?' The answer is easy — you planted too late. Peas like cool weather."

Ed, of course, has some tips we could all benefit from — after all, he and his wife Louise still have 20 bags of shelled peas in their freezer from last season. As you might expect, he amended his soil in the fall with leaf compost, horse manure and lime. So he's ready to plant. He puts in a 3-foot-high, 10-foot-long wire fence and sows his seeds about 2 inches from the fence line on both sides. Then he measures another 11 inches from the first row and sows a second row on each side. He plants about an inch deep. Ed starts with disease-resistant Green Arrow and the long-yielding Lincoln, which take 60 to 70 days to mature. When they germinate he fills in with peas that mature more quickly like Maestro and Thomas Laxton. And he throws in some sugar snaps and some snow peas, which both have edible pods.

You also should know that peas aren't just good to eat. They're good for the earth. Like all legumes, they gather nitrogen from the air and release it back into the soil. Except for Louis XIV's indigestion, I don't know of any fault you can find with peas.

I don't have a green nightgown, but I'll try to plant them on St. Patrick's Day.

April

In the house, my seed-starter sets are full. Soon the first tiny green shoots will amaze me as they always do. Outside, spring steps along in a sparkle of freshly green lawns and trees whose buds swell into leaf. April's Easter parade marches through the month. It is a gentle time, soft and lovely with the rebirth of the garden. Forsythia paints yards and parkways the color of sunshine, and daphnes sweeten the air. The symbolism of the Easter lily and the deliverance of Passover define the days. My beloved daffodils are glorious, and battalions of tulips start their move toward May. Yellow and orange and red and white and pink and purple. Striped and speckled and fringed and fragrant. And everywhere I go, pansies are smiling.

Starting From Seeds

Seed-starting sets like the one above give your vegetables and flowers a jump start indoors.

In the beginning, there was the seed. Well maybe not in the very beginning, but at least 360 million years ago. That's how far back experts have traced "true seeds" with protective, if incomplete, coats. And they've traced fully encased seeds back to the Cretaceous Period some 100 million years ago. That's when the last dinosaurs were roaming the Earth. The giant reptiles died out but the tiny seeds made it big. Some people find the disappearance of dinosaurs difficult to fathom — I subscribe to the giant-comet-or-asteroid-hitting-the-Earth theory — but I think the survival of seeds is even more amazing. Charles Darwin got it right when he called the origin of seed-bearing plants an "abominable mystery."

I rarely press a seed into the earth without at least a passing fancy about the miracle it represents. "Convince me that you have a seed there," Henry David Thoreau said, "and I am prepared to expect wonders." Seeds come in a variety of shapes and sizes. They're found surrounded by fruit or loose in pods, and they come in thousands of forms — almost square like corn seeds and round like cherry pits and helmeted like acorns and crescent-shaped like marigold seeds and plumed like dandelion seeds. They're as big as coconuts and as little as the mote-sized seeds of orchids.

And they know how to travel. Dandelion seeds float in the wind like parachutes and cornflower seeds zoom like feathered shuttlecocks and coconuts sail across the sea. And there are the rocket-seeds. Mild-mannered impatiens explode their seeds, and people who study this sort of thing say witch hazel can shoot its seed as much as 40 feet. Other seeds stick to clothing or fur or attract birds and animals that eat the casings and spread the seeds about the earth. Lotus seeds have been known to survive entombed for centuries and still germinate.

The real miracle about a seed is what's inside it. A seed is a self-contained fertilized ovule that holds a plant embryo and enough stored food to get it from dormancy to germination. There are two kinds of seed-bearing plants — gymnosperms such as pines and firs, whose seeds are naked, and angiosperms, which have covered seeds and produce flowers. The earliest seed-bearers were gymnosperms, while three-quarters of today's seed-bearing plants are angiosperms.

An equally accurate and more poetic definition of a seed was given by my heroine Celia Thaxter more than a century ago in "An Island Garden": "The genie in the Arabian tale is not half so astonishing. In this tiny casket lie folded roots, stalks, leaves, buds, flowers, seed-vessels, surpassing color and beautiful form, all that goes to make up a plant which is as gigantic in proportion to the bounds that confine it as the oak is to the acorn."

It is a good time to muse about seeds. It's true that you can start some seeds like broccoli and lettuce indoors as early as February, and you can plant peas and spinach outdoors as early as mid-March. But indoors and outdoors, April is the heart of the seed-starting season — especially for such quintessential suburban crops as tomatoes and eggplants. Starting times are decided by counting back from the last frost date — on Long Island, that's usually around the middle of May, but I'm a nervous Nellie when it comes to the tender young seedlings I've pampered indoors. Usually, I wait until Memorial Day before putting any of them outside in the real world.

At my house, April is when we get to work at our potting table. It has a galvanized steel top and we bought it to put outside. But I decided it was too nice to leave to the elements and we put it inside instead in a sunny mud room. And that's where our seed-starting takes root. I love the paraphernalia for indoor sowing — our Styrofoam seed-starting sets, peat pots, soilless sterile medium and all those wonderful seeds.

Most of our seeds are the ones we ordered from catalogs over the winter. We fill in with selections from nursery shelves and I've gotten some nice seeds from a local hardware store. And we save seeds — especially Brandywine tomatoes and an heirloom I know only as Assunta's giant plums. My friend Assunta Tucker, the lady bountiful of Lindenhurst, gave me some of her heirloom seeds from Italy several years ago, and I think of her every time I plant their descendants. If you save seeds, you're better off saving the seeds of open, or naturally pollinated, varieties rather than hybrids. With hybrids you can't be sure of what you'll reap — they're not as likely to reproduce true to type.

If you don't want to buy seed-starting sets, you can use the cell-packs from last year's annuals, Dixie cups or egg cartons. Celia Thaxter even used eggshells to start her favorite Shirley poppies. Or you can try the cut-off bottoms of plastic soda bottles. Whatever you use, make sure there are drainage holes in the bottom and remember to sterilize plastic trays in bleach and water before you use them. I find that store-bought seed-starting mix works best — and helps prevent the damping-off fungus that can do in seedlings. A good rule of thumb when sowing is to cover the seed with moist mix twice as deep as its thickness. Generally speaking, temperatures in the 60-70 degree range are ideal for germination. Don't overwater — the soil should be moist, not saturated.

If your system calls for irrigating from the bottom, don't let the containers sit in water for more than 10 minutes. The idea is for the seedling's roots to reach down and look for food. Making roots is more important than top growth. Fertilize with fish emulsion or liquid seaweed at one-quarter strength each time you water. And let there be light. For good results, use fluorescent bulbs — set just a few inches above the foliage so the plants don't stretch and get leggy in their search for light. Keep the lights on about 14 hours a day, and turn the seedlings every other day so one side doesn't get too much of a good thing.

Don't forget about acclimating, or hardening off, your tender infants before you actually plant them in the great outdoors. Just put them outside for a few hours each day over the course of a week and make sure they're inside by nightfall.

As the plants grow, remember the seeds they started from. And every once in a while, stop and wonder at the sweet mystery of it all.

Giggling In the Garden

My stepfather raised a lot of hell in my childhood, but we made peace in the last years of his life. On Easter, I planted pansies on his grave. I figured he could use a little joy. That's what pansies do — I think of them as the smiling flowers.

They're happy faces in the garden world and their smiles are contagious. Like today, when the world — or at least its mechanical components — was conspiring against me. For a while, it seemed like I'd broken the on-off button of my computer, and then the printer jammed. The oil gauge on my car had to be replaced, and I discovered too late that I'd programed the VCR to record "Ally McBeal" on a warped tape. So I went outside and looked at my pansies, and I couldn't help myself — I started to grin.

At my house this spring, pansies and their smaller, daintier cousins, violas, are lifting spirits all over. The buttery yellows and creamy mauves were put in last spring. The baby blues and pale purples were planted in the fall. And the lovely lavenders and vibrant violets are new additions. Pansies popping out of a window box on the garden shed and winking from a miniature wheelbarrow outside the sliding glass door in the kitchen. And everywhere I walk, they look up at me and giggle from the garden beds.

My favorites are the dreamy, frilly Antique Shades near the pool, and the tricolored lavenders with yellow eyes and the velvety purples that are so deep they almost look black. They mix and mingle with drifts of daffodils along the front walk. The purples and yellows accent each other and they're perfect spring colors.

There are all kind of pansies, a k a *Viola x wittrockiana*. Botanically speaking, all pansies are violas, but not all violas are pansies — even though they're often marketed as miniature pansies. Violas usually flower longer than pansies, but their blooms are smaller.

Pansies, as we know them, are the result of a ménage à trois between the wild Johnny-jump-up (*Viola tricolor*), the large-flowered yellow perennial *V. lutea* and a big blue Dutch species, *V. altaica*. Pansies go by all kinds of quaint and colorful monikers like heartsease, three-faces-in-a-hood, love-in-idleness, none-so-pretty, tickle-my-fancy, cuddle-me-to-you, kiss-me-at-the-garden-gate, meet-her-in-the-pantry, and ladies' delight. But whatever the name, it's all in the same family.

The variations in their little cat faces are what make pansies delightful. It's hard to resist delicately fragrant 2- to 3-inch flowers with 5 velvet-soft overlapping petals. They come in every shade and combination imaginable of blue, purple, lavender, yellow, red, white, orange — every color except green. Solid colors and bicolors and tricolors, plus endless patterns of stripes and blotches.

Big-blossomed pansies with blotches — that's what the smiles on their flat faces are called — didn't show up in the garden until the early 19th Century. They caused a sensation in Victorian England where all-pansy gardens were the rage and plants were passed on as family heirlooms. By 1845, one magazine listed 354 named varieties.

But even before then, the flower was never anonymous. Shakespeare and Milton recognized the charming wild viola known as Johnny-jump-up and used the name pansy — derived from the French word pensée, for thought. In "Hamlet," Shakespeare had the lovesick Ophelia whisper, "there is pansies, that's for thoughts." In "Lycidas," Milton wrote of "the Pansy freaked with jet," alluding to the blossom's perky black face.

Throughout history, pansies have come to symbolize loving thoughts. Napoleon, when he was banished to Elba, promised his supporters: "I will return with the pansies in the spring." To keep his memory alive, Bonapartists passed out leaflets with the exiled leader's face superimposed on a pansy. And as far back as Celtic and Elizabethan times, pansies were picked for use in love potions and heartbreak cures and treatments for depression.

Napoleon returned   at least for a while — and so do pansies. I still can't believe how gleefully last year's pansies came back. They looked a little scraggly for a while, but by the time the crocuses were whispering of spring, they were looking up again.

For sure, pansies are no shrinking violets. They can take cool temperatures, which is why early spring and fall planting is best. If you wait till late spring and all you find are leggy plants with floppy flowers, pinch them back before planting. I know it hurts, but you're helping the pansies. The more flowers you pick, the more blooms you'll get. And you can make a little bouquet for the house.

My Johnny jump-ups have seeded themselves all over the place. They've jumped up in the cracks of my brick patio and front walk. And they've done a grand jeté into the path that meanders along the perennial beds outside the living room window, where they've made merry among the tiny white flowers of a groundcover called mazus.

I'm smiling at all my pansies these days. And they're returning my appreciation.

Chores Galore

CLEAN UP perennial beds. Rake up debris and fallen leaves and toss them in the compost heap.

GIVE your compost heap a good turn so that it gets aerated and starts cooking.

WAIT TO MULCH cleaned-up beds. May is soon enough. The soil should be thoroughly warmed before it's covered.

HEAP lots and lots of compost on new beds. Old ones are satisfied with an inch or two each year.

SCATTER California poppy seeds on a bare patch of ground.

FEED famished roses. They're hungry when they wake up — a sprinkling of Epsom salts is a nice pick-me-up that will help shoots develop.

STAKE peonies before they get too big and flop over.

SHARPEN your lawn mower. You should start cutting the grass when it's about 3 inches high, but don't water it until the last week of May.

CONSIDER a mulching mower if you mow your own lawn. The finely chopped clippings will degrade quickly and feed both grass and soil.

SOW another crop of spring peas. Mid-April is the last call.

PUT IN seeds of hardy annuals. Alyssum, nigella, larkspur, cornflowers and sweet peas can be sown right in the garden. Snapdragons germinate in two weeks and should be pinched to encourage branching. Baby's breath should be sown successively for longer blooming. Calendulas can go out later in the month. But wait on impatiens — they like warmer days and nights.

TRY chives. Plant them now so they'll be blooming by May.

GIVE roots of container-grown trees and shrubs a chance. Disentangle them and fan them out in the planting hole so they get a good foothold.

PLANT a tree for Arbor Day, which is the last Friday of the month.

PRUNE summer-flowering shrubs that bloom on new growth — like rose of Sharon and Pee Gee hydrangeas. Do it early in the month and you won't sacrifice flowers.

START weeding. Sorry about that, but the sooner you get out there, the easier it will be to keep things under control.

TRANSPLANT trees and shrubs, but don't fertilize them when you do.

COLOR your fields strawberry. Planting time is the middle of the month. Sparkle, Catskill, Fletcher and Redchief bear fruit in June and July. Ozark Beauty and Geneva are everbearing varieties — they produce fruit in June and again from August to October.

PLANT 2- or 3-year-old asparagus roots.

SOW marigolds and nasturtiums indoors.

BRIGHTEN UP with cool-weather plants like primroses, ranunculus, dianthus and stock.

Hoo-Ha Time For the Radish

My husband loves to tell about the victory garden he planted as a child during World War II. Fueled by patriotism but lacking the slightest bit of gardening knowledge, he hoed up a small patch of ground and put in a single crop — a packet of radish seeds he'd brought home from school.

Then he watered and waited. He didn't wait very long. You should understand that he had never planted anything before and that he lived in Queens on a street where the houses were not connected but built very close together. The next morning, when he saw radishes strewn all over the garden, it never occurred to him that the nice woman next door had tossed some store-bought radishes out her window in an act of inspired whimsy. My husband was and still is a very ingenuous soul. He had read "Jack and the Beanstalk," and he didn't expect any giants, but he did figure it wouldn't take more than a few days for whole radishes to appear. He thought he had really done something for his country. He thought that was how radishes grew.

Over the years, he's learned otherwise. But he still grows radishes and tries to get in two crops a season. He likes to start out with Easter Egg Mix, which takes only 25 days to produce a rainbow of oval red, white, lavender, pink and purple beauties.

There are no instant miracles in the garden, but radishes are pretty impressive just the same. Believe it or not, there are sleek daikon radishes from Japan that can grow as long as 2 feet and weigh as much as 70 pounds. Radishes go back only 1,000 years in Japan but were grown in China as long ago as the Seventh Century BC. And the ancient Greeks made gold replicas of radishes as offerings to Apollo in his temple at Delphi.

In medieval England radishes were touted as cures for kidney stones, facial blemishes and intestinal worms. A 17th-Century apothecary named John Parkinson recommended them for salads and said they sharpened the palate for the consumption of meat. The Pilgrims brought radish seeds with them to the New World.

All things considered, it's about time we paid more attention to radishes. They're 94 percent water, low in calories and have almost as much potassium as

sweet and mild and can be used for feeding livestock as well as people.

One of the nice things about radishes is that they're not particular about where they put down roots — my husband even stuck some in shallow containers with marigolds. Of course, if you want shapely vegetables, it's best to plant them in loose, well-drained soil. That goes for early radishes, which should be harvested before the dog days of summer, as well as the longer-season varieties, which can be started in early August, since they need warm soil during germination, but short, cool days toward the end of their growing period.

When it's time to plant a crop for fall picking, work some compost into the soil and sow seeds about one-half inch deep and 2 inches apart in rows 18 inches apart. Water lightly and when the seedlings are an inch high thin them to 4-6 inches apart. The later varieties like more room than early radishes, which need to be thinned to only 2 inches apart.

If you're smart, you'll plant small amounts of seed every 10 days or so starting in early spring. You should have a steady supply of plump juicy radishes well into July. Harvest them when they're under an inch in diameter. If you planted too many radishes for tonight's salad, pull them up and trim the leaves close to the root and store them in a plastic bag in the refrigerator. They'll keep for about three weeks.

Of course, if it's a Sakurajima you're storing, you may have to think about a new refrigerator..

bananas and half the ascorbic acid of oranges.

We've made a big hoo-ha over other vegetables. Potatoes are part of Long Island's history, freshly picked corn rules the summer and tomatoes are part of our suburban landscape. Even arugula and radicchio had their 15 minutes of fame. But when was the last time anybody ever made a fuss over a radish?

As far as I'm concerned, radishes deserve a fanfare of their own. It doesn't matter whether they're round or oval or hot or mild. They taste great, and they're relatively easy to grow whether they're short-term crops like scarlet Cherry Belle or red and white Flamboyant that mature in 21 to 30 days, or longer-season varieties like Round Black Spanish or pure white Sakurajima, which need 50 to 70 days and are best planted in midsummer for picking in autumn.

Incidentally, Sakurajima is the daikon that grows to 5 pounds in 70 days and can hit 70 if left in the ground long enough. Nichols Garden Nursery in Oregon offers the mammoth Sakurajima in its seed catalog, proclaiming it "the largest radish in the world." The catalog also notes it is

Crisp Additions To the Salad

Your salad bowl doesn't have to be without homegrown radishes for very long if you try some midseason or longer-season varieties. Asian radishes, which mature in 45 to 60 days, can even be sown in early summer, since they've been bred to resist bolting during hot weather. And you can leave longer-season varieties in the ground for a few weeks after they mature, as long as you harvest them before the first hard frost. Remove their tops and bury them in a root pit or in a box of damp sand stored in a cool, dark cellar. They'll keep for about two months.

APRIL CROSS — a white daikon that takes 60 days to mature and will reach a length of 18 inches and a diameter of 3 inches before becoming pithy.

BLACK SPANISH LONG — a zesty-flavored, 10-inch-long radish that matures in 60 days and must be peeled before it's eaten.

GERMAN BEER — a white radish 3 inches in diameter that is often served peeled and thinly sliced with salt at the annual Oktoberfest in Munich.

MISATO ROSE — a turnip-shaped radish with a pale green and white exterior and a rose-pink interior that can be sown from August to October and weighs up to 1 1/2 pounds at maturity in about 60 days.

SUMMER CROSS — a sweet white daikon that is heat- and drought-tolerant and resists fusarium wilt, a fungus that blackens foliage and kills roots.

WHITE CHINESE — a mild, carrot-shaped variety that matures in 50 to 60 days.

Vegetable Planting Guide

Here are vegetable planting times for the metropolitan area, as recommended by Cornell Cooperative Extension. These are considered the best times to obtain optimum results, based on more than 15 years of experience by local gardeners.

Legend:
- Sow seeds directly in the garden
- Sow seeds or plant transplants
- Plant transplants

Vegetable	April	May	June	July	August
Basil		■	■	■	
Beans (bush)		■	■	■	
Beans (pole)		■	■		
Beets	■	■			■
Broccoli	■			■	
Broccoli rabe	■	■		■	
Brussels sprouts	■				
Cabbage	■			■	
Carrots	■	■		■	■
Cauliflower	■			■	
Celery	■				
Chinese cabbages	■			■	
Collards	■	■	■	■	■
Corn		■	■		
Cucumber		■	■		
Dry beans*		■	■		
Eggplant		■	■		
Greens**	■	■			
Kohlrabi	■	■			■
Leek (seeds)	■	■			
Lettuce	■	■			■
Melons		■	■		
Mustard greens		■	■	■	■
Onions (sets)	■	■			
Parsley	■	■			
Parsnip	■	■			
Peas (bush or pole)	■				
Peppers (hot or sweet)		■	■		
Potato (eyes)		■	■		
Pumpkin		■	■		
Radish	■	■			■
Rutabaga	■	■			
Shallot (bulbs)	■	■			
Spinach	■				
Squash (summer/winter)		■	■		
Summer spinach		■	■		
Swiss chard		■	■	■	
Tomato		■	■		
Turnip	■	■			■
Turnip greens					■

* Black-eyed peas, chickpeas, fava beans, kidney beans, lima beans, pinto beans, soybeans. ** Arugula, chicories, cilantro, corn salad, cress, dandelion, endive, escarole, mesclun.

Dazzling Daffodils

William Wordsworth may have been lonely as a cloud when he became spellbound by "a host of golden daffodils" and wrote his famous poem. But it was a little different for me. I found daffodils when I got fed up with squirrels. Or at least with squirrels treating my tulip beds as a free-lunch counter.

The squirrels that consider my trees a playground were consuming the tulip bulbs I'd put such effort into planting. And that was just in the fall. In the spring they devoured the flowers of the survivors. Then I learned squirrels don't eat daffodils. It was the beginning of a beautiful friendship.

I still plant tulips — but I treat them like annuals. I also cover the newly planted beds with wire mesh and douse them with blood meal, which I sprinkle again when the first green shoots appear. But my spring romance is with daffodils. The show starts in March and continues into May. By Mother's Day, I walk out my front door and see a host of daffodils that are not just golden but every shade of yellow from pastel to sulphur. Plus pink and white and apricot and orange.

Wordsworth's sister Dorothy wrote in her diary that the daffodils she and William spotted as they walked "tossed and reeled and danced, and seemed as if they verily laughed with the wind ..." I know what she meant. Daffodils make me happy. They simply scream spring. They show up when you're absolutely starved for color.

They're gorgeous by any name. Actually, daffodil is the common name for *Narcissus*. The American Daffodil Society says it's OK to call all narcissi daffodils, but the Dutch aren't as accommodating. They reserve the word daffodil for bulbs of the Trumpet variety — the big-flowered plant with a single bold bloom per stem and a trumpet as long or longer than the flower petals. They class everything else as narcissi. I call them all beautiful. And there are more than 5,000 varieties.

There are, of course, the classics — the pure yellow daffodils that inspired Wordworth's muse and gladden my own heart. But thanks to caring hybridizers, there are fields upon fields of daffodils to discover when it comes to sizes and shapes — from tiny yellow Tête-à-Tête, which is all of six inches tall, to the imposing golden giant, 18-inch-high Dutch Master.

The color combinations are dazzling. There are a host of wonders like Pomona, with white petals and red trumpets, or Easter Bonnet, with cream petals and ruffled salmon trumpets, or Kissproof, with 20-inch stems, apricot petals and a deep-orange cup. Or Professor Einstein, a relative genius of a daffodil with pure white crepe-paper-like petals and a large flat orange-red cup.

In my own garden, the daffodils that warm my winter-cold heart include Tête-à-Tête, white and cream Ice Follies, pink-cupped, white-petaled Salome, sulphur-yellow Minnow, and Mount Hood, with white petals and an ivory-yellow trumpet that changes to pure white. And I dote on multi-flowered Sundial, which has fragrant deep golden blooms. I'm checking the catalogs carefully for shades of pink and coral and orange and ever more interesting shapes — like *Narcissus bulbocodium,* which looks like an old-fashioned petticoat and is appropriately nicknamed "the yellow hoop petticoat." Or flamboyant Papillon daffodils with split cups that look like butterflies. I'd love to see Lemon Beauty fluttering in my garden next spring, with its star-shaped yellow heart against ivory petals. Or Palmares with an apricot-pink cup.

I felt happy just looking at a photo of Petit Four, which has white petals and a frilled double apricot-pink trumpet. It was the same with Tahiti, a tall, double bloom of gold and orange-red, and Thalia, known as the orchid narcissus with glistening white flowers. Also Actaea, the so-called "poet's narcissus" with white petals and a golden cup with a bright red edge. And aptly named Cheerfulness, whose gardenialike, double-white flowers practically say "have a nice day." It smells good, too. Which is something else I'm sniffing out — daffodils with fragrance.

There's one more thing I should tell you about daffodils. They require minimal care and keep on blooming season after season as long as you don't cut back the foliage until it turns yellow and falls over. They preen in pots and in formal plantings, but as far as I'm concerned, they're at their most delightful in drifts. Just the way Wordsworth saw them.

An Early

Joann Knapp's garden is truly an early spring garden — one that starts in February with snowdrops and winter aconite and is finished flowering in June. Joann explains why. "After the mountain laurels bloom, everything's green. I hate to garden in the heat of summer."

The result is that at the Knapp house in Locust Valley, spring is a season and a half. On an afternoon of tentative sunshine in early April, the garden unfolds in the valley below a hillside on Joann's 2-acre property. Even in a spring when everything is coming up early, the profusion of blooms is eye-catching. Viewed from a distance, the shapes and colors are splashed against the darker canvas of the slope like an impressionist painting. There is no lawn, no Belgian block, no picket fence anywhere to be seen. The ambience is not so much suburban as natural woodland.

Don't get me wrong. I like suburban gardens. Belgian block, picket fence and lawn are very visible on my own property. But the charm of Joann's garden lies in its naturalness — in the way it suits its setting. Drifts of daffodils and carpets of *Scilla* sparkle where one might expect a lawn. Magnolia trees bloom in front of the house and on the hillside. Yellow bell-shaped merrybells with crinkled leaves that look like they need ironing and a fragrant blue species hyacinth gambol near the primrose bed. Single-flowered and double forms of *Sanguinaria,* or bloodroot — which Joann says the Indians used to make rust-colored dye — grow in a raised bed across the path from the primroses. The double bloodroots, *Sanguinaria canadensis* Multiplex, which spread only via underground rhizomes — push out of the ground like thumbs, and their grayish leaves unfurl around half-dollar-sized white flowers. White *Trillium* combines with Virginia bluebells and dainty white bleeding hearts — *Dicentra*

Spring Show in the Woods

cucullaria — also known as Dutchman's breeches.

And of course there are lovely primroses. Joann and her husband, Fred, are partial to primroses — on this particular day, in fact, Fred is at a national primrose convention in Seattle. I love the bold and beautiful Polyantha cultivars in my own yard but I am equally charmed by the *Primula japonica* and *Primula sieboldi* and the *Juliana* hybrids that Joann and Fred raise. They have a subtle, delicate beauty.

I'm also taken with *Jeffersonia diphylla*, named after the third president of the United States, which has kidney-shaped leaves that are split in two parts like butterfly wings and an ephemeral white flower. May apples are coming up and ferns are unfurling and an Asian species of Jack-in-the-pulpit is just days away from popping into bloom. Magnificent andromedas are in full splendor. I love my own ordinary white *Pieris japonica*, but I purely lust for Joann's pale pink Christmas Cheer and bright rosy Flamingo.

None of this is the result of happenstance — the garden is planned that way. "We're plant collectors, and most plant collectors don't have very attractive gardens," Joann says. "They plant like buckshot — one plant here, one plant there. But I wanted a pretty garden, so I started clumping things together."

Plant selection and timing are essential to the Knapp garden. Many of Joann's favorites are native eastern wildflowers — single and double bloodroots, trilliums, Virginia bluebells, May apples. But she doesn't close the garden gate on non-natives. In fact, she likes growing wildflowers like *Jeffersonia* and *Shortia galacifolia* or Oconee Bells next to their Asian counterparts. "Plantwise, the East Coast of the United States and Asia are a much better match than the East and West Coasts of this country," Joann says. "We have similar conditions, like the same prevailing winds and ocean currents, so you can have fun growing different species of the same genera."

Different species abound. It's as if Joann is

putting on a show of little vignettes that come and go. As one scene fades, another blooms center stage. One scene features star magnolias and andromedas and Korean azaleas in combination with early spring bulbs like glory-of-the-snow, and *Cornus mas,* or the Cornelian cherry tree, which has clusters of tiny golden flowers that bloom on leafless branches. When the daffodils and hellebores steal away, the spotlight will shine on yellow magnolias — Elizabeth and Yellow Bird.

Joann's garden flowers and fades and finally turns to green. By the end of June, after the rhododendrons and the mountain laurels have done their thing, the oaks and American beeches and a stand of marvelous tulip trees will have leafed out, and the garden will be a woodland.

It helps that both Fred, a retired Grumman engineer, and Joann, who has served in a variety of capacities at Planting Fields Arboretum in Oyster Bay from slide librarian to coordinator of volunteers, are constantly learning about horticulture. Their property includes a rock garden, complete with trough gardens, and every summer they go west into the mountains to places like Crater Lake in Oregon and Mt. Rainier in Washington. They travel by trailer and study and photograph tiny alpine plants that grow above the tree line. "This year we're going into the Canadian Rockies," Joann says. "But the older we get, the higher we drive. We used to hike more."

All of which makes the Knapp garden a classroom for flower lovers. I know that during my visit I learned something about a natural garden — about native wildflowers and woodland plants. And I didn't feel as if I was in a "garden." It was as if I'd stumbled on a spot in the woods where nature had gathered its flowers. Which is exactly what Joann and Fred wanted. "This is just a piece of woods that two people have been playing with for 20 years," she says.

> ❛ *After the mountain laurels bloom, everything's green.* ❜

At left, Joann and Fred Knapp on their 2-acre hillside property in Locust Valley.

The Lilies Of the Field

The botanical symbol of Easter forever blooms in my memory — fragrant white flowers bordering the pulpit where the minister of my childhood, imposing in a long black robe, spoke of renewal and rebirth. I was touched not only by the story of the Resurrection but also by the trumpet-shaped flowers of the Easter lily. They seemed so perfect.

If it blooms forever in memory, the Easter lily of spring blooms only for little more than two weeks in life. But even for that brief moment in time, it's nice to know that something can be so perfect and so pure and so white and so clean.

There are many religious and literary references to Lilium longiflorum, the stately white flower we know as the Easter lily. It is a flower for the ages. Ancient myths hold that white lilies sprang from the milk of Hera, the Greek queen of heaven. Another story is that they were born in Eve's tears when she was banished from the Garden of Eden.

Or that they grew in the Garden of Gethsemane, where drops of Christ's sweat fell to the ground in his time of agony before He was betrayed. Sometimes, Lilium longiflorum has been called the "Madonna lily" because of its association with the Virgin Mary. In many early religious paintings, saints are shown offering white lilies to Mary and the Infant Jesus.

There's a saying that goes, "To gild a lily is to attempt, foolishly, to improve on perfection." It's not easy being perfect and the Easter lily is no exception. Lilium longiflorum is native to the southern islands of Japan, and until World War II most Easter lily bulbs came from that country. After Pearl Harbor, the supply was cut off and a band of Oregon horticulturists expanded what had been a hobby for them.

Now more than 95 percent of bulbs destined for the holiday market are produced by just 10 farms in the so-called "Easter Lily Capital of the World," a narrow coastal strip along the Oregon-California border banked by redwood forests. The area has a year-round temperate climate, rich soil and plentiful rainfall. And growers with lots of patience. It takes three or four years in the field before the bulbs are ready for the greenhouse. And they are never dormant — just like babies, they need constant care.

An Easter lily bulb starts as a bulblet on the underground stem of the mother plant. It is taken away from mom at harvest time in late September-early October and planted in a new field to start its own life. The following season, the growing bulb — now called a "yearling" — is dug up again, planted in yet another field and nurtured into maturity for the market.

But it is still a bulb — the perfect lily is yet to come. Left alone in the field, Lilium longiflorum blooms in the summer. Making it an Easter lily is tricky business, especially since the holiday occurs on a different Sunday each year depending on the vernal equinox. Easter falls on the first Sunday after the first full moon of spring, anywhere between March 22 and April 25.

It's almost as if time were a target and nursery operators aim for a bull's-eye. "It's the most labor-intensive crop to grow if you want them for Easter," says Eric Keil of Otto Keil Florist in Huntington, which wholesales 28,000 pots in the tristate area for the holiday. "It's especially tough when you have an early Easter."

The perfect lily requires perfect timing and temperature. At Hicks Nurseries in Westbury, head grower John Patterson starts worrying about Easter lilies in October, when he receives a shipment of about 1,000 bulbs from the Oregon fields. From that moment on, he follows a precise timetable to get his lilies ready for churches and dinner tables across Long Island. The bulbs are potted, and around Nov. 1 they start a six-week stay in an 8-foot-high, 30-foot-long storage box at 40 to 45 degrees. Just before Christmas they go into the greenhouse, where the temperature is carefully monitored for 100 to 110 days to force bloom.

Within two weeks, a bulb sends out basal roots and then stem roots and is on its way to lily-hood. Once the buds develop, Eric Keil explains, the plant takes about two weeks to flower. If the buds are opening too quickly, the pots have to be moved back to a cooler location.

If all goes as planned, the lilies should be in full splendor by Easter Sunday. It's pretty amazing. A *Lilium longiflorum* bulb is handled about 40 times before it leaves the Easter Lily Capital in the Pacific Northwest. Then it's fussed over in the greenhouse. And if you want to extend its bloom in your house, a little more fussing is required. Keep your Easter lily near a window for bright indirect sunlight. The temperature should be between 60 and 65 during the day, slightly cooler at night. Water only when the soil feels dry, and remove withered flowers. When the plants are through flowering, keep the pot in a sunny location and keep on watering.

If you want to grow *Lilium longiflorum* in your yard, wait until May when you don't have to worry about frost. Plant the bulbs three inches deep in a well-drained bed that gets a lot of sun and spread the roots out and down. Plant bulbs at least 12 to 18 inches apart and mound three inches of topsoil over the bed. When the foliage fades, cut back the stems. If you're lucky, your Easter lily will perform an encore later in the growing season, but chances are you'll have to wait till the following year.

Of course, the flowers won't show up until summer. But the appearance of *Lilium longiflorum* in your own garden around the Fourth of July should still be perfect.

When I was a kid I thought about Easter lilies only at Easter. Now I can see them in all their glory in my own backyard.

May

Whoever coined the phrase "the merry month of May" must have been a gardener. May is the standard-bearer of spring, a time when the earth revels. Sweet woodruff in the May wine and garlands on the maypole. Magnolias grace the season and azaleas wrap it all up in pink and white and red and purple. Forget-me-nots remind us of their loveliness in gentle blues. Lady's slippers fit perfectly. Lilies of the Valley nod hello and lilacs bid us adieu.

And as if in apology for the bare branches of winter, the trees trot out their best colors. Crab apple trees dress up in red and dogwoods glory in pink and white. Japanese cherry trees smile in the spring breeze until a carpet of soft petals blankets patio and lawn.

Gardeners crowd nurseries to choose from the kaleidoscope of local color and patiently press seedlings into clay pots and window boxes and hanging baskets. And May carries on.

Impatient With Impatiens

This is the time of year when garden centers are bursting with impatiens and geraniums. But believe me, that's not all there is. It's not that I want to banish these hallmarks of suburbia. I'm not one of those horticultural snobs who wouldn't get within a trowel's reach of impatiens. There's good reason why impatiens are probably the nation's most popular annual. They splash color from spring till frost. They grow like weeds. They even like a little shade. And they're versatile. They're happy in containers or hanging baskets or in the flower border. You can depend on impatiens. But I've become impatient with impatiens of late — maybe it's a case of too much of a good thing.

I guess the point is that in the garden as well as in life it's too easy to fall into a rut. It's that way with annuals — we can't seem to see beyond

Deadheading

In the garden, deadheading means new life. It keeps your annuals blooming. Use forefinger and thumb–or sharp pruners or scissors and remove all the faded flower parts. Don't just pluck off the spent petals but make sure you remove the seed head. The basic precept here is that the less energy the plant puts into seeds, the more flowers it will produce. And the fuller and healthier the plant will be. So deadhead as soon as the flowers fade. Also, eliminating all those mushy blooms helps keep botrytis and other fungal diseases out of your garden.

How To

May

Kathy Pufahl in one of her greenhouses in Riverhead. An annuals specialist, she challenges gardeners to develop a sense of adventure.

the red geraniums and pink impatiens for the pink geraniums and red impatiens.

What I'm espousing here is a spirit of adventure. There's a world of annuals beyond impatiens and geraniums — and light-years away from red salvia for that matter. It's filled with opportunities — like ruby-red Egyptian star cluster and hot pink trailing verbena and anise-scented sage with its gentian-blue flowers. Not to mention *Asclepias*

curassavica, the blood flower milkweed with clusters of yellow, orange and red blossoms that butterflies and hummingbirds can't resist. Or *Angelonia angustifolia* Blue Pacific, a violet-and-yellow showstopper that does a good imitation of an orchid.

That world unfolds at Kathy Pufahl's Beds & Borders nursery in Riverhead, where you won't find the water beds and mattresses callers some-

High-Performance Plants

SHRUBS	Genus, Species	Common Name	Mature Height
Berberis thunbergii		Rose Glow Barberry	6 ft.
Cornus alba sibirica		Red-twig dogwood	7 ft.
Corylus avellana contorta		Harry Lauder's walking stick	8 ft.
Cotinus coggyria purpureus		Purple smoke bush	10 ft.
Cotoneaster horizontalis		Cotoneaster	Low spreading
Fothergilla gardenii		Fothergilla	8 ft.
Hamamelis mollis		Chinese witch hazel	6-20 ft.
Hydrangea arborescens Annabelle		Annabelle hydrangea	5 ft.
Hydrangea quercifolia		Oakleaf hydrangea	8 ft.
Ilex verticillata Winter Red		Winterberry holly	9 ft.
Rhus typhina laciniata		Cutleaf staghorn sumac	15 ft.
Salix alba		Twig willows	7 ft.
Spiraea bumalda Goldflame		Goldflame spirea	3 ft.
Viburnum dentatum plicatum		Doublefile viburnum	15 ft.
TREES			
Acer griseum		Paperbark maple	20-40 ft.
Acer palmatum		Japanese maple	Dwarf-25 ft.
Amelanchier arborea		Shadblow	6-20 ft.
Betula nigra		River birch	40 ft.
Cornus Kousa		Kousa dogwood	20-30 ft.
Crataegus viridis		Green hawthorn	25-35 ft.
Malus floribunda		Japanese crabapple	15-25 ft.
Malus sargentii		Sargent crabapple	10 ft.
Prunus Okame		Okame cherry	25 ft.
Stewartia pseudocamellia		Stewartia	20-40 ft.
Syringa reticulata		Japanese tree lilac	30 ft.

M a y

times try to order but where you can find toadflax and corn cockle and giant wild parsnip and strawflowers and — here's a name to stir the imagination — exotic love. Of course, Kathy has made a career out of wholesaling annuals and tender perennials, especially those not often seen on your street or mine. Incidentally, a tender perennial is one that would make it year-round in a warmer clime but is too fragile to survive our winters. So it gets treated as an annual.

"Gardeners are always looking for something different," says Kathy, who has a degree in biology but always dug plants. She was working in one of the first nurseries on Long Island to specialize in perennials when she decided to branch out on her own. She wanted a different niche and picked annuals.

"My timing was great," she says.

Though they are not conifers – the truest four-season choice – these garden possibilities do more than your average plant. Some fill a difficult gap in the season, others offer multiple seasons of interest by showing off more than once a year.

Seasonal Interest

Spring	Summer	Fall	Winter	
	●	●		Purple foliage developing pink and white splashes; red fruit
●	●	●	●	White spring flowers; variegated foliage all season; red twigs in winter
●			●	Long, birch-like tassles early spring; very contorted winter shape
●	●	●		Wine foliage all season; cloudlike summer flowers
●	●	●	●	Spring flowers; red fruit fall to winter
●	●	●		Fuzzy white early spring flowers; nice foliage turning fiery in fall
	●	●	●	Late-winter yellow or orange flowers; handsome foliage with yellow fall color
	●	●		Long-lasting cream to green flowers
	●	●		Long-lasting summer flowers; wine purple fall foliage; cinnamon peeling bark
		●	●	Profuse bright red berries last into late winter
	●	●	●	Red fruit, hot fall foliage, gnarled mature form
●	●	●	●	Colorful twigs in winter
●	●	●		Chartreuse foliage all season; rose summer flower
				White spring flowers; red fruit, wine fall foliage
	●	●	●	Nice foliage; fall color; peeling cinnamon bark
	●	●	●	Red foliage all season; good fall color; interesting winter shape
●		●	●	White April flowers; small dark fruits; yellow fall foliage; smooth gray bark
●	●	●	●	Triangular leaves; yellow fall color; peeling white-pink bark
●	●	●	●	White June flowers; large red fruits; hot fall foliage; mottled bark
		●	●	Lasting red fruits and silver-gray bark
●	●	●		Pink to white May flowers; red or yellow fruit into fall
●		●	●	White May flowers; red fruit; good horizontal shape
●		●		Pink flowers late March; colorful fall foliage
●	●	●	●	White flowers in July; fiery fall foliage; camouflage-pattern bark
	●		●	White flowers after all other lilacs; shiny bark

I love success stories — Kathy started her business more than 10 years ago with a single greenhouse. Now she has 12 greenhouses and a new potting machine. She propagates 60 percent of her stock and ships several hundred thousand containers of annuals and tender perennials to nurseries from here to Connecticut.

"Retailers will tell you, 'If it doesn't flower in May, forget it,'" Kathy says, "but we've challenged the conventional wisdom. People are more sophisticated, and they're drawn to the unusual, whether it's in flower in May or not. You have to get people to cross the line from geraniums and impatiens to other things. And the message is simple: Just try it."

Which is good advice for all of us. I was knocked out by a hanging moss basket Kathy had put together. "People ask me all the time, are you

High-Performance Plants

	Genus, Species	Common Name	Mature Height
ANNUALS			
	Amaranthus caudatus	Amaranth	2-6 ft.
	Atriplex hortensis	Red orach	4-5 ft.
	Canna hybrids	Canna	3-6 ft.
	Coleus hybrids	Coleus	1-3 ft.
	Dahlia hybrids	Dahlia	1 $\frac{1}{2}$ -5 ft.
	Foeniculum vulgare Redleaf	Copper fennel	3-4 ft.
	Gomphrena globosa	Globe amaranth	1-2 ft.
	Pennisetum setaceum Rubrum	Fountain grass	2-3 ft.
	Perilla frutescens	Perilla	3 ft.
	Salvia leucantha	Mexican bush sage	3-4 ft.
	Verbena bonariensis	Tall verbena	3-4 ft.
PERENNIALS			
	Artemisia species/hybrids	Artemisia	1 $\frac{1}{2}$ -4 ft.
	Aster species/hybrids	Aster	1-6 ft.
	Bergenia cordifolia	Bergenia	1 $\frac{1}{2}$ ft.
	Clematis maximowicziana	Sweet autumn clematis	10-30 ft.
	Fern species/hybrids	Ferns	$\frac{1}{2}$ -6 ft.
	Geranium macrorrhizum	Bigroot geranium	1 ft.
	Helleborus species/varieties	Hellebore	1-1 $\frac{1}{2}$ ft.
	Hosta species/varieties	Hosta	$\frac{1}{2}$ -3 ft.
	Iris sibirica	Siberian iris	3 ft.
	Miscanthus sinensis	Silver grass, maiden grass	5-8 ft.
	Pennisetum alopecuroides	Fountain grass	2-4 ft.
	Pulmonaria saccharata	Lungwort	1 ft.
	Rudbeckia species/varieties	Coneflowers	2-6 ft.

supposed to put this plant with that plant," Kathy says. "And all I can say in response is, 'Well, do you like it?' Approach it as an adventure. If you don't like it, change it."

I wouldn't make a single change in the basket, which contained a cascading variety of coleus called *C. rehneltianus* Compact Red with petite reddish-purple leave edged in yellow, a trailing verbena named *V. canadensis* Apple Blossom with pink-hued petals, an Australian blue fan flower more properly known as *Scaevola aemula* Blue Wonder, and a nutmeg-scented geranium — not your ordinary, garden-variety geranium, but *Pelargonium fragrans* with small gray-green leaves and white flowers.

Kathy held a leaf of the pelargonium to my nose and the nutmeg scent was so strong it made me want to run for a glass of eggnog. And she said

Seasonal Interest

Spring	Summer	Fall	Winter	
	●	●		Red foliage and plumes summer through frost
●	●	●		Purple foliage all season
	●	●		Bronze, red and variegated leaf forms colorful all season; late flowers
	●	●		Colorful foliage all season
	●	●		Red-leaf forms colorful all season; flowers late summer to frost
●	●	●		Bronze foliage all season
	●	●		Pink, purple, white or red flowers late summer through fall
	●	●		Reddish foliage and plumes all summer to frost
	●	●		Purple foliage all season
	●	●		Late summer to frost, purple spiky flowers
	●	●		Summer through frost, airy purple flowers
○	○	○		Silvery foliage all season
	○	○		Pink, white, blue or purple flowers late summer through frost
○	○	○	○	Magenta to white spring flowers; shiny evergreen or near-evergreen foliage
	○	○		Late summer through fall cloud of fragrant, small white flowers
○	○	○	○	Handsome foliage all season; some have honey autumn color; others near-evergreen
○	○	○	○	Handsome near-evergreen foliage with red fall color; pink or white late spring flowers
○	○	○	○	Late winter to spring flowers; some with evergreen foliage
○	○	○		Showy foliage, often variegated, all season; white or purple flowers summer or autumn
	○	○		Purple or white early summer flowers; outstanding grassy foliage goes gold in fall
	○	○	○	Green or variegated foliage summer-fall; summer plumes; stays gold in winter
	○	○	○	Green foliage turns yellow-almond in fall to winter; cream, pink or tan summer plumes
○	○	○		Very early spring flowers, pink blue or white; variegated foliage all season
	○	○	○	Long-lasting daisy flowers; seedheads look nice right through winter

that coleus is back in style — although it's not quite the same plant Victorian gardeners doted upon. Today's coleus is heat- and sun-tolerant and it emphasizes foliage rather than flowers.

Kathy mentioned several other trendy annuals and tender perennials — she calls them "hot numbers." One of her personal favorites is the South African daisy, or *Arctotis*, with gray foliage and salmon or dusty-pink flowers that close up in early evening. "It's a gorgeous daisy. It does well in containers, in the flower bed, in heavy soil, in light soil. It just keeps doing its thing right through to a heavy frost."

And she loves *Agastache*, a fragrant tender perennial related to salvia — especially Tutti-Frutti, which has rose-purple blooms filled with nectar that attract hummingbirds. And the salvias themselves. Not the red salvias that go back to the first split level but *S. farinacea* Victoria Blue with pencil-thin 18-inch-tall spikes and *S.* Indigo Spires, a purple-blue hybrid that peaks in August and lasts till frost. Indigo Spires sounds absolutely

Chores Galore

TAKE care when you shop for annuals. Look for strong, well-proportioned, stocky seedlings. Buy "green" — that means without flowers. Young plants get stressed out if they have to make blooms in the confines of a cell-pack.

PATIENCE, patience. Wait until Memorial Day to plant heat-loving vegetables like tomatoes, peppers and eggplants. Harden off seedlings — gradually exposing them to the outdoors — before putting them in the ground.

BURY the stems of tomato seedlings so that only one or two pairs of leaves are above ground. Do the same with peppers, but not eggplants, which should be planted at the same level they were grown in cell-packs.

GIVE veggies a good serving of compost and space to grow — 2 feet for tomatoes, 18 inches for peppers and eggplants. Protect stems from cutworms with collars fashioned from Dixie cups and yogurt containers — cut out the bottoms and sink them 2 inches into the soil.

SUPPORT your tomatoes. Try 6-foot-tall 2X2s, bamboo or metal stakes, wire cages, broomstick handles or trellises made out of heavy-gauge 6-inch wire mesh and well-anchored posts. Loosely tie the growing stems to the stake with figure-eight loops of soft cloth, horticultural ribbon or strips of pantyhose.

Speaking of panty hose, here's another stocking stuffer. Keep slugs out of flowerpots and container gardens by slipping the pot into an old nylon stocking. The slimy beasts won't be able to slither up the pot, but water will still drain out.

YOU can't grow chips but you can grow your own salsa — plant cilantro, hot peppers and a few tomatillos, a tomato-relative with green golf-ball-sized fruit that is a constant in Mexican cuisine.

START a summer cutting garden of zinnias, dahlias, snapdragons, cosmos, calendula and chrysanthemums. For cut flowers that are head and shoulders above the rest, plant sunflowers and tithonia.

MULCH azaleas, rhododendrons, pieris with an acid mulch like pine needles or oak leaves. Don't forget to water newly planted trees and shrubs deeply.

SOW seeds of pumpkins, cucumbers, summer and winter squash. Make sure these heavy feeders have well-prepared soil loaded with compost and rotted manure to sustain them through the season. Give them plenty of room to run, or select bush varieties — available in all but the pumpkins.

UNTANGLE compacted roots of container-grown plants and seedlings so they'll spread out quickly in their new home. Cut damaged or crushed roots of woody plants with sharp pruners so they'll soak up moisture.

PLENTY of pesto is one of my mottoes. Sow a generous row of basil seeds.

CREATE a bed around trees and shrubs in the lawn to avoid "lawn mower blight," wounds caused when the mower bumps into the trunk. Mulch to conserve moisture.

ADD color and height to the garden. Let climbing nasturtiums scramble up tomato cages and pole beans hug corn stalks. Plant beans around each corn stalk, one to two weeks after the corn seeds are in, and the beans will add nitrogen as well as lovely blossoms to the garden.

EDGE beds and borders with a flat, square-headed garden spade or half-circle edging tool to keep the lawn from encroaching.

FERTILIZE the lawn for the first time on Memorial Day. Mark the calendar: Labor Day and Thanksgiving are the next feeding times.

PLANT herbs in a whiskey barrel, hanging basket, window box or strawberry pot if you don't have room in the garden.

MULCH cool-weather vegetables to keep down weeds. Spinach and lettuce appreciate having cooler roots. But hold off mulching heat-lovers like tomatoes and peppers until hot weather arrives.

BE CAREFUL out there — wear a hat and sunblock. Watch out for ticks.

majestic with 2-foot-high spikes on a 4-foot-tall woody base. "There are more than 900 kinds of salvias, and to just think of ordinary old red salvia does a disservice to the entire genus."

Kathy's suggestions keep coming. *Ipomoea* is big, especially *I. batatas* Blackie, or sweet potato vine, a plant with purple foliage that shows off well with other hot numbers like chartreuse *Helichrysum* Limelight and *Verbena* Homestead Purple. And don't overlook *Gomphrena haageana* Aurea, or globe amaranth, with apricot pompon-like blossoms that make lovely dried-flower arrangements.

There's also lantana, which has become a regular in my garden — and not just because there's a variety called Irene. If you're just inching over the line from impatiens and geraniums to the new world, you might find comfort in *Zinnia linearis* White Star, a low-maintenance, disease-resistant creeper that loves hot weather. And you can go wild with *Petunia integrifolia*, a magenta-pink flower on trailing stems that never needs dead-heading.

Finally, Kathy recommends an upright fuchsia called Gartenmeister with coral-pink tubular blooms and dark foliage that likes shade and "blossoms like crazy." And guess what? It mixes perfectly with white or salmon impatiens.

Arctotis **or South African daisy is one of Kathy Pufahl's favorite, easy-to-grow annuals.**

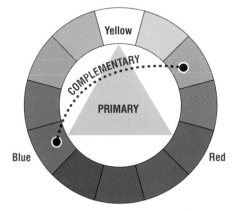

Color Wheel

Primary colors are red, blue and yellow. Secondary colors -- green, orange and violet -- are created by mixing pairs of primary colors in equal amounts. Complementary colors are opposite each other on the color wheel and make bold partners. Analogous colors are adjacent to each other and have a gentler relationship. Pastels and whites perk up shady areas. Hot hues like yellow seem closer than they are; cool shades like blue appear to recede. Use plants with silver leaves or cream-colored flowers to separate clashing colors and bring harmony.

When Flowers Bring Memories

The Japanese cherry tree behind the house has finished blooming but its petals still cover the patio. I hate to sweep them up, not only because they extend the splendor of the tree in flower but because they carry meaning beyond their beauty.

It is not simply the tree in bloom that touches me. It's not just what it stands for in my yard; it's what it stands for in my life. When the tree turns pink, a door opens onto two special Sundays of springs past.

One was my husband's 65th birthday, when his children gathered and his friends sang and I played the accordion — an instrument I usually keep buried among the ghosts of my childhood — and read entries from a diary his mother kept when he was a little boy.

The other moment was a brunch for breast cancer survivors I had written a book about. They were my sisters, brave and gracious and caring, and they sat on the patio beneath the pink curtain of the flowering cherry tree and celebrated life.

The special flowers of our own times are there for all of us. They bring back whole moments and the thoughts and feelings that created them. More than that, they can bring back people.

Snapdragons remind me of Slavko Krause, the neighbor who must have been a farmer-gardener in his native Yugoslavia and who nurtured his devotion to the land in the small patch of earth he tended next to my family's house in Bridgeport, Conn. He had an impressive compost pile but it was his snapdragons that gave dimension to Slavko — a bald man with glasses who wore plaid flannel shirts and let my sister and me play in his yard where a hillside glowed with the tall and fragrant flowers.

And there are times when all I have to do is walk past lilacs on a warm spring day and I see my grandmother. A tall lilac bush grew in our backyard in Bridgeport. None of us were gardeners — on the contrary, we were plant philistines who even made fun of Slavko's compost pile because we didn't know any better — but my grandmother loved the lilac bush and was constantly cutting blooms and bringing them inside. I can see her now with the flowers in her hand — a heavy woman with white hair who wore black sensible shoes and called me by my Hungarian name, Irénke.

I have a lilac bush along my driveway. We did some serious pruning, but the shoots are green now and I know the blossoms will return.

It's the same with another plant in my yard, a groundcover, actually. I'm waiting for the sweet woodruff to send up its tiny white flowers. They're even more than memories — they're keepsakes.

A few years ago, a lovely lady named Lorraine Pollitt showed me around her garden and gave me her recipe for making May wine with sweet woodruff. She also shared her friendship. And she gave me a pot of sweet woodruff to plant. Lorraine died of cancer a year after I met her. I have yet to make the wine, but the potful has grown into a sizable patch in the shade garden.

It is nice, perhaps, to press flowers in books, but it is the ones we press in our hearts that matter most. We planted rose of Sharon last year and when it bloomed my husband stood in front of it and smiled a smile that was almost that of a child.

He told me rose of Sharon grew on a trellis outside the small home in Queens where he grew up. He had barely moved into the house when a neighborhood bully accosted him beneath the trellis and called him a "Jew ———" and punched him in the face. It is not an easy memory, but then life is not always easy either. My husband endured and so did the rose of Sharon. "I still loved to stand beneath the trellis," he told me. "And I learned to fight back."

Delphiniums take me back to my junior year of college at the University of London. My dormitory was in a working-class neighborhood whose drabness was relieved by small frontyard gardens where blue delphiniums stood out. The red and pink hibiscus plants that summer in pots on our patio steps are a reminder of our annual Christmas get-away to Bermuda, where the flowers bloom in hedges year-round.

And part of the joy I take in the daffodils and tulips that dance around our house in spring stems from the memory of a trip to Holland when I saw the tulip fields that grow not far from the North Sea and visited the famous Keukenhof gardens, where bulbs of all kinds bloom across acre after acre.

The trip ended in Amsterdam, where we visited the Van Gogh museum and saw paintings we'd never seen before and strolled in the flower market along the canal and walked in the rooms where Anne Frank found a way to embrace life. We thought about love and hate and life and death and the ugliness we should never forget. And we thought, too, about all the places where beauty grows.

In the author's garden, the
Japanese cherry tree is a
reminder of special moments.

47

Color Coordinated

"**Y**ou'll know the house when you see it," Nancy Angermaier tells me. We're talking on the phone and I can almost hear her smile. I understand why the minute I spot the white gingerbread cottage in Bay Shore with the purple trim and the purple porch and the purple house number — and the garden to match.

The truth about Nancy is all out there. And then she comes through the purple front door and makes the point in person — she's wearing a lavender dress and white sneakers with purple laces. You've heard of the lady in red and the woman in white. Meet Nancy Angermaier. Or as she's known to her friends: "Purple Nancy."

Purple is a passion that dominates the decor of Nancy's life inside and outside. "I love anything as long as it's purple," she says. Which means just that — anything from a cutting board to a compost bucket or a couch to a candlestick. We'll get to the garden soon, but her 100-year-old house is a study in the secondary color born of the union of red and blue.

The velvet couch in the living room is precious in purple and the wooden floor in the kitchen is painted purple. Nancy has purple pot holders, purple picture frames, purple bath towels, purple serving platters, purple curtains, purple rugs and purple walls. She uses purple paper clips and purple file folders and purple scissors. She even has a purple electric fan and a purple tea kettle and a purple yo-yo and a purple leather bar stool and a purple mouse pad. "I have drawers devoted to purple socks and purple shirts," she says, "and of course I have a special shelf for purple shoes. Sometimes I go purple shopping." Why am I not surprised?

Obviously, Nancy, a sign language interpreter for the New York City school system and a fledgling landscape designer, is no shrinking violet when it comes to her favorite color. It's all right there on her license plate — PURPLBCH, for purple and another of her passions, the beach. Purple is a bold, brave color that seems to fit her nature. She's a breast cancer survivor, and she'd like me to mention that she's single. Naturally, anyone who's interested had better like purple.

Nancy says her love of purple was part of a spiritual awakening that occurred 18 years ago after she went through a divorce. "I was on my own for the first time in my life, and I had to find out who I was. I found out I was purple. I just like the color. It makes me happy. It's a signature at this point."

Her autograph is all over the garden. It looks as if it was born to the purple in its various hues from lavender to magenta —with a dash of pink and a splash of white artfully blended in.

Nancy is a skilled gardener with a lot of ideas. She uses a rainwater collection system for irrigation, and she built raised beds for her vegetable patch out of recycled plastic lumber. Her compost bin is made out of the sides of a baby crib, and she grows interesting plants such as a eucalyptus tree — purple sage thrives beneath it — and a salad bowl of vegetables through the season, all of it flourishing in front of the purple and white shed that holds her purple-handled hoe and spade and several purple buckets. And she also raises artichokes in the shade of a purple umbrella.

The color theme carries across her sunbaked third of an acre. Purple whirlygigs and purple plant brackets. Purple patio furniture and, needless to say, a plethora of purple plants. "The first thing I did when I moved in five and a half years ago was tear up the lawn," Nancy says, "and the garden started to evolve. I'd been living in apartments, and I was thrilled to have dirt. I'd gardened as a kid in Merrick with my dad. I was the youngest of four and I was his helper."

As you might expect, she grows lavender lavender and violet violets and lilac lilacs. And more. Lavender crocuses and purple chionodoxa and violet tulips and amethyst hyacinths sing of spring. Then irises join the chorus — and alliums and phlox and tree peonies and delphiniums and daylilies and coneflowers and clematis chime in. I wish I had the bower of wisteria that shades her front porch. Of course, first I'll have to get a front porch.

Come summer, a groundcover of ice plants spills starry purple pink flowers over a rock wall that Nancy built herself. Ice plants remind me of my annual Christmas vacation in Bermuda, and I'm especially partial to the *Verbena bonariensis*, a self-seeder with lilac-colored flowers and willowy stems that I grow in my own garden.

A dark pink canna strikes a pose next to a clump of purple fountain grass known botanically as *Pennisetum setaceum* Rubrum. Purple butterfly bushes dance near pink rose of Sharon and white cosmos and purple *Platycodon*. And along the driveway, morning glories and passion flowers and clematis are true to the color scheme. So is *Malva sylvestris*, with its purple and white blossoms. The giant purple-black leaves of taro provide a tropical note.

Seasons come and go, but purple is practically forever. By September the fading lavender blooms of love-in-a-mist will seem wistful near a vigorous *Ipomoea* Blackie, a sweet potato vine that is such a deep purple it verges on black. As autumn advances, purple asters will stand bold against a backdrop of white Montauk daisies. And there's double-blossomed *Datura*, a fragrant and spectacular flower more commonly known as angels' trumpets. She's not sure of the variety name but says, "I stopped dead in my tracks when I saw it. It has three shades of purple."

So it goes in Purple Nancy's garden. I'm almost disappointed that she doesn't have a purple cow. In any case, I can't resist fooling with the silly verse that a rhymster named Gelett Burgess wrote a century ago.

> I never saw a purple cow,
> It's not a thing I'd fancy;
> But I can tell you, anyhow,
> It's just the thing for Nancy.

Nancy's passion for purple blossoms everywhere — in front of her gingerbread cottage at left; top, in a cozy spot in her side yard; center, in a bouquet of fresh-cut flowers; bottom, in a border where other bold colors accent her favorite shade.

Keeping History Alive

T here is a sense of timelessness about Marjorie Kern's garden. Time past merges with time present and runs into time to come. The garden unfolds on the very tip of Kings Point, where Long Island Sound meets Manhasset Bay. Sands Point sits to the east and the Throgs Neck and Bronx Whitestone Bridges cross the horizon to the west. Earth and water embrace like spring and summer. The house and grounds share the mood. The house was built before the Civil War by John Alsop King Jr., a prominent financier and the king of Kings Point.

In the 1920s, the estate belonged to Richard Church of Arm & Hammer baking soda fame, who threw a party for the whole village every Fourth of July with fireworks bursting from barges. Marjorie Kern believes F. Scott Fitzgerald must have found inspiration here for "The Great Gatsby" — that he may have been thinking of the place known as The Point when he wrote of a marble pool and of blue gardens where "men and girls came and went like moths among the whisperings and the champagne and the stars." And where James Gatz who wanted to make today out of yesterday stared across the water at Daisy Buchanan's green light.

"But when the movie people came to look the place over they decided it wasn't grand enough," Marjorie says, remembering when the 1974 film was in the works. "They used one of the 'cottages' in Newport instead. Oh, I would have loved having Robert Redford around the house."

The Point whispers of the past, the history of a family and of a time remembered. Marjorie's parents, the late Herman and Sybil Brickman, bought the waterfront estate in 1947. Herman Brickman was an industrial arbitrator and accomplished sportsman, and a photo gallery on a corridor wall shows tennis greats Sidney Wood and Don Budge and Alice Marble holding their rackets. In another photo, Marjorie's then young sons, John and Russell Handler, greet Eleanor Roosevelt; she has come to The Point as the guest of honor at a benefit for the Wiltwyck School. A collection of glass paperweights and English and Italian china and a glittering chandelier contrast with snapshots of Marjorie's grandchildren and an embroidered cushion that says,

"One who plants a garden, plants happiness."

Just beyond a baby grand piano, a door opens into an enchanted conservatory where Marjorie plants happiness. Clivia shows off bright orange blooms, and a grapefruit tree stands next to a cut-leaf philodendron with thick mottled bark that looks like snakeskin, and a Norfolk Island pine threatens to break through the glass ceiling. Marjorie Kern — a tiny woman with pale blond hair and glasses who is wearing a short green skirt and high white boots — reaches in among the scented geraniums and picks up one of her horticultural specialties. It's a living wreath that she made years ago out of sedums.

Marjorie does much more than make wreaths out of living plants and herbs. She's a Renaissance woman of the garden, a woman who studied with Margaret Mead and was a bona fide Martha Stewart before Martha Stewart invented herself. Who makes dried flower arrangements and her own potpourri from the heirloom roses in her garden and starts foxgloves and petunias and salvia from seed and grows dandelions, organically, for salads and lectures on everything from the history of herbs to edible flowers and orchids.

"Herbs are my strong point," she says. She discovered them years ago when she studied the Elizabethan era and found that Elizabeth I was 69 years old when she died. "That was quite old for those days," Marjorie says, "especially with typhus and such diseases and no antibiotics, and I wondered what did she do to survive so long. Well, she loved strawberries — and she was a devotee of herbs. She turned moats into herb gardens. And so I've made myself an ambassador of herbs."

All around the house that sits on the edge of the sea, herbs, azaleas and history rule. Great towering trees cry out to the past. A copper beech that John Alsop King had transported from Belgium and is the largest of its kind in the state. A weeping beech whose branches form a canopy for family weddings. And blue Atlas cedars that cast their color over the grounds and that Marjorie and her son John think inspired the blue lawns and gardens of Gatsby's mansion.

But it is the azaleas that dominate the landscape on this drizzly spring day that conjures up a soft and misty mood pregnant with the past. They are so rooted in this 18-acre estate, almost majestic and yet so fleeting in their pink and white and lavender loveliness. They form a living wall of color at least 8-feet-high at the end of an expanse of lawn. And they line a weathered marble path past the copper beech and the weeping beech and the tallest river birch on Long Island to the formal flower and herb gardens and the lily pond and beyond to the potager and the vineyards.

"Mr. Church planted the azaleas," John says as he reaches into a bush of pink blooms and unhooks a worn metal tag that reads "*Linearifolia* 1929." And his mother smiles. "Every day when the azaleas are in bloom I open the front door and I can't believe my eyes."

Azaleas are clusters of color throughout the landscape and they surround the aged marble swimming pool that waits to be filled with water. The Olympic-sized pool, built by Richard Church, consists of more than a million hand-laid squares of blue and white marble. Even empty, it is a work of art. John Handler and his wife and two daughters live in a cliff-mounted, many-windowed pavilion between the pool and the sea on the tip of Kings Point that follows the actual curves of the land's end.

Now mother and son point out peach, apple and fig trees and bloodroot and mint and borage and chives and the fading blooms of jonquils around the pool. And the glossy green leaves of more azaleas — a variety that will bloom magenta in June. The azaleas are a metaphor for the timelessness of Marjorie Kern's garden. "It is a privilege to live in a place where nature paints such a stunning picture every day," she says.

It is hard to know for sure where Scott Fitzgerald dreamed the dreams that led to "The Great Gatsby," where he first thought of the green light at the end of Daisy's dock and decided that James Gatz would come a long way to the blue lawns of West Egg — where he thought of all of us reaching for the future while we "beat on, boats against the current, borne back ceaselessly into the past."

But I look at the wind-tossed sea and the wall of azaleas and think that it could have been here — where earth and water embrace like spring and summer, and time past merges with time present and runs into time to come.

> *It is a privilege to live in a place where nature paints such a stunning picture every day.*

At left, Marjorie Kern at her Kings Point estate. Her azalea collection dominates the garden. Below, an azalea ready to bloom.

Anna Feile in the display gardens at the State University at Farmingdale.

Mother's Day With Anna Feile

The first time I met Anna Feile, my insecurities were showing. I was a fledgling tiller of the earth and she was the grande dame of Long Island gardening. And to make matters worse, even though she was 88 and used a cane to compensate for a hip injury, I could barely keep up with her.

This was on a drizzly spring morning a few days before Mother's Day at Atlantic Nursery and Garden Shop in Freeport — the place that was Anna's life's work. As our tour gained momentum, I tried to slow her down by asking her to name her favorite plant.

I think she saw through me but she smiled

and pointed in succession to a patch of purple pansies and yellow daffodils and a golden *Fritillaria* Crown Imperial. Then she shook her head. "Of course when the roses bloom," she said, "I think, oh yes, that's it — how could I have forgotten? — roses are my favorite. I've never come close to answering that question. Whatever plant is in bloom is my favorite. It goes on that way all through the season."

It went on that way all through the following Sunday when she answered the phone and offered advice on what blooms when and put out the ham and turkey sandwiches she made for her 50 employees like she always did on Mother's Day. It went on that way all through the more than 50 years that Anna Feile lived with plants and loved plants and sold plants at Atlantic.

Anna, who never married, had no children of her own, but she had nieces and nephews who loved her and the affection and respect of the Island's horticultural community. In a sense, her children bloomed all around her in the nursery she'd come to as a young woman from Germany so many years before.

On that wet spring day when I got to know her, Anna walked around the 2-acre nursery like a proud parent basking in the perfection of her progeny. She grinned back at the tulips and pansies and rhapsodized over the fritillarias. She admired the white blossoms of an andromeda and touched the evergreen branches of a dwarf eastern white pine that the late Jim Cross, a horticultural pioneer, had named after her.

"If I'd had the time, I could have been a good horticulturalist," she said.

"What do you think you are?" I asked.

"A good nurseryman," Anna answered. "A plantsman."

And then she laughed — and I knew I'd found a friend and mentor and something more in this small silver-haired woman with a smile as sweet as the flowers that filled her nursery. Anna Feile died in May of 1998 at the age of 90. I can think of no one in the garden world it makes more sense to remember on Mother's Day.

I admired Anna for her patience and her knowledge and for helping women of later generations — my own included. Anna would not have used the word to describe herself, but she was a feminist long before the term became popular. It was in 1940 that she came to help her brother Karl in his new nursery — a 40-foot-long strip along Atlantic Avenue. " 'Just for the spring season,' he said, but I fell in love with the work and never left."

If the nursery was love at first sight, Anna came to it with trepidation. She knew little about plants. "My mother gardened," she told me. "We had vegetables in the back and flowers in the front, but my brother helped her. I had the assignment of cleaning the house. I was in my early 30s when I came to the nursery, and in those days my hair, my nails, everything had to be just so. In those days, oh my, a lady didn't walk across the street without putting on a hat and gloves."

Before she knew it, Anna had exchanged her white gloves for garden gloves. Suburbia was in its infancy, and the system of growing and selling plants in containers had not yet revolutionized the nursery business. Every tree and shrub was balled and burlapped, every single annual and perennial was grown in the ground. Anna would walk into the field with customers and dig up the plants they selected and wrap them in newspaper.

"The problem was that they never wanted the one on the end of a row," she remembered. "You'd get a dozen petunias for 35 cents, and it was never the 12 plants growing right next to each other. No, it was this one over here and that one over there. And of course it had to be a baker's dozen and 'Oh Anna, you didn't count this little one, did you?' "

It testifies to Anna's strong sense of self that as times changed, she had no hang-up about politically correct labels. She thought of herself as a nurseryman. To Anna, it was the name of her profession. A profession that honored her. The Long Island Nurseryman's Association named her Nurseryman of the Year in 1968, and seven years later she was the first woman to be elected the group's president. She was inducted into the New York State Nurseryman's Association Hall of Fame in 1981.

And on her 90th birthday, the State University at Farmingdale gave her the Ram's Horn Award, the school's most prestigious honor, for her decades of dedication to the horticulture industry. They also gave her a birthday cake inscribed "Anna — the Fairest Rose of All."

I'll second that. Especially on Mother's Day when thoughts of Anna bloom in the garden.

"There's so much to learn," I told her on that day when we walked around her nursery in the spring rain.

Anna smiled. "Don't be afraid to take chances," she said. "The garden is a very forgiving place. And learn your Latin — you'll never be taken seriously if you don't know the Latin names of plants."

I take chances nowadays and I'm much better with the Latin. But I still wish Anna were around to help.

SUMMER

June

Like the poet — in this case James Russell Lowell — says, "What is as rare as a day in June?" Clematis and morning glories climb fences and trellises, and peonies astound me in their pink and red and white perfection. Phlox tiptoes across the borders of my flower beds, and rhododendrons come into their purple suburban majesty. But above all, June is the month when the queen of the garden reigns supreme, thorns and all. It is the month of grandifloras and floribundas, of ramblers and rugosas, of miniatures and hybrid teas. The sun ascends to the highest point it will reach all year, and the heat begins to still the afternoons of weeding and watering. As the sun bears down, the sweet smell of the rose signals the start of summer. I taste the joy of fresh peas and think how fortunate I am to be a gardener.

The Queen Of Flowers

For longer than I like to admit, I was intimidated by roses. If anyone had promised me a rose garden, I would have said forget it. Caught up in fear, I took an adversarial position. Sort of my own war of the roses. Not only were roses the royals of the garden, but they acted like it. They were all finicky, pampered, prickly, spoiled and demanding. If you didn't pay them constant fealty — fussing and fretting and dusting and spraying — they were likely to swoon and keel over. Or develop canker dieback, powdery mildew, crown gall or black spot. Or fall victim to aphids, thrips, spider mites,

J u n e

those roses that require molly-coddling, well, take a good look at them. They just may be worth the fuss.

Especially if you walk through a rose garden in June. If any flower is part of the life and legend of the garden, it's the rose. As everybody knows, roses are newly sprung in June and can be found in No Man's Land and Picardy and Washington Square. There's a yellow rose in Texas and a rose in Tralee.

Roses have been in cultivation for at least 500 centuries, and their ancestors existed ages upon ages ago. Fossils show that wild roses grew in what is now Colorado 40 million years ago, and botanists believe they were springing up in China at least 20 million years before that. The Greek poet Sappho called the rose "the queen of flowers." Confucius and Chaucer wrote about roses and so did Shakespeare and Yeats. King Midas counted roses as well as money — according to legend, he grew 60-petaled roses in his garden.

And the rose fancier I get the biggest kick out of was the Empress Josephine, who established the mother of all rose gardens on her estate at Malmaison in France. When she died in 1814, she had collected just about every known variety. Many of the roses we admire today were born in that garden. As the story goes, she always carried a rose so she could raise it to her face when she laughed. She wasn't being coy — she was hiding her bad teeth.

Roses have long been a standard of beauty — Chaucer wrote that Cleopatra "was as fair as is the rose in May." And there's the whole roses-are-red thing. If love, it is a flower, we all know what the flower is. There's nothing quite so romantic as a single rose from someone you love. Not that there's anything wrong with a dozen. I certainly found myself looking at the world through rose-colored glasses the day I got four dozen roses from Willie Nelson because he liked a story I had written about his second wife — or maybe she was his third. That was years ago in Texas, where everything is a little overdone, but I kept those flowers on my desk until they disintegrated.

My attitude about growing roses is very different now, although the change did not come all at once.

If there was a defining moment, I guess it was a day in June of 1996, when I went along on a rose-rustling expedition to an old cemetery in eastern Pennsylvania with Stephen Scanniello, the curator of the Cranford Rose Garden at the Brooklyn Botanic Garden. Stephen is a renowned authority on roses, but what impressed me most was his constant enthusiasm and his quickness to admit what he didn't know. "I haven't a clue," he said now and then as we explored the cemetery, where roses rambled over graying headstones, "but it's a lovely rose."

I learned a great deal that day, especially about old garden roses, which are also known as heirloom

From bud to bloom, roses are the standard of beauty in the garden.

scale or Japanese beetles. And if you handled them wrong, watch out — they drew blood.

I now realize that I was acting out of ignorance as well as fear. As is usually the case when such forces are at work, I was developing a prejudice — a bias against roses. A reverse snobbery stemming from a lack of knowledge and the right perspective. Certainly all roses require some care and feeding — proper planting and watering and fertilizing and sagacious pruning. There will always be high-maintenance roses, but easy-care varieties are also available for gardeners who want to grow the national flower in their own yards without prepping and primping. As for or antique or heritage roses. Maybe it was the faded look of the headstones combined with the seasonal glory of roses that grew before La France, the first hybrid tea, made its debut in 1867. And the old roses cascaded and billowed and looked like bushes instead of just standing around like skinny models showing off their perfect outfits. A lot of modern hybrids are bred for the size and color of their flowers and are not very fragrant. On that cloudy day in the cemetery, the scent of roses made me want to cry. It reminded me of my grandmother's perfume.

Other rose lovers inspired me. Like my friend, Nelson Sterner, director of horticulture at Old Westbury Gardens and one of the country's premier rosarians. Nelson, a "confirmed roseaholic," supervises the All-America Rose Selections trial garden right here in our own backyard at Old Westbury. It's more proof that Long Island is a hotbed of roses. There are close to a dozen classes each of old roses and modern roses, and new cultivars are developed all the time. Every year, major growers select their finest new roses for evaluation in 23 trial gardens set up by All-America Rose Selections Inc., a Chicago-based non-profit organization.

The Old Westbury garden is a half-acre plot nestled between the bluebell walk and the wildflower meadow. Each July and November, Nelson scores more than 200 roses. If you're a rose, getting an AARS medal is like winning the Miss America Pageant – you need more than just a pretty face. "We judge them on everything from the form of the buds and the color of the blooms to their fragrance and foliage, and their winter hardiness and disease resistance," Nelson says.

I also learned from growers like Marvin Eilenberg of East Meadow, who got tired of mowing his lawn and dug it up and replaced it with roses. Marvin's blooms are perpetual winners at the Long Island Rose Society's annual show in June at Planting Fields Arboretum. Or like Roseann Kozloff of Wantagh, whose majestic white Secret with pink edging won a King of the Show. "The thing is not to be intimidated by roses," she told me.

And I haven't been. I can't say everything is coming up roses at my house, but I'm taking chances. And playing it relatively safe, too. I've had good success with Flower Carpet roses, which were developed by a German breeder who put in 25 years perfecting disease-resistant hybrids. When it comes to pruning, one hard cut-back in late winter will do the trick. And they're highly resistant to black spot and mildew and don't require chemical sprays.

Last season, Flower Carpet Pink tumbled out of big terra-cotta pots on my patio. Flower Carpet White looked like just exactly that. And it had plenty of company. Soft pink Simplicity and its cousin, White Simplicity, which are floribundas that have to get by on

looks because they're only lightly fragrant. And Sea Foam, a creamy white rambler that makes a glorious ground cover. And then there was a delicate-looking rose called The Fairy, with pastel pink buttonlike flowers that were still blooming when russet leaves swirled on the ground and the earth grew cold.

Nearby, Bonica — which in 1987 was the first shrub rose awarded the AARS label — showed off with clusters of salmon-pink blossoms. And the corners of the fence were enhanced by tree roses — Winsome and Lights of Broadway and Jean Kenneally, a miniature with 22-petaled apricot blooms. Queen Elizabeth was regal on the fence's two arbors. A creamy pink rose grew in an adjoining bed. I found it in a nursery in Pennsylvania the day I went rose rustling with Stephen Scanniello. I can't find it in my books, but it's labeled Bride's Dream, and it's just that — I wished I'd known about it when I was getting married. I might have carried it down the aisle.

There are so many roses to choose from when you're planning a garden. Hybrid teas seem to be everybody's favorite modern rose because of their large flowers, but I'm partial to floribundas and climbers and shrub roses. Hybrid teas are beautiful but they can be finicky.

As for old roses, I'm fascinated by gallicas, which originated from an ancient wild rose that was a religious symbol of the Medes and Persians in the 12th Century BC. And romance books are spotted with mentions of damask roses, which are among the most fragrant of the queens of the garden. As befits their station, perhaps, they bloom only once a year and are exceptionally prickly. Something else you should know is that roses don't have thorns, they have prickles. A striped gallica called Rosa Mundi is named after Henry II's mistress, Rosamund. He hid her in a labyrinth, but his jealous wife, Eleanor of Aquitane, found her and had her murdered.

So many roses are testaments to people who are and were. There's Elizabeth Taylor and Princess Di and Princess Grace and Maria Callas and Catherine Deneuve and Gertrude Jeykll and Dolly Parton. Men, too, are remembered in roses — Victor Hugo and John F. Kennedy and Bing Crosby and Sir Walter Raleigh and Henry Hudson. Long after people forget there was ever a car called Chrysler Imperial, they may still know the rose. And it's nice to have a rose named Peace — a yellow and pale pink beauty referred to as "The Rose of the Century" that was shipped to America on the last plane out of France before the Nazis invaded.

So plant your roses while you may. And pause for a moment to reflect on this line from a poem by George Eliot: "I wish the sky would rain down roses." What a lovely thought.

Caring for Roses Month by Month

January
• Curl up by the fireplace with a good rose catalog and make your wish list. If you're thinking organic, try easy-care disease-resistant cultivars such as Simplicity, Bonica, Golden Showers, Carefree Wonder or Iceberg.

February
• Get ready to cut. Pruners should be sharp and well-oiled so they'll make neat even cuts. I love my Felco pruners. They're not cheap, but they're worth the price.

March
• When the forsythia blooms, it's time to prune. Remove all dead and diseased wood, as well as weak canes, and make your cuts at a 45-degree angle about a quarter-inch above an outward-facing bud.

April
• When you see a couple of inches of growth on your roses, you can remove winter mulch – but not before the middle of the month or your bushes might get nipped by a late frost.
• Take a soil test. The ideal pH for roses is between 5.6 and 6.6.
• Apply fertilizer early in the month and reapply every 6 weeks.
• Plant bare-root roses – remember, roses need 6 hours of direct sunlight a day. Soak bare-root roses overnight in tepid water, prune twiggy canes and trim roots.

1 Dig a hole 18 inches deep and wide, build a pyramid of soil and compost in the center and spread roots over the slope. Make sure the bud union is one inch above the soil. Backfill the hole by two-thirds, holding the plant in place and working soil around the roots.

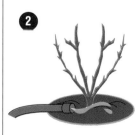

2 Fill the hole with water, let it drain, then finish backfilling and tamp down gently with your hands. Water thoroughly.

3 Mound 6 inches of soil around and over the plant to protect canes from drying out. When buds sprout, remove the soil mound.

May
• Mulch to conserve water, smother weeds and keep roots cool and moist. Use soaker hoses or a drip system for deep watering – your rose garden needs at least one to two inches of water a week. But make sure you water the soil, not the leaves. Wet foliage, particularly after sunset, encourages black spot and other fungal diseases.
• Plant potted roses anytime now through fall. Here's how:

1 Dig a hole twice as wide and deep as the container. Remove the rose from its pot and gently loosen roots. Position the rose in the hole so the bud union is an inch above the ground.

2 Backfill the hole and firm the soil with your hands.

3 Water and mound 6 inches of soil around the canes until growth begins.

June
• Enjoy your roses. For long-lasting bouquets, cut roses early in the morning. Have a bucket of water on hand and recut the submerged stem ends underwater. Whether you're collecting flowers to bring inside or deadheading faded blooms, cut the stem above the first 5-leaf cluster.

July
• If rose growers have a nemesis, it's the fungus known as black spot. This plague thrives in summer humidity. Prune out diseased portions, getting rid of foliage 3 to 6 inches from the ground and removing spindly canes. Soak pruners in bleach before using on other plants. Don't add black-spotted leaves or any other rose debris to the compost pile.

August
• Fertilize your roses for the last time by the middle of this month, no later than six weeks before the first possible frost.

September
• Stop deadheading on Labor Day.
• This month's cool nights and warm days are the perfect breeding ground for powdery mildew. Fight it with a homemade organic weapon – mix one tablespoon of baking soda in a gallon of water and add a few drops of horticultural oil or a splash of soapy water. Spray on infected foliage.
• Enjoy the autumn blooms of beauties such as Jardins de Bagatelle, Secret, Escapade and Gertrude Jekyll.

October
• Clean up beds and refresh your mulch to a depth of 2 inches: First, fold in this season's mulch to aerate the soil, expose hidden insect larvae to the cold and bury fungal spores deep under the soil surface. Then collect oak leaves, run a lawn mower over them and spread them around your roses.

November
• Another chance to plant bare-root roses. Mound topsoil around the canes of all newly planted roses up to about a foot high to protect against deep freezes and destructive winds. Give the same TLC to any established bushes that are weak or needy.

December
• Instead of dumping your Christmas tree, lop off the drying branches and lay them carefully over your rose beds once the ground has frozen.

Moving Away From

For weeks, I looked forward to seeing my rhododendrons in bloom. I watched the flower buds getting bigger and bigger. Swelling until bits of color peeked through. Finally, they're out. Color bearers in a pink and white and mauve parade marching around suburbia.

And I'm taking a second look at them. A hard look.

Doubt set in when I started talking to rhododendron fanciers. "I know what kind of rhododendrons you have," one told me. "You have those mauve things." To the cognoscenti, my mauve rhododendrons — known botanically as *Rhododendron* Roseum Elegans — are not very elegant. To put it in a pistil, they're plebian. The kind that developers plop down everywhere. The kind you probably have.

The experts were polite, but I could tell what they were thinking.

"Most homes on Long Island have Roseum Elegans," explained rhododendron hybridizer Frank Arsen of Lindenhurst. "Landscapers use them because they're cheap and easy to get and they grow fast — 6 to 8 inches a year. If you don't have a green thumb, plant Roseum Elegans — you can't kill it."

"There's nothing wrong with them," his wife, Gay, added amiably. "They're just so common. A friend called to tell me about a million-dollar house someone was building in Lloyd Harbor. 'Guess what they planted?' she said. 'No, don't tell me,' I said, 'not Roseum Elegans!' "

When the Arsens showed me their own plants, I realized the rhododendronites are not just sniffing in elitist disdain. If they sniff anything, it's apt to be a rhododendron aristocrat like Scintillation, which has a delicate fragrance as well as frilled, light-pink blooms with a faint white star and yellow-green speckles. And not a hint of mauve.

I sensed there was another world out there. A world rooted in history. Fossil records show rhododendrons reach back at least 50 million years. In 1800, only 12 species were being cultivated; today, there are more than 900 species and thousands of varieties.

It's a world now bursting with Windbeam, which has apricot-pink flowers that fade to pure white flushed with salmon, and Wheatley, with a light fragrance and rose-pink frilled flowers touched

with yellow-green in the throat. Or P.J.M., whose pinkish-lavender flowers show up early and whose small leaves continue the display by turning mahogany-copper in late fall.

A world that keeps 80-somethings Frank and Gay in bloom.

Frank, who planted nasturtium seeds in wooden cream-cheese cartons as a child in his native Astoria, and Gay, whose mother grew marigolds on their fire escape in Washington Heights, have been raising rhododendrons on their 60-by-153-foot property for more than 30 years. They also raised two sons, and Frank says the kids are fine, but "I get more satisfaction out of the rhododendrons."

The Arsens are longtime members of the New

Mauve

bookkeeper. The other was Gay Arsen.

Frank ran paternity tests to figure out the parentage of the sister seedlings. The responsible party turned out to be the yak's neighbor, a deep-pink rhododendron called Henrietta Sargent. By then, Frank was a committed hybridizer — learned in the art of emasculation, in which the petals are removed so the plant is no longer attractive to bees. And skilled in the science of hand pollination, in which the stamen, or male part, of one plant is placed on the pistil, or female part, of another plant to produce seed. This gets sticky, but we're talking about a real birds-and-bees affair.

Frank has made countless crosses since, producing trusses of many shapes and sizes and colors. If you want to move beyond Roseum Elegans, you should know that truss is the proper name for the flower clusters. It may not be poetic, but it is botanically correct.

June is a month for rhododendrons as well as roses, and Gay Arsens are blooming now in the couple's yard. As you might expect, rhododendrons should be planted in spring or fall. Gay recommends a spot that will get some sun — dappled shade is ideal. Since rhododendrons are shallow-rooted, do not bury them too deeply. And don't forget they like acid soil, so make sure the pH is in the 5.5 range. The hole should be twice the diameter of the root ball and the same depth. Mix in at least half as much compost and peat as soil, then set the plant in the hole at ground level so the delicate roots can breathe. Mulching is essential — Frank recommends shredded oak leaves, old wood chips or pine bark.

The best thing you can do for your rhododendrons now is pinch off the faded truss, which puts the plant's energy back into making flowers for next year. Then you can prune, if necessary. The Arsens prune their pink Scintillation and red GiGi into tree shapes, and for added attraction they underplant them with Solomon's seal, columbine, double bloodroot and hosta.

The couple will have rhododendrons flowering into August. "How could you see something so perfect and not say, 'I've got to have it?' " Frank says. "It's the growing of seed and the anticipation of the results that keep us going."

Frank and Gay Arsen live for next year's blooms. So should we all. It will keep us young.

York chapter of the American Rhododendron Society, and it wouldn't be unfair to call Frank a rhododendron patriarch. He's a hybridizer and has even created a floriferous beauty that blooms rose and fades to white and is named after the woman he's been married to for almost a half-century.

It happened in the 1960s, when Frank planted seeds from a rare Japanese *R. yakusimanum*. He expected the yak juniors to look just like their parent. But the bees in his backyard were busy pollinating. The seedlings that cropped up all showed variations. Two were so striking that Frank decided to name them. One was a pink lovely he called Agateen, named for a product of the lacquer factory where he was an assistant chemist and Gay was a

At left, Gay and Frank Arsen surrounded by the rhododendrons in their garden. Below, the multiple colors of rhododendrons in bloom.

These purple- and green-leaved basils are two varieties of kitchen herbs grown at Peconic River Herb Farm in Calverton.

The Wheel Of Herbs

It probably helped that it was a hot humid day when scents hung in the air like vapor. I was at Cris Spindler's Peconic River Herb Farm, and fragrance was all around me. I love herbs. Especially kitchen herbs, which tease the palate as well as tickle the nose. No wonder dill was once venerated as a charm to ward off witches, and sages in ancient Arabia associated the herb of that name with longevity. Marjoram was said to be treasured by Aphrodite, the goddess of love, and the very word "chamomile" makes me calm.

Herbs smell too good not to have magical properties. Anise, which the ancient Roman Pliny recommended as a powerful breath freshener if chewed in the morning, smells like licorice. Oregano smells like oregano. Or maybe like pizza. Mint smells like mint. And basil, well, basil smells — and tastes — like heaven.

Basil is probably my favorite herb — and not just because of its graceful green foliage or what it does for tomato sauce. Basil has genuine cachet. Its character is born of tradition. Basil is a sacred plant in its native India, and it's long been associated with romance. One old belief was that a pot of basil on a woman's balcony was a sure come-hither sign. Another was that all a man had to do was give a woman a sprig of basil and not only would she fall madly in love with him but she'd never leave him.

There are several varieties of basil, and Cris had a nice assortment on hand at her place in Calverton. Genoa Green, which is your basic basil for sauce and pesto. Lettuce-leaf basil with crinkly leaves for sandwiches. An All-America Selections winner named Siam Queen, which shows a pretty light lavender flower, and Rubin, a very productive red number. Not to mention Thai basil that smells like anise and African blue basil that's used in Indian cooking and dwarf varieties like Spicy Globe and Greek Mini that do well in containers. "The minis are so adorable," Cris said. "In Greece they're on everyone's windowsills."

At my house, basil and sage and rosemary and cilantro and oregano and thyme and dill fill an herb wheel in the center of my front-yard garden. The wheel is 8-feet in diameter and more than takes care of our needs. The location is sunny and the herbs thrive — the hardest part is remembering to keep cutting back the growing tips so the herbs don't flower and go to seed.

And in a larger sense, herbs grow in other places in the garden. I call them flowers, but what's in a name? The question of what is an herb is tackled in The Herb Society of America's "Encyclopedia of Herbs & Their Uses:" "Botanists describe an herb as a small, seed-bearing plant with fleshy, rather than woody, parts (from which we get the term 'herbaceous') ... In addition to herbaceous perennials, herbs include trees, shrubs, annuals, vines, and more primitive plants such as ferns, mosses, algae, lichens and fungi. They are valued for their flavor, fragrance, medicinal and healthful qualities, economic and industrial uses, pesticidal properties and coloring materials (dyes)."

Cris' definition is more succinct. She says an herb is "any herbaceous plant that has a useful purpose." That makes sense to me. In fact, many herbs are so integral to the flower garden that most of us don't even realize they were once monopolized by doctors and cooks. I'm thinking about plants like yarrow, lady's mantle, Russian sage, sweet woodruff, lemon verbena, lungwort, dame's rocket, anise hyssop, bee balm, foxglove, purple coneflower. Lavender is used for soaps and sachets and perfume and potpourri. A rose is a rose is an herb when it's dried for potpourri. Or used as an astringent or in bath oils. Of course, it takes 60,000 rose petals to make one ounce of the pure essential oil that goes into toilet waters and perfumes and scented soaps.

Then there are medicinal herbs like comfrey, which is used to soothe athlete's foot and insect bites. And don't forget dyer's herbs like angelica for green and Saint-John's-wort for red and tansy for yellow.

But I'm interested in the kitchen. I want my wheel to turn with culinary herbs. Before we put in the front-yard garden, I grew herbs in pots right outside my kitchen. Dill was at my doorstep, rosemary was in reach and thyme waited for me. The only time I had to go farther afield was when I wanted mint to flavor iced tea or garnish cold strawberry soup. Then I foraged among the mint forest that ran wild along my driveway. You should know that mint is more invasive than crabgrass, and my advice is not to plant it in the ground — not even in pots — but to confine it to containers or whiskey barrels.

It was hard confining myself to the usual choices at the herb farm. For instance, I got sage, but not just the garden-variety sage with its lemony, pleasant-ly bitter taste that perks up everything from poultry to potatoes. I also took home some golden sage, a showy little number with yellow and green variegated leaves — "use the leaves whole on pasta," Cris told me. And yes, I chose lots of Genoa basil, but I'm also trying lemon, cinnamon and purple basil. Purple basil sounds like fun — it turns pasta pink.

And, I threw in some nasturtiums. After all, you can eat them. The peppery leaves and pretty flowers, treasured in England centuries ago as a treatment for scurvy, are chock full of vitamin C. But I like them in soups and salads, and I'm going to try them on cheese sandwiches. You can use the seeds as substitutes for capers. And besides, a garden is a garden. They look terrific.

Chores Galore

STAKE dahlias, lilies, gladioli, cannas. Put up trellises or teepees for morning glories, moonflowers and other vines. Cucumbers and summer squash can also be trained to climb.

SHEAR back pansies, Johnny-jump-ups, petunias, creeping phlox and dianthus. It's the kindest of cuts — designed to help them bloom again.

DON'T forget to start seeds of biennials such as forget-me-nots and foxgloves as well as perennials like columbines and coreopsis. Sow in a cold frame or prepared seed bed and keep moist. They'll be ready for a permanent location in early fall.

BRING houseplants — except African violets — outside for a summer vacation. Let them relax in partial shade till they get used to the sun and wind.

PULL out early spring lettuce and arugula, add compost and resow with beets, carrots, beans, or heat-resistant looseleaf lettuce. Sow lettuce seeds every two weeks to keep the salad bowl full all summer.

DIRECT-SEED zinnias, sunflowers, tithonia, cosmos and dwarf marigolds for late summer color.

REMOVE faded blooms from spring-flowering bulbs, but let the foliage wither away on its own. This sends food back into the bulbs for next spring. Dig up and discard old tulips that were a disappointment.

MULCH flower and vegetable beds to cut down on weeds and conserve water.

PRUNE flowering shrubs — weigela, spirea, deutzia — as soon as they've finished blooming.

KEEP planting gladiolus corms all month for a summer-long show.

THIN carrot seedlings when they're 3 inches high. Thin again to about 2 inches apart when the tops begin to touch. Be ruthless, the survivors will flourish and fatten.

DIVIDE crowded clumps of primroses. Dig and divide overcrowded bearded irises. Carefully dig up the rhizomes and cut back the foliage halfway. Trim out soft, damaged or shrunken portions and replant in clusters. Don't bury the rhizomes — they should be partially exposed above-ground.

HARVEST fresh strawberries.

FERTILIZE peonies after flowers fade.

PLANT white alyssum or drifts of lobelia under your roses.

PICK Japanese beetles off roses, marigolds, flowering plums. Show no mercy. Drown them in rubbing alcohol.

PLANT zucchini seeds in mid-to-late June to avoid the attack of the killer squash vine borers.

Days of Vines & Roses

Above, among the many vines that decorate the garden, is the passion flower with its showy petals. At right, climbing rose and clematis.

When I was dealing with chemotherapy a few summers ago, my oncologist Paula Schwartz and I talked about more than breast cancer. We talked about Long Island delis and California resorts and friends and families. We talked about the dangers of diet sodas and HMOs. And we talked a lot about the joy of flowers. It made sense — we're both gardeners.

It was there in a world of blood counts and chemo drugs that I sensed the potential of a vine called mandevilla with gorgeous hot pink flowers. It's one of Paula's favorite flowers and her enthusiasm was contagious. After that, one vine led to another. Clematis climbed the fence and roses clambered over the arbors. Morning glory soared up the cedar obelisk in the center of the herb garden and passion flowers stunned me with their splendor.

Vines add a whole new dimension to the garden — up and away and over and about and around and around. They grow on picket fences and utility poles and stone walls and old tree stumps. They grow on arches and arbors and tepees and trellises. I just bought a new trellis handcrafted from cedar poles and wisteria branches. So I've been thinking a lot

about what I'll garland it with — and about vines in general.

Like clematis, which has been called the queen of climbers and has had a hold on gardeners for centuries. The ancient Romans grew it on the walls of their houses because they believed the blooms offered protection from thunderstorms. Its common name reaches back to a time when the pharmacist for Queen Elizabeth I cultivated clematis and, in deference to her majesty, called the flower lady's or virgin's bower. American Indians used the blossoms and leaves as horse medicine. And Thomas Jefferson grew clematis at Monticello.

The vine belongs to the buttercup family and its luscious flowers come in just about every color. With a little planning, clematis of one kind or another can bloom in your garden from spring to frost. But not all clematis are trellis material. Not if your trellis is only about 5 feet high like mine. The early blooming vanilla-scented *Clematis montana*, known as anemone clematis, reaches a height of 20 feet, and the sweet autumn clematis, or *C. paniculata*, tops even that — it can grow another 10 feet or more.

Clematis texensis with bell-shaped scarlet flowers is more in line with my thinking. The drought-tolerant species with fluffy seed heads in fall grows about 6 feet tall. I'm also considering white Henryi and lavender-blue Ramona, both hybrids introduced in the late 1800s, and *Clematis x jackmanii* with dramatic 6-inch purple blossoms that keep going in sun or shade until frost.

I didn't forget to start moonflowers — *Ipomea alba* — from seed this spring. Moonflowers are the nocturnal counterparts of morning glories — *Ipomea purpurea*. They open at dusk and perfume the evening with their sweet fragrance. By sunrise, the funnel-shaped flowers have closed for the day, leaving their cousins to bring glory to the morning. The genus *Ipomoea* offers other vines that take to trellises — cardinal climber with crimson pentagonal blossoms that hummingbirds adore and cypress vine with feathery leaves and star-shaped scarlet flowers.

And there are passion flowers. I write often of little miracles in the garden, but a passion flower in my own yard — wow! With showy petals, a corona of brightly colored filaments, and a raised stalk in the center of each flower that bears the ovary and stamens, the passion flower looks too perfect and complex to be real. For centuries it has been seen as an allegory for the Crucifixion — the stamen symbolizing the cross and the fringed corona standing for the crown of thorns. The stigma represents the nails that impaled Jesus and the red stains and five blood-colored anthers suggest his wounds.

The best known species of passion flower include *Passiflora caerulea* — a slightly fragrant blue beauty that is the parent of several hybrids. *P. alata* has four-winged stems, egg-shaped leaves and drooping bowl-like, carmine flowers whose coronas have purple, white and red zones. *P. x caeruleoracemosa* is a vigorous climber with 5-inch-wide flowers and *P. x alatocaerulea* has 4-inch-wide flowers that are pinkish purple and white outside and have white interiors and violet filaments.

There are more vines than I can mention. Perennial vines. Annual vines. Vines with tiny suction cups that cling to solid surfaces. Vines that reach out and grab hold with curling tendrils. Vines that twine their entire stems around a support. Vines with names like porcelain berry and love-in-a-puff and trumpet vine and black-eyed Susan vine and cup-and-saucer vine and goldflame honeysuckle and purple hyacinth bean. Not to mention flame flower and flag-of-Spain and canary creeper.

Like I said, I've been thinking a lot about which vine to choose for my new trellis. The trellis itself is so charming that I wasn't sure I wanted to cover it. Not unless I could come up with a knockout vine. And then I thought about the summer of my chemotherapy and my friend Paula Schwartz.

I just might try mandevilla.

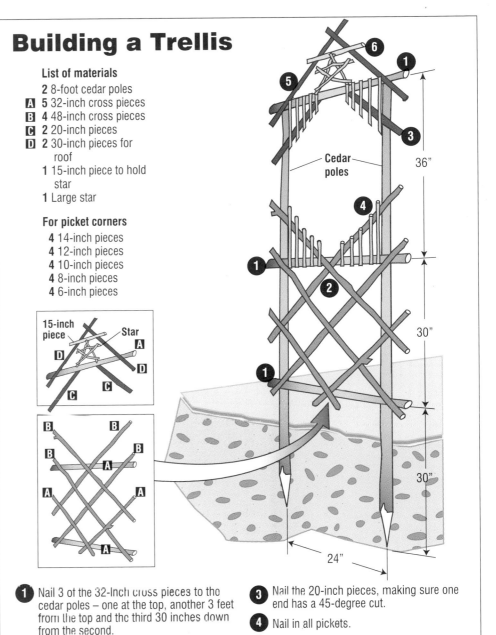

Building a Trellis

List of materials
2 8-foot cedar poles
A **5** 32-inch cross pieces
B **4** 48-inch cross pieces
C **2** 20-inch pieces
D **2** 30-inch pieces for roof
1 15-inch piece to hold star
1 Large star

For picket corners
4 14-inch pieces
4 12-inch pieces
4 10-inch pieces
4 8-inch pieces
4 6-inch pieces

Cedar poles

36"

30"

30"

24"

15-inch piece   Star

1 Nail 3 of the 32-inch cross pieces to the cedar poles – one at the top, another 3 feet from the top and the third 30 inches down from the second.

2 Nail two 48-inch pieces to make an X. Continue the lattice with the remaining 48-inch and 32-inch pieces.

3 Nail the 20-inch pieces, making sure one end has a 45-degree cut.

4 Nail in all pickets.

5 Nail on roof pieces. Place nails about an inch apart for stability.

6 Nail in 15-inch piece and hang star from it.

SOURCE: Laura Schneider

Green

About 20 years ago, Dan Koshansky threw some soil and a few cucumber seeds on his compost pile. It was just a whim, but it produced the best cucumbers Dan ever ate. The result was much more than a salad — it was an epiphany. Dan Koshansky turned into an organic gardener.

Today the retired Long Island Rail Road conductor has three compost bins going — not those fancy store-bought ones with plastic covers and turning handles but a simple 8-foot circle of green vinyl-coated fencing stuck in the ground. And his vegetable garden takes up a 50-by-50-foot plot in his side yard in Uniondale.

There are 20 tomato plants thriving in wire cages — Roma, Beefsteak, Big Beef, Husky Gold, Rutgers. There are 72 stalks of corn, 15 heads of cabbage, 10 heads of cauliflower, 12 asparagus plants, 30 heads of lettuce, 200 garlic stalks and one jalapeno pepper plant, because, as Dan observes, "who needs more?" There are onions, okra, beets, broccoli, bok choy, celery, lima beans, pole beans, peppers, two 50-foot-long rows of potatoes, eggplants, radishes, basil, parsley, fennel, coriander — and two strawberry patches. That's not counting the cucumbers, cantaloupes, pumpkins, zucchinis and honeydew melons he'll plant soon — or the peas and scallions he's already harvested.

The plants are green and healthy. And none of them has ever been touched by a chemical. Even the seeds came from organically raised plants.

All of which seems appropriate for an elder statesman of the Organic Gardeners of Long Island club who has been known to wear a T-shirt the color of broccoli that proclaims him "Green Thumb Grandpa."

"He starts in January and ends in December,"

Dan Koshansky with Simpson head lettuce from his organic garden.

Thumb Grandpa

says Mr. Organic's wife, Olga, who agrees there's nothing quite like a vine-ripened tomato or an ear of just-picked corn but who politely stays inside when Dan shows off his vegetable patch on a 90-degree day. "We're chained to the garden. You can't go anywhere. It's like having a pet ... Some women complain about being a golf widow or a baseball widow; well, I'm a garden widow."

Dan gets up at daybreak to labor among his vegetables just like he did when he was a kid on his father's 7-acre truck farm in East Meadow. But his approach is drastically different. "My father got cow manure from the dairy farms nearby, but he wasn't organic — he used chemicals."

And so, to tell the hard truth, did Dan. "Malathion, Diazinon, I forget the names now. But if you could spray it, I used it." Until the day of his epiphany at the compost heap.

"Those cucumbers were better than the cucumbers I was growing in my garden" — the ones that had been chemically fertilized and sprayed but were still plagued by beetles and aphids and squash vine borers. "I used all those poisons and still got bad results."

He never used them again. "It's not that hard to be an organic gardener," says Dan, who has even grown peanuts and cotton in Uniondale. "So you have to pick beetles off your lettuce. So the outer leaves of your cabbage get nibbled a bit. You have to learn to share with the bugs. You have to be philosophical."

Get your philosophy straight — then go after your bugs. Search the undersides of leaves for white cylindrical egg masses and crush them before they turn into hungry leafminers. Pick off that striped cucumber beetle munching your beans, that carrot beetle nibbling your beets, that June beetle stalking your strawberries, and then do what Dan does: "Step on it so it doesn't come back."

If you can't beat the bugs by hand, try organic controls. Dan's arsenal includes plant-based pesticides such as Rotenone, made from the root of a South American legume, and Pyrethrin, a natural derivative of pyrethrum daisies used to control a variety of pests like aphids and asparagus beetles. He also uses insecticidal soaps and horticultural oils and *Bacillus thuringiensis,* or Bt, a bacterium that kills caterpillars and the larvae of moths and butterflies without harming humans, honey bees or earthworms.

Slugs used to bring out the dark side of this soft-spoken church-going grandfather who keeps computer files on how his garden grows. He'd stalk the slimy devils with a chopstick-sized harpoon of his own invention. "Funny thing," he says. "I don't get that many slugs anymore." When he does, he treats them like beetles.

When corn borers or armyworms tunnel into those sweet-tasting ears, Dan suggests a tried-and-true homemade remedy. Apply a couple of dabs of mineral oil with a medicine dropper to the tip of the ear after pollination has occurred and the silk has turned brown.

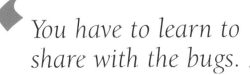

You have to learn to share with the bugs.

Finally, Dan nurtures his soil. "If you start with good soil, you won't have many problems." That's why he always has a batch of compost cooking — although he never turns his brew. In the spring and fall, he rototills the brown, crumbly compost into his garden. Afterward, he rakes in lime to sweeten Long Island's naturally acid soil. He doesn't mulch much unless he has a surplus of lawn clippings, but he always puts a mat of black plastic in his tomato beds. And he makes his own organic fertilizer — mixing one part each of cottonseed meal, ground rock phosphate and greensand with two parts each of bone meal and dried blood.

"You plant a seed, and you get a big bush, and then you get a half a bushel of tomatoes," he says. "A garden is magic. Why would you want to put poison on it?"

Memories Of Dad

Rain is falling on the small garden in Wantagh, where red roses climb a white trellis and purple clematis colors a stockade fence. The rain grays the sky and finds its way through the spreading branches of pine trees and drenches the pink and white impatiens beneath them. It battens down the yellow yarrow outside the front door and collects in the broad leaves of the hostas and soaks the vegetable beds along the side of the house. The rain would not have dampened Bill Tallman's spirits. If it was good for the garden, Bill was happy.

It seems fitting to remember Bill Tallman on Father's Day. Bill was a modest man and his garden is a modest garden. But its significance exceeds its borders. Bill died suddenly of an aneurysm in January of 1998, but he still lives in his garden. For his wife, Alice, and two daughters, Bill lives in every leaf and tendril and blossom. The garden he planted has been evolving ever since he moved into the small cape on a corner more than 40 years ago when the house was new and there was a cornfield at the end of the street.

For most of his life, Bill worked in an insurance office in Manhattan and he couldn't wait to get home to the garden. Over the years, he put in fledgling evergreens and a birch tree. He planted seedlings that grew into sheltering pines and a crab apple tree that announces spring with its blossoms. A rhododendron still blooms outside the window of the bedroom where his daughter Alice dreamed the dreams of childhood.

"My dad was always in the garden doing something," says Alice Ford of Wantagh, who is now grown up with two children of her own. "He'd cut the grass first thing Saturday morning and then we'd go to the garden center. There were always roses on the side of the house and fresh vegetables and strawberries."

Alice remembers how she and her younger sister, Dorothy Torres of Malvern, Pa., came to know the garden as a constant in their lives. She smiles. "I helped him pull the weeds. But I could never have a swing set or a sandbox or a swimming pool,

because that would take away space from the garden. He loved the feel of the earth. His parents had always rented, but this land was his to do with as he wanted and no one could take it from him."

Thunder rolls outside the house where Bill Tallman's wife and daughter look at photographs of gardens past and family parties, and read the journal that recorded what he planted and when. Like Bill was, the journal is understated — an account of the down-to-earth business of working the earth. "5/24 — Planted cukes and basil in Bed #2," reads an entry for 1997 in the last spring of his life. "5/26 — Planted: French yellow marigolds & red begonias in front circle; zinnias in front of bay window; rose-colored impatiens around clump of birch …"

Lightning flashes, the rain lets up. Alice Tallman puts on a jacket and leads the way into the garden where every plant is neatly labeled. Japanese anemone, dianthus, liatris, tithonia, nepeta, dwarf cannas. The garden is Bill's legacy. Through the dark winter that followed her husband's death, Alice had longed more than ever for spring and the reappear-

ance of the perennials she and Bill had planted.

"It was a comfort to me when the astilbes and hostas and hydrangeas started coming back," Alice says. "I couldn't wait to go out and put in the peppers and tomatoes, and I could feel his presence when I was out there working. I could hear him saying, 'Come on, Alice, it's time to get going.'"

It's not as easy for Alice to get going as it was when she and Bill nurtured the garden together. "I followed his lead. I know he wanted to root-feed certain plants this spring, but I didn't get to it. I guess they'll be okay for another year."

Life blossomed when Bill retired in 1987. He took the master gardener class through the Cornell Cooperative Extension of Nassau County, and then Alice followed his lead. Gardening branched out beyond the plot in Wantagh. The Tallmans worked the phones for the extension's plant information center, giving advice to the horticulturally confused. They conducted soil tests and plant clinics at flower shows and other extension events. And with a small group of other master gardeners, they tended the greenhouses at Nassau County Medical Center, where every year they started thousands of geraniums and other annuals by seed for the hospital auxiliary to sell.

In 1993, the tall, white-haired man received the extension's first Master Gardener of the Year award. In return for their training, master gardeners give back 150 hours of volunteer service. By 1997, Bill had clocked more than 1,000. On a warm spring afternoon a few months after Bill's death, his fellow master gardeners gathered at the extension gardens in Plainview and dedicated a bench in his honor. "In Memory of William Tallman, Dedicated Master Gardener," the plaque says. The bench faces the rose garden, and a birdbath and a rose-shaped stepping stone were placed nearby.

But he will be remembered most in the small garden in Wantagh, where his grandson Sean is playing in the rain. Sean is only 2. His 5-year-old brother, Kyle, wants to plant a tree in the garden where he worked with his grandpa. He has a little trowel and a pair of garden gloves Bill Tallman bought him.

It's Father's Day and life goes on in the garden.

Above, Bill Tallman donating his time at the Nassau County Medical Center greenhouses. At left, Alice Tallman, her grandson, Sean Ford, and daughter, Alice Ford, cultivate the garden Bill left behind.

July

The dog days of summer are upon us. According to the ancients, they stem from the heavenly journey of Sirius, the dazzling Dog Star. Their belief was that as the sun begins to decline after the summer solstice, it gains new power from Sirius. Here on Earth, the dog days are synonymous with the season's warmest weather — when even gardeners heed Noel Coward's admonition that only mad dogs and Englishmen go out in the noonday sun. But it's lovely in the morning and in the fading afternoon as the blooms of summer hold us enthralled.

In July, the fireworks are in the garden as well as the sky. Pink hollyhocks and sunny Heliopsis flash and sparkle. White baby's breath ignites gently and Sweet William shoots red and pink and white traces across the yard. And in the evening after the heat of day, it's a wonderful time to stay on the patio as the barbecue coals turn to ashes and fireflies light up the dark and the sun fades into night.

July

The Garden of Health

I wish I could have known my husband's parents, who both died before we were married. He says they would have liked me. He's sure they would have gotten used to the fact that I'm a year younger than my oldest stepdaughter and that I'm not Jewish. The only thing he's not sure of is how they would have reacted to the time and money we've put into re-landscaping our yard.

"They'd probably go into shock," he says. "I can just hear them — 'The two of you spend money like it grows on trees.'"

Actually, trees were part of the package. Three river birches and a Kousa dogwood and a crape myrtle. My husband said his parents never bought so much as a houseplant in their lives. "When I bought my first house, my father said I should get some nice bushes," my husband told me. "He said I should go along the parkway at night and dig them up."

We could have had our kitchen remodeled for what we've spent on re-landscaping and had enough left over to start on the bathrooms. We could have — and probably should have — taken out a home equity loan to redo the yard.

I tell you this not to extol our ability to spend money but because it says something about what our garden has come to mean to us. I think about this on a bright July day when our garden is at its best. I think that when my husband kids about how his parents would have reacted, he's expressing his own wonder at what we've done and where we are.

We began a few years ago by undermining the very bedrock of suburban landscaping. We pulled out all our foundation plantings — the yews and arborvitae and ilexes and rhododendrons and azaleas that surrounded our 45-year-old house. Sure, the Roseum Elegans that shrouded the den windows were mauve majesties in spring, but I could barely see beyond them to the freshwater pond that ripples at the edge of our backyard. And the view from our picture window was a collage of evergreens.

The diggers arrived on a May morning. When they were done, more than 100 shrubs stood in a long green line along our driveway, their roots encased in burlap. I looked at their ranks and thought that at the very least I had liberated my house from an occupying army. For the first time in the five years we had lived there, we saw what our foundation looked like. It was below grade.

We knew from the start that we needed professional help and we found it in the person of landscape designer Conni Cross. We liked her because we'd seen her own garden. Because she and my husband told each other their life stories five minutes after we'd met. And because she didn't overwhelm us with complicated sketches. Conni carries her blueprints in her head.

We made a wish list of all the things we would do with our yard if money really grew on trees. "We love each other and we love our yard," we wrote, "and we want it to reflect that."

"Nothing elaborate," we wrote. "Just a simple wonderland."

Conni found new homes for all the displaced shrubs around the periphery of our front yard. The new look was natural and informal — the beds curved and asymmetrical. Shrubs ran along the sides and front of the lawn and shaded the front in a graceful scallop. We had privacy from the road, but we could see out the picture window. The river birches and the Kousa dogwood graced the front border. The crape myrtle stands right by the gate to the backyard, reminding us of the streets of one of our favorite cities, New Orleans.

Meanwhile, back at the foundation, extras we hadn't counted on suddenly seemed necessary. We regraded and built a low stone wall about 10 feet from the house. We installed a drip irrigation system with a control box that looks like the bridge of the Starship Enterprise. To help with the drainage, we installed a dry well. We went for a small koi pond. And in the back of the house, we remodeled the patio — replacing rotting railroad ties and crumbling brick with stonework and redesigning steps to provide more space for large flowerpots.

As that summer was ending, new plants took their place in the back-of-the house beds that were once home to pond-blocking behemoths. *Anemone japonica* Honorine Jobert bloomed white near the silvery silhouettes of Russian sage. *Sedum* Autumn Joy deepened to russet and greeted the fall. And in

and Joy

the front, dwarf azaleas and rhododendrons stood amid slow-growing evergreens. And a special boxwood — *Buxus sempervirens* Graham Blandy — propagated by Conni's late husband, horticulturalist Jim Cross, stood proudly. Conni hugged the boxwood when it was planted, and we make sure it gets a lot of love.

The following season, we took Step 2. We put what money we had left where our hearts were. We dug up a 40-by-40-foot section in the center of our front lawn and replaced it with a vegetable and flower garden. It was planted in the early summer of 1997 when I was fighting the wild seed in my own body. I'd had my lumpectomy and I was undergoing chemotherapy. In a summer that was not without sadness, the garden in my front yard stood for tomorrow — for crops to come and flowers to bloom. We named it the Garden of Health and Joy.

From the start, our new garden had a lot going for it. Sunshine pours down like golden rain and we have excellent soil. "You have great soil," Conni told us. "I'd kill for your soil." I was very proud of my dirt.

The design is simple — an herb wheel in the center, four vegetable beds around it, a border of flowers like cosmos and cleome and Oriental lilies and asters and phlox and salvia and snapdragons for cutting, a 4-foot-high green picket fence with vines growing along it and an outer border of roses and baby's breath and more salvia. There are pine bark paths, and arbors where climbing roses grow. And a cedar obelisk that my stepchildren bought their father for his birthday. The obelisk stands in the center of the herb wheel. Passion flowers and morning glories grow up the tower and an irrigation pipe runs through it. Twice a week, the spray head rises out of the obelisk and waters the whole garden. Sometimes, we turn it on manually to entertain guests or just to amaze ourselves.

Full sun and water and rich soil have conspired to create little miracles in a garden that grows by leaps and bounds and bounties. Hibiscus flowers as big as dinner plates, hollyhocks taller than I am and lacecap hydrangeas as blue as a summer sky. The marvel of mandevilla and clematis. The scent of lavender. The fuschia flowers of gomphrena and the red and green leaves of Swiss chard. Peas and lettuce and bush beans and tomatoes in an abundance I can barely believe.

I sit in the garden sipping tea and the morning sun reminds me of the light of Southern France on a day when my husband asked me to marry me and I said

"uh-huh" and our lives rooted together through days of rain and days of roses. Butterflies come to visit and I have seen hummingbirds among the flowers.

By October of the year we planted the garden, I had finished chemotherapy and radiation. The following summer, the garden was even more verdant. I am a breast cancer survivor. The phantom stirs fear every time I go for a checkup but I cling to my tomorrows. I cherish my Garden of Health and Joy.

I think about what my husband and I wrote about wanting our garden to reflect love.

It does. I suspect his parents would approve.

At left, a quiet place to sit amid the flowers. Top, Belgian block defines the garden beds. Above, the garden in bloom.

Some Like It Dry

The sweltering days of summer are upon us and all over Long Island plants are wilting in the heat. Leaves are turning yellow; flowers are thirsty. But not in a small garden at the Cornell Cooperative Extension of Nassau County, where drought is no blight. I'm talking about the extension's xeriscape garden.

Xeric plants are by nature drought-tolerant. The name — pronounced as if the first letter were a "z" — is derived from the Greek word xeros, meaning dry. Xeriscape gardening comes down to water conservation, or what my friend Richard Weir calls "good, common-sense horticulture." Richard is the extension's horticulture educator, and xeriscape is one of his fields of expertise.

The whole idea of the special demonstration garden at the extension's headquarters in Plainview is to see how well plants get along with little more moisture than what comes naturally from above. So these scorching days are a real test. A few plants are having some problems, but most of them are passing with flying colors. I thought you might find their report cards interesting and get some ideas about drought-tolerant plants you'd like to try in your own garden next season.

It's a hot July morning as Richard and I stroll through the xeric garden. My immediate thought is that anyone who doesn't believe in xeriscaping is all wet. The garden looks as if it's been under regular irrigation, which, of course, it hasn't.

"Everything looks good," Richard says with a certain pride. But he points out that the plants have been given a good grounding. As with any garden, soil preparation is paramount — starting with compost to make the soil more porous and mulch to improve moisture retention. A generous heaping of organic matter — 6 to 8 inches — is rototilled into the planting beds, and the garden is mulched to the rafters with cocoa or buckwheat hulls.

"There's a presumption that you can just stick a xeric plant in the ground and forget about it," Richard says. "That's not so. All plants need water until their root systems are established."

It's clear right away that the plumbago, or *Ceratostigma plumbagnoides*, is very well established. The brilliant blue flower clusters next to the bright green leaves are stunning. I know from my own garden what a treasure this plant is — I have it in a sunny shrub border with variegated euonymous and boxwoods, and I also grow it in pots on my somewhat shady patio. "Sun or shade, it's the best ground cover there is," Richard says. And it will go on well into fall.

A *Euphorbia* called Chameleon is nearby. The euphorbia's purple leaves and specks of yellow-green flowers looked terrific so near the lemon balm, or *Melissa officinalis* All Gold, an herb that certainly enhances a perennial border. And Chameleon is not just another pretty face — it reseeds itself without getting weedy. It's also set off by the narrow dark green leaves of *Saponaria lempergii* Max Frei at its feet. In June and July the perennial *Saponaria* is a mass of clear pink flowers that don't need deadheading.

To my eyes, the standout in the xericscape is the *Agastache*. I like each of the three types that Richard shows me. The licorice-scented blue-flowered species *A. foeniculum* known as anise hyssop that is a native of the dry, sunny Southwest; Firebird, with willowy foot-tall spikes of coppery flowers, and Tutti-Frutti, with scented gray-green leaves and raspberry-red blooms.

If the *Agastache* is thriving, I'm wilting. The heat is making me dizzy. Sweat runs down my back and I pull my hair into a ponytail. I wish I could look as cheery as the *Melampodium*, which Richard calls a "proven winner." Just a decade ago it wasn't even known in this country. It's a daisy-like annual that comes from Mexico, which should tell you something about its xeric nature. It made a big splash in Plainview this season. "A good tough plant," Richard says. And he recommends another toughie: Aztec Sun, a new cultivar of the smoldering Mexican sunflower *Tithonia roundifolia*.

Richard can't help singling out a shrub called Spanish broom, or *Spartium junceum*, even though its blooms are gone. "We lost part of it this winter," he says, "but it came back with a vengeance." The golden-yellow wisteria-like flowers bloomed throughout April and May. "The flowers were so wonderful and heavy we had to stake it."

There are other success stories. *Laurentia* Blue Stars, an annual that looks just like its variety name, and *Portulaca* Sundial Peach — a 1999 All-America Selections winner. *Gaura lindheimeri* Siskiyou Pink, a summer-long bloomer, and *Anagallis monelli* Skylover with blue, saucer-shaped flowers. *Viburnum*

Conoy, a shrub with a springtime show of white flowers, and a barberry called William Penn with arching branches and lustrous leaves that turn bronze even though it's an evergreen.

I can't keep my eyes off a bold beauty sprawling along the border's edge. With its paper-thin yellow flower, the plant resembles a poppy, but it has prickly foliage like a thistle. The plant list in the garden guide identifies it as *Argemone*. Richard got the seeds from the Royal Horticultural Society in England, which described it simply as "a dry-loving plant." And that's what *Argemone mexicana* — with the perfect common name of prickly poppy — has proven to be. "It was so thrilled with the drought," Richard said, "it grew by leaps and bounds."

And he gives straight A's for *Angelonia*, which sure looks like a class leader to me. Last year the purple variety was impressive — the blooms went until frost without deadheading. This season the white is a knockout. The cup-shaped flowers, which should do well in containers, show no signs of stress. "It speaks for itself," Richard said.

I answered with a nod. After an hour in the garden where water is a controlled substance, my throat is parched. I race to my car and jack up the air conditioner. I twist open a bottle of Poland Spring that I've brought along in a cold pack and guzzle the icy liquid. It's not easy being xeric.

At Left, *Argemone* thrives in a dry spell. Above, a colorful border shows that xeriscapes can be beautiful.

77

A Fluid Landscape

Above, a cedar bridgewalk leads across the pond to the front door.

A small stream runs through the woods and becomes a waterfall that tumbles down huge rocks, hesitating in three basins on the way and finally falling into the pond. The day is blazing and humid, and the tree-shaded waterfall and the shimmering pond are cool just to look at. Mossy rocks nestle along the edges of the water and the bushes that surround it are mirrored in its depths. A chipmunk scurries into the shelter of the large trees nearby and dragonflies dance above the water.

Baby fish feed in the bogs at the edges of the pond, safe from the gluttony of their larger companions. There are dozens of big fish, a species of carp known as koi, and they dart and flash through the pond like parts of a constantly changing kaleidoscope.

The pond is soothing in summer. But it is easy to imagine it in other seasons — reflecting the azaleas and rhododendrons of spring, filled by the russet leaves of fall, silvered by the frost of winter. With oaks and evergreens running up a nearby hillside, the pond is the very embodiment of a forest oasis.

But the tall stand of bamboo at the head of the pond grows out of four giant white pots. The crosswalk of large stepping stones that seem as if they're floating in the water are actually attached to concrete-filled Sonotubes anchored in cement. A biological filter hidden by rhododendrons and azaleas feeds the 20-foot-long stream and the 7-foot-high falls with 5,000 gallons of water per hour. The mossy rocks and the boulders along the shore are part of a 40-ton shipment trucked from New Jersey. The four bogs strategically situated around the pond were built by hand and filled with soil and sand and gravel to accommodate hardy aquatic plants like parrot feathers and lizard tails and pennywort.

And the staggered cedar bridgewalk held in place with plastic wood leads to the front door of a white stucco contemporary home in Muttontown. This serene waterworld is a 20,000-gallon paradise in what used to be a sea of grass. It has replaced a suburban front lawn.

The very concept is calming. Where power mowers once droned, fish splash. Talk about refuges from the tensions of traffic and the bustle of daily life in the 'burbs — even on the gilded North Shore. It is what koi pond owners like me dream of. By comparison, the 400-gallon pond bordering my brick front walk is a puddle — one, I might add, that comes with two fat goldfish, three Israeli koi, a water-

fall with a 3-inch drop and a persistent leak. My husband and I enjoy showing it off to visitors whose landscapes are strictly terra firma. But standing on the stepping stones of this secluded sanctuary, all I could do was gape.

For me, the forested pond in Muttontown is the stuff of dreams. I pause on a stepping stone — there are nine, incidentally — and dream of doubling my little puddle so it would be just big enough for another koi or two, so I would have space for a bog where I could plant blue irises or marsh marigolds or water poppies.

Even then, of course, it would only be a teacup compared with the pond around me — with its

Above, a 7-foot-high waterfall cascades down moss-covered rocks.

July

rounded naturalistic shape that reaches a length of 40 feet and a width of 35 feet. It is 4 feet at its deepest point, more than enough to accommodate the koi that seem in constant motion. As you may know, koi are a special breed of carp developed by 18th-Century fish farmers in Japan. They're called nishikigoi or living jewels, and there are koi swim-

ming in international circles that are as valuable as precious gems. One rare koi sold in Japan a few years ago for $1.2 million.

Koi names are harder to pronounce than the Latin names of plants, and there are so many of the living jewels sparkling in the pond by the stucco house. There are red and white Kohaku, yellow gold Ogon Yamabuki, red and black Hi Utsuri, white and black Bekko, and Tancho, which is white with a red dot and is revered in Japan for its resemblance to the Rising Sun.

"Here's your ice cream," says a short, white-haired woman named Erika who has come out of the house to toss two pieces of whole-wheat bread into the pond. She explains the bread is a daily treat for the koi, which eat special fish food as their regular diet. The koi practically jump over each other and attack the bread with slurps and smacks. I remember learning that koi have teeth in the back of their throats and can crush snails and spit out the shells.

"We keep adding plants and fish," says Erika, who calls the house and pond home but prefers to remain anonymous. In the 20 years she and her husband, Hermann, have lived on the 3-acre property, they have transformed both house and grounds. They expanded the house from a two-bedroom cottage to a two-story contemporary, and they added a swimming pool and gazebos in the backyard and carved out rhododendron-bordered paths through the woods. But something was missing.

"I always wanted a little pond," Erika says.

In a moment of pure inspiration, Hermann suggested they place it on the front lawn. "My husband has the greatest ideas."

At which point they met Bob Bon Giorno, Long Island's koi king. At his Suburban Water Gardens in Dix Hills, Bob grows 20,000 aquatic plants a year and stocks about 3,000 koi — both American-bred and imports from Japan and Israel. He grows water hyacinths and water irises and water lilies and just about every other plant with the word water in its name — water clover and watercress and water lovage and water plantain. "I grow at least 100 varieties of water plants," Bob told me the first time I met him. "That's counting water lilies as one variety — there are 40 varieties of tropical lilies and 25 hardy varieties."

We were in one of Bob's greenhouses and he pointed out the hosta-like leaves of water plantain with white blooms that resemble baby's breath and the spiky cobalt-blue flowers of pickerel rush and the huge foliage of a hardy lotus with buds bigger than my fist. "There are almost as many water plants as there are terrestrial plants," he said, and he named a few more — zebra rush and blue reed and arrowhead and horsetails and parrot feathers and cardinal flowers and giant papyrus and umbrella palm.

So when Bob Bon Giorno met Erika and Hermann, he knew "it shouldn't just be a pond with a lawn wrapped around it." He saw the whole lawn as a water garden with stepping stones and bridge-walks and bogs and waterfall. That was a year ago. Excavating began in May, and three months later the pond looked as if nature had put it there.

From any viewpoint, the natural look of the pond is what sets the mood. Even from inside the house, the views offer a sense of tranquility — from a glass-enclosed room on the first floor to an upstairs bedroom where a treadmill faces the koi's domain. And at night, lights turn the water garden into an illuminated painting — catching the fish in their glow and shining on the white calla lilies and the cranberry taro and the giant Egyptian paper plant and highlighting the waterfall.

A small outdoor table and chairs are set outside the front door of the white stucco house. I think about how nice it would be to sit there and sip iced tea in the heat of summer and lose myself in the music and magic of the waterfall and the peace of the pond.

At left, red-veined *Caladium* nestles among rushes and water hyacinths. Above, shimmering koi dart among stepping stones.

Chores Galore

PREPARE the garden for your vacation. The garden shouldn't suffer while you're having a good time. Move containers to a spot with dappled light that's close to a water source. Hook up an automatic timer to the hose. Or charm a good neighbor into watering — offer ripening veggies or cut flowers as a thank-you.

PRUNE rambler roses. They're not like other roses — they bloom on last year's wood. Keep your cuts to dead wood and last year's growth, which won't flower again. Prune climbing roses as soon as they're through flowering. This promotes new growth.

PEP UP your pepper plants by pinching off the first blossoms so energy goes into the roots and foliage. You'll have a more productive plant in a few weeks. When ready to harvest, cut — don't pull — peppers off the plant.

PINCH back hardy chrysanthemums for the last time.

PERK up container plants by giving them a sip of diluted fish emulsion or seaweed fertilizer every two weeks. Reshape shaggy plants in hanging baskets.

PULL out spent pea vines and bush beans that have stopped producing. Springtime broccoli, too. Compost the remains.

MOISTEN the compost pile.

Decomposition slows down if the pile dries out.

RAISE your mower to its highest setting, preferably for a 3-inch-high lawn. This will prevent turf from burning in hot weather.

WATER carrots and root crops to ensure sweetness. Don't let cucumbers turn yellow or they'll get seedy and lose their crunch.

HARVEST melons when the half-inch disk at the base of the stem starts to pull away from the fruit. If it slips off with a little pressure, the melon is probably ready. Or conduct the sniff test — ripe melons should have a mouth-watering fragrance.

SET up a soaker hose on low pressure to water trees. Water slowly and deeply once every other week if it doesn't rain.

TAKE softwood cuttings of shrubs like butterfly bush, weigela, mock orange. Cut just above a leaf node, trim back to three sets of leaves, dip the stem in water and then in rooting hormone powder and insert it in potting soil, with two nodes beneath the soil. Label and date. Place pots in homemade propagation tents made of plastic bags. Keep soil moist. They should root in a month or two.

PICK blueberries in the morning after dew has evaporated. Cut out raspberry and blackberry canes after fruiting.

REPEAT the gardeners' mantra: Weed, water, mulch.

Inviting the Butterflies

My husband likes to tell about the July morning when I ran into the kitchen yelling "Quick, quick. Come outside — there's a pearly crescent on the coreopsis!" When we got outside, he gave me this wise-guy smirk. "Oh, there's a butterfly on a flower. Why didn't you say so? I thought there were Martians in the yard." He tells people that was the day he realized I was heavy into gardening. But as I remember, he stopped to watch until the tawny brown butterfly left the yellow bloom.

Just about everybody enjoys watching a beautiful butterfly land on a pretty flower. It's one of nature's best pas de deuxs. After all, butterflies are free, which is why it's so nice when they linger for a while in your garden.

Of course, since they come and go of their own volition, you have to provide inducements. You have to give them good reasons to hang around.

What it comes down to is this: Butterflies like to drink. If you want pearly crescents and mourning cloaks and monarchs and swallowtails and silver-spotted skippers to visit, you need to turn your garden into a juice bar — filled with plants that provide sugary sweet nectar for the gods of the insect kingdom. Plants like cosmos and coreopsis, lantana and liatris, *Buddleia* and bee balm.

It's a matter of butterfly biology and botany, too. Freud could have had a figurative as well as literal field day with *Lepidoptera*, as butterflies and moths are called. Almost from the minute a male butterfly completes his metamorphosis and emerges from the pupal case and stretches his wings, he's got that famous one thing on his mind. He's fixated on finding females. If you see two butterflies stuck together, they're probably getting it on. The process can last from minutes to hours.

After that, he goes out looking for more action while she concentrates on finding plants on which she can lay her eggs. For both male and female, all this calls for a lot of flying around, which takes energy. Butterflies draw their energy from sugary, carbohydrate-rich nectar. And many of them have their favorites. Eastern tiger swallowtails like thistle, for instance, while clouded sulphurs sip clover and monarchs drink milkweed.

Which brings us to the botany. As they satisfy their life forces, the butterflies are flitting around pollinating plants.

So the idea is to make your garden butterfly-friendly by offering plants that provide nectar for the adults and accommodations for the eggs, which turn into larvae or caterpillars. These are eating machines that repay the plant for its hospitality by gobbling up its foliage — sort of trying to eat themselves out of house and home. Cabbage whites, for instance, are not all sweetness and light — they love to nibble on cabbage, broccoli and other crucifers during their larval stage. Fortunately, natural predators such as birds and spiders keep the caterpillar population under control.

When the caterpillars turn into butterflies, they're on the move. They know what they're looking for. Butterflies have a great sense of smell, and their eyes don't bulge for nothing. Their eyes are composed of thousands of separate lenses set so closely together that a butterfly can see all around itself without turning its head. And unlike humans, they can see into the ultraviolet end of the spectrum, so they're able to hone in on the invisible guides around the center of a flower that reveal where nectar is stored. When male butterflies want to signal their mates, they flap their wings, which are equipped with special scales that reflect ultraviolet rays like a prism to produce tiny flashes of lightning. That's how they got their name, *Lepidoptera*, which is of Greek origin, meaning "scale-winged."

All butterflies are drawn to colorful blooms with scented reservoirs of sugary nectar. And there are a few other things you should know: Butterflies are cold-blooded and need sunlight to warm the muscles they use to fly. And their wings are delicate machines prone to tearing in gusty winds. So plant your butterfly garden in a sunny place that is sheltered from wind. Plan a spring-to-fall succession of irresistible scents and colors — butterflies are especially drawn to large splashes of red, orange, yellow or purple

flowers. And strive for a diversity of heights as well as a variety of plants — everything from ground-hugging sedums and alpine pinks to stately Joe Pye weed and Mexican sunflowers. Create a shallow mud puddle to provide these winged beauties with salt and other necessary nutrients. And remember — insectides kill butterflies, too.

The rewards are breathtaking. I sit in my garden and watch a black swallowtail sail in on the breeze and stop to sip nectar from the pink phlox. Its proboscis is deep into the flower and the double band of yellow on its wings and the smudge of iridescent blue on its tail shimmer in the sun. Sometimes cabbage whites flutter down like snowflakes onto my cutting garden.

I've seen silver-spotted skippers flitting among yellow lantana. And I feel like I'm getting a royal visit when regal monarchs light on my *Buddleia*, so accurately known as the butterfly bush. When I'm down, I can't help but smile at the sight of a yellow eastern tiger swallowtail with its black stripes waltzing around my purple coneflowers.

Perhaps Robert Frost described butterflies best. He called them "flowers that fly."

Butterfly Fountain

As Elton John sings, "Butterflies are free to fly, fly away, high away, bye bye." But don't worry, if you provide the right refreshment for these flying flowers, they'll be back. Here are some menu suggestions:

LATIN NAME	COMMON NAME
Achillea species	Yarrow
Agastache foeniculum	Anise hyssop
Asclepias tuberosa	Butterfly weed
Aster species	Aster
Buddleia davidii	Butterfly bush
Clethra alnifolia	Sweet pepperbush
Daucus carota	Queen Anne's lace
Dianthus barbatus	Sweet William
Echinacea purpurea	Purple coneflower
Echinops rito	Globe thistle
Eupatorium purpureum	Joe Pye weed
Heliotropium arborescens	Heliotrope
Hesperis matronalis	Dame's rocket
Lathyrus	Sweet pea
Lavandula angustifolia	Lavender
Liatris spicata	Gayfeather
Nicotiana species	Flowering tobacco
Phlox paniculata	Summer phlox
Rudbeckia hirta	Black-eyed Susan
Scabiosa caucasica	Pincushion flower
Sedum spectabile	Sedum Autumn Joy
Solidago species	Goldenrod
Syringa vulgaris	Common lilac
Tagetes species	Marigolds
Tithonia rotundifolia	Mexican sunflower
Zinnia elegans	Zinnia.

And don't forget some nibbles for the larvae — dill, parsley, Queen Anne's lace and fennel for swallowtails; milkweeds for monarchs; burdock for painted ladies; violets and pansies for fritillaries and spring azures; willows for mourning cloaks. Plus all-round snack food like dogwoods, hollyhocks, lupines, nasturtiums, plumbago, potentilla and wisteria.

The Vegetable Patch

When to Plant

Here are vegetable planting times for crops that do well in the fall garden. Count weeks backward from the first frost date to determine when to plant.

ARUGULA 6-8
BEETS 10-12
BOK CHOY.......................8-10
BROCCOLI.....................10-12
CARROTS 10-12
CAULIFLOWER 10-12
CHINESE CABBAGE 10-12
COLLARDS 10-12
KALE..................................7-9
LETTUCE 6-8
MESCLUN GREENS 6-8
PEAS 10-12
RADICCHIO 10-12
RADISHES 8-10
SPINACH 6-8
TURNIPS 6-8

I don't make sandwiches without lettuce these days and we eat salads at every meal except breakfast. I'm beginning to wonder about lettuce omelets. The trouble is that we erred on the side of plenty this spring. We planted too much lettuce at the same time. And of course it all came up in unison.

As you've probably surmised, the romaines, icebergs and butterheads are about to turn bitter and bolt. They're like Venusians that have been masquerading as humans — now they're shedding their outer skin and they're about to reveal their true identity. Flower stalks are pushing up through their centers. Believe it or not, lettuce is a member of the daisy or *Compositae* family — cousins of chrysanthemums and black-eyed Susans.

Tomatoes may like it hot, but lettuce is like me

— it hates the heat. So we're giving it away and eating it faster than the rabbits my husband hounds out of the garden. By the second week of July, all the heads will be gone, leaving ugly gaps and wasted space in the rows. Meanwhile, it doesn't help that we've picked the last peas from our spring planting and the beans are going fast. We need replacements. It's time to start planning fall crops.

The truth out there in the vegetable patch is that life begins in July and August as well as March, April and May. It can even begin in September. Plant now and instead of letting your garden waste away in the fall, you'll be giving it new staying power. When your tomato vines start to wither and the sheen is off the eggplant, you can take heart in broccoli and cabbage and cauliflower, and how about kohlrabi? And you can enjoy more lettuce and peas, too. This year we're planning a fall garden. We're certainly going to try more lettuce. I like the sound of frost-tolerant varieties like Rougette du Midi, a miniature red butterhead, and Winter Density, a cold-hardy romaine.

If you want to be harvesting vegetables when autumn leaves start to fall, you have get out there now. One of the tricks to planting a fall garden is knowing the expected date of the first frost, usually around the second week of October. Or check your seed packets for the number of "days to maturity." Then count backward.

For instance, arugula and spinach should be sown directly in the garden about six to eight weeks before frost. Arugula is a Mediterranean native and spinach comes from Asia, but they have a lot in common. Both take about 40 days to go from a garden seed to your salad bowl, and both like cooler weather. Certain varieties of spinach like the aptly named Indian Summer are bred especially for fall planting. Kale — the most cold-hardy and easiest to grow of the cabbage clan — requires seven to nine weeks before frost, broccoli and cauliflower about 10 to 12. But of course, if you buy transplants, you can put them in a little later.

There's a stewpotful of vegetables for the second planting season. Crops to sow from seed this month include cabbage, collards, Swiss chard, rutabaga, carrots, beets, endive and broccoli raab — which resembles common broccoli with blue-green leaves and upright growing habit but has small tasty florets at the end of slender shoots instead of a large head at the center. Broccoli raab is a mainstay in my neighborhood Italian restaurant, where it's prepared in the traditional way with olive oil and garlic. Speaking of garlic, if you plant it in the fall a few weeks before Thanksgiving, you'll get bigger bulbs and higher yields next spring.

Carrots and radishes and beets can be sown throughout the coming weeks, up until two months before frost. Remember — with carrots, the secret is to plant them in deeply turned, fertile soil. I haven't had much luck with carrots because my soil is heavy and I'm too lazy to dig that deep. So I'm thinking about 2-inch Thumbelina carrots that don't require such fine soil.

Just because you worked the soil in spring, don't think you're off the hook in midsummer. The leafy vegetables of autumn are heavy feeders, so lots of compost and organic matter should be worked into the soil before planting. Don't forget to water — remember you're working with soil that is already warmed up. A fresh layer of mulch makes sense because it helps retain moisture. And stay on top of the weeds because they compete for nutrients. Also, it's a good idea to rotate crops to discourage pests and disease. So don't sow a new crop of peas in the place where you just pulled out the vines from your first planting.

Plant now and you can harvest sweet-tasting vegetables until the frost is on the pumpkin and it's time to put in cover crops such as rye and oats and buckwheat and hairy vetch to replenish the soil through the winter.

But that's another season. For now, I've got lettuce omelets to think about and a new crop of peas to plant.

Good and Evil in the Garden

It makes sense to know what's bugging your garden. Here's how some insects line up:

BAD BUGS

Aphids – Green, pink, black, yellow, brown or dusty-gray, pear-shaped insects with long antennae. Suck sap from new shoots and buds of trees, shrubs, annuals, perennials, vegetables – withering leaves and flowers. Sticky honeydew encourages sooty mold fungus. Crush with your fingers, knock off with jet of water, send in natural predators like lacewings and lady beetles, spray plants with insecticidal soaps or pyrethrins.

Japanese Beetles – Metallic green with coppery wing covers and long legs. Pig out on leaves, stems and flowers of many plants, especially roses and daylilies. Larvae – plump white grubs with brown heads – devour grass roots. Hand-pick beetles in early morning and drown in soapy water, control with parasitic wasps, apply parasitic nematodes or milky spore disease to lawn to kill grubs.

Colorado Potato Beetles – Orange with black and creamy white stripes. Orange, humpbacked larvae have a row of black spots on each side. Both chew leaves and stems of tomatoes, potatoes, eggplants, peppers, petunias. Crush bright yellow egg masses, spray larvae with San Diego strain of Bt, drown adults in soapy water, use straw mulch or floating row covers, rotate crops.

Tomato Hornworms – Scary green caterpillars up to 4 inches long with black horn on the tail and white diagonal marks on sides. Consume leaves and sometimes fruit of tomato plants. Hand-pick from foliage, enlist parasitic wasps, spray with Bt when caterpillars are small.

Lace Bugs – Small, flat bugs with lacy wings. Suck plant juices from rhododendrons, evergreen azaleas, Andromeda, Kalmia, and others. Spray with insecticidal soap.

Spider Mites – Minute, pale green, golden or red with 8 legs. Prefer conifers, especially dwarf Alberta spruce, as well as beans, melons, apples and plums. Spin cobwebs around leaves, suck plant juices. Mist to suppress reproduction, plant nectar-rich plants to attract natural predators like lady beetles.

Slugs – Garden's arch-enemy. Soft-bodied mollusks that slither by night and leave a trail of slime. Attack almost any plant, especially tender young seedlings. Trap in shallow pans of beer buried at soil level, protect seedlings with diatomaceous earth.

GOOD BUGS

Braconid Wasps – Cream-colored larvae eat aphids, cabbageworms, hornworms, corn borers, and other pests. Adults inject eggs into host insects, where larvae develop. Attract with small-flowered nectar plants like dill, parsley and yarrow.

Lacewings – Fragile green insects with tiny heads, big eyes and transparent wings. Spindle-shaped larvae munch on aphids, whiteflies, thrips and other soft-bodied insects. Lure with purple coneflowers, yarrow, shasta daisies.

Lady Beetles – Adults and larvae snack on aphids, mealybugs, spider mites. Shiny, round adults are reddish orange with black spots. Larvae look like mini-alligators.

Darrel Henry's garden blooms with memories as well as vegetables.

Gardening On a Different Island

The long, narrow patch of earth is a long way from his island in the sun, and there are no banana trees or mangoes or papayas growing in the beds. But beans and carrots and cantaloupes and cabbages flourish in the carefully tended field, and for Darrel Henry the garden in the apple orchard is a reminder of home.

The island of Jamaica lives in the musical cadences of his speech and fills his memories of childhood and young manhood and his family's 15-acre farm. He has six brothers and five sisters, and they all had chores. Darrel took care of the pigs and goats and cows and planted sugar cane and hoed the rows of vegetables. "I used to like milking the cows," he says. "The first pint in the morning was for me. I'd drink it right then and there. But planting was always my thing. We grew many of the same vegetables as here, but there you can farm 12 months of the year. Ever since I can remember myself I've been planting."

The heft of the earth in his hands, the sun on his brow and the nearness of the sea have always been comforts for Darrel. And ever since he came to the United States almost two decades ago when he was already in his 30s, he has tried to keep these things in his life. They are as much constants as the memories of his late mother and the taste of the fresh milk that marked the mornings of his boyhood.

Now, he lives alone in a small house on an orchard where he nurtures trees and harvests fruit in East Northport. It is not Jamaica but it is on the north shore of a fish-shaped island. "This is like the country," he says as he stands in the middle of his vegetable bed next to the eggplants that are already in lavender blossom. "I could never live in New York City. I grew up in the country. Country is country wherever you go."

The sound of traffic on a nearby road seems muted in the orchard, where white blossoms color the spring and peaches scent the summer and red and gold apples brighten the fall. The sea, steely gray instead of aquamarine, is only a few miles away. And the 25-foot-by-85-foot garden on the edge of Richters Orchard is Darrel Henry's anchor.

"I can't imagine life without fresh vegetables," he says as he shows off the fledgling fruit of his summer squash and the tomato cages he makes out of wire and wooden stakes. He strolls about the garden he started years ago not long after he came to Richters. He noticed an unused sunny spot near the edge of the orchard just beyond a row of Galas and sandwiched between the Russets and Fujis. It seemed a perfect place for a garden and that's what Darrel turned it into. In his manner, his smile, Darrel Henry is a gardener at home. With a look of pride, he brushes his hand across the aromatic leaves of a clump of thyme on a day when if the sun is not the golden orb of the tropics, it is hot and strong nevertheless.

Minutes before, he had been equally at ease working in the orchard with Andy and Lou Amsler, the brothers who run Richters, thinning apples off the trees so the remaining fruit can grow full and round and juicy. "We've been working together a long time," Andy says.

Darrel laughs. "I call their parents Mommy and Daddy."

In the winter, Darrel stays in Florida and he and the Amslers keep in touch by phone and occasionally they come down to visit. He has a vegetable garden in Florida but it is small compared with the beds in East Northport, where the first dew-kissed cantaloupe of the season is reserved as a birthday present for Lou's young son, L.J.

The greatest joy Darrel reaps from his garden comes from the harvesting and eating of his own produce. "I eat meat, but seven days a week I cook vegetables — dinner wouldn't be the same without fresh vegetables." He loves the fire of the Scotch bonnet peppers like the ones his family grew on the farm — "if you can't take hot, don't eat them" — and he relishes the string beans that are his favorite vegetable. "I like to eat steamed beans with peppers and eggplants more than anything. Or I take hot peppers and carrots and beans and eggplants and onions and I steam them with butter and salt and pepper, and I'm all set."

But there is a pleasure that comes before the harvest. "I love watching things grow. Something is always growing from my hand. It's a way of life. I don't understand how some people walk around with hands and they don't plant anything. If I look outside and don't see something growing, I think, 'What's wrong?'"

In the evenings after work, the garden is where Darrel counts his blessings: 67 bushes of beans, 81 onion plants, 22 heads of cabbage, 7 tomato vines and lots of okra and scallions and carrots and celery and beets and turnips and broccoli and cucumbers. And it is where his life comes together.

"I grow here, and this is where I'm happy," he says. And the banana trees and the mangoes and the aquamarine sea and the burning sun of Jamaica are memories and that's OK. "There are a lot of ways to be at home when you're not at home. When I'm here in my garden watching things grow, I'm at home."

 Something is always growing from my hand. It's a way of life.

In Rachel's Garden

History grows in Rachel's Garden. It grows in the yellow flowers of tansy and the licorice-scented leaves of anise and the silvery stems of wormwood and the red hips of the apothecary's rose. It grows on a small patch of land where the warmth of the sun and the scent of old roses and lavender wafting on the breeze seem to slow down the rush of time. The sounds of modern suburbia — trucks rumbling by and cars honking — melt away in Rachel Mulford's garden.

It is a place that speaks to another time — and in its own quiet way to the noisy holiday we celebrate this month. The Fourth of July when we mark the birth of a nation and the spirit of the people who fought for liberty and the freedom to till their own land.

Rachel, the wife of a Revolutionary War major turned farmer and weaver, lived in East Hampton in the 1790s. The farmhouse still stands on a sunny sweep of land next to the Home Sweet Home Museum. Rachel lived in the two-story saltbox just off the main thoroughfare with her husband, David, and their four children and six slaves. The Mulfords had a few cows and horses and a smokehouse and cornfields, and Rachel may have had a garden.

"This is the garden Rachel could have had, might have had, should have had," says Isabel Furlaud, curator of the site for the East Hampton Garden Club. Isabel got the idea for Rachel's Garden several years ago when she noticed that the impatiens planted on the property were out of step with old times.

Isabel researched Rachel Mulford as well as her horticultural time and set the garden in 1790 when Rachel was 39 and had just given birth to her fourth child. East Hampton was a dusty cow town with no general store or doctor or apothecary. A garden was a matter of survival in this new land. Sustenance was the point, beauty nothing more than a by-product.

The result of Isabel's research is a garden typical of Rachel Mulford's milieu and of Long Island in the wake of the war — with quince trees for jelly in each corner and four raised beds to warm the soil and an arbor for hops and grape vines, and a twig teepee for scarlet runner beans. A garden where every plant had a purpose and every flower had a function.

Rachel's Garden blooms with plants that would have supplied most of her family's needs. The vegetable bed is a greengrocery of staples such as deer tongue lettuce and red orach and lamb's quarter for salads. Not to mention purslane, which 20th-Century gardeners might call a weed, but Rachel and her sisters tossed in the salad bowl and kept on hand to alleviate toothaches. There's sorrel for soups and summer savory to keep the bugs away from a bevy of beans — Jacob's cattle beans and wren's egg beans and soldier beans and Hutterite beans. Also, squonter squash and rattail radish, and cardoons and skirrets, both of which have edible roots that Rachel would have boiled, baked or stewed.

Another bed is a pharmacy of medicinal plants — winter savory to relieve stomachaches and asthma, marjoram for earaches and vervain for gout. "Saint-John's-wort was the Prozac of its day," Isabel says, "and anise was an early Viagra — the books say it promotes 'bodily lust.' "

Color is the crop in a third bed, devoted to dyes for weaving. Mullein for yellow and woad for blue and black-eyed Susan for olive green and dock for orange and southern wood for black and lady's bedstraw for red. The fourth bed holds housekeeping supplies such as pennyroyal to repel ants and fleas, larkspur to get rid of lice, bayberry for candles, lemon balm for furniture polish, thyme for mouthwash and lamb's ears to ward off witchcraft.

In Rachel's Garden, every plant is rooted in history. Moonwort was brought over on the Mayflower. Honeysuckle was a favorite of George Washington. The boxwoods along the east border are cuttings from Mount Vernon. The roses go back for generations — old pink moss roses that date to 1696 and maiden's blush roses circa 1738. Roses, incidentally, were used for perfume and potpourri.

Gardening for sustenance was hard work, and life wasn't easy. David Mulford died in 1798 at the age of 44, leaving his wife just two cows and the furniture that had been her dowry. She left Long Island for Connecticut, and her fate is not recorded. But, thanks to Isabel Furlaud and the East Hampton Garden Club, history lives on in the garden Rachel Mulford might have tended. And on the Fourth of July, its plants say much more than fireworks.

At left, the recreation of the East Hampton garden "that Rachel could have had, might have had, should have had."

89

August

Summertime and the living seems easy in August, the last full month of the season. The heat of summer lingers, gathering in the garden. Watch out for still-hungry rabbits and walk carefully past the poison ivy. August is a good month for drinking iced tea or lemonade and watching butterflies in the fading afternoon when you're talking a break from weeding and dividing daylilies and trimming tomato vines. Gladiolus strut and hydrangeas show off and water lilies romance ponds. The flowers that have been gracing the summer seem almost opulent, and it's easy to believe that the blooming will go on forever.

Pat Sayers of Huntington in her garden of 3,000 daylilies. On LI, these low-care plants bloom from mid-June to early September.

The Perfect Perennial

The daylilies of the field come in many colors and textures and shapes and sizes. Some of them have ruffled edges and red eyes, others have spidery petals and purple eyes. There are daylilies that look like trumpets and daylilies that resemble peonies and daylilies shaped like stars. They blossom across the rainbow from almost white through yellow and orange to dark purple and deep red-black. Hybridizers are trying to come up with blue daylilies.

There are more than 35,000 named varieties and the genus name sums up the charm of each and every one. *Hemerocallis* comes from the Greek,

meaning "beautiful for a day." Each bloom lives and dies in the course of a day, but a single plant produces a plethora of buds that flower for weeks.

All that, and daylilies are edible as well as ornamental. They don't have to be staked or sprayed. They thrive in sun or shade and will survive in almost any soil, except solid clay. They're almost disease- and insect-free. In a world where everything from kids to cars to houses requires vast expenditures of money and attention, daylilies stand out by virtue of self-sufficiency. They are truly low-maintenance plants.

On Long Island, these herbaceous perennials bloom from mid-June to early September.

Considering all their virtues, it's no wonder that their devotees are among the most passionate of gardeners — such as Pat Sayers of Huntington, who has invited me over on this muggy summer morning to meet her daylilies.

Pat said our mutual friend, Roswitha Waterman of Cold Spring Harbor, had suggested she call. Roswitha is Long Island's duchess of daylilies and an international authority on *Hemerocallis*. She lectures on her favorite flower from Old Westbury Gardens to the Palmengarten in Frankfurt, Germany, and she calls daylilies "the perfect perennial." If Roswitha suggests, I listen. Besides, Pat piqued my interest by telling me that she tends 3,000 daylilies that she's hybridizing.

So here I am sweating in a field somewhere in Huntington (Pat swore me to secrecy about its exact location). I watch as Pat stoops and snaps off the pollen-laden stamen of one plant and sweeps it across the pistil of another. Then she reverses the procedure in a process called backcrossing — she dusts pollen from the second plant onto the pistil of the first.

"I'm hoping that the petals of this yellow daylily will elongate and come out further," she says, pointing to the second plant. She'll have to wait and see — it takes three years for daylilies to mature into their adult characteristics. Pat grins. "By then I'll be on to something else. It's like Christmas all the time."

As I watch Pat bend to her flowers, I think that some of the nicest and most dedicated people I know are gardeners. They are people like Pat, who takes time out from a busy profession as an interior designer and is in her daylily field every morning at 7 — pollinating and photographing and generally keeping tabs on her crosses. I catch her enthusiasm and think that it would be nice to check with her in three years and find out if a yellow daylily with longer petals is growing in my new friend's garden. I've learned how important it is to have expectations, small as well as great. They are among the joys of gardening.

Of course, it is easy to be joyful in Pat's field. A sea of daylilies shimmers around me. The variety of shapes and hues is stunning. And what is even more stunning is the fact that virtually all these plants are the result of her own hand-pollination. After Pat completes a cross, it takes 61 days for the seeds to ripen. She collects them in the fall after the protective pods turn brown and pop open. She dries the seeds on her dining room table for 14 days, then chills them in a refrigerator for 10 weeks. By January, they're growing inside under lights. "They look like grass when they come up," she says.

Dealing With Daylilies

Daylilies benefit from being dug up and divided every five or six years. It rejuvenates the plants and your efforts will be rewarded next summer when you're greeted with even more cheery faces to lift your spirits. The best time to divide daylilies is in late summer or early fall after they've finished blooming. Here's a primer on how to divide and plant a daylily:

1. With a spade, loosen the clump on all sides, digging down about 10 to 12 inches to free as many roots as possible. Lift the clump from the ground in a single ball. Shake and wash off excess dirt with the hose on full force until you can see the individual fans – small plants consisting of fibrous roots, a crown and foliage that make up the clump.
2. Drive two pitchforks placed back to back into the middle of the root mass and push in opposite directions to pry the clump in two. Pull each section apart, dividing the clump into

smaller and smaller chunks. Each chunk should have at least two fans to ensure blooms the following year.
3. Wash the fan and cut the foliage down to about 12 inches.
4. Dig holes 18 to 24 inches deep and about one foot apart in a sunny, well-drained bed. Enrich the soil using Roswitha's own recipe – peat moss, a handful of super-phosphate and a handful of a mixture she concocts using two parts dehydrated cow manure and one part bone meal.

5. Build a mound of soil in the middle of each hole and spread the roots around it. Fill in the hole, covering the crown – the union of roots and stalk – with no more than 1 1/2 inches of soil.
6. Water well. And keep watering.

In the spring, they are ready for the field — a giant laboratory where Pat is working to produce better colors, taller plants, more-ruffled edges. She's tinkering to create plants with double blossoms and more buds and stronger scapes, or leafless stalks, and multiple branching. She's been playing with daylilies for the past nine years and has created two new hybrids that are registered with the American Hemerocallis Society: Passion's Promise, a vibrant red daylily with a gold edge, and Pink Margarita, a double with a green throat. She hopes to introduce Passion's Promise to the market for sale soon as well as register three more daylilies.

The *Hemerocallis* hybridizer surveys her field with inner vision. "I have a photographic memory for form and color. I look at a plant and I know its genealogy — what its parents and grandparents look like. Some turn out to be pretty little things — but nothing special. Some are dogs, and some show real promise."

Real promise is in the eye of the hybridizer. Pat breeds her daylilies for everything from strength and vigor to height and form. She points to the far end of the field at a yellow daylily that reminds her of the colors of the sun setting on the Seine and that stands head and shoulders above the rest. "It's 53 inches high," she says proudly.

Then she turns to a daylily right in front of her. "Here's a purple baby with elongated petals and a yellow throat, but there's already something like it called Peacock Maiden on the market. But it doesn't recurve like this." She shows off the petals that curve backward in a circle. "Maybe I can get the petals longer and curlier and then I'll have something."

An eggplant-colored daylily catches her eye. "Four years ago I bought a pretty unnamed seedling I was in love with. It had three blooms on it, and I've been trying ever since to get more." She bends and counts the buds on just one stalk. "I'm up to 29 on a single scape."

Every day, there are new discoveries and delights in the field in Huntington.

"Oh wow, this is the first bloom ever for that daylily."

"Look at this one, look at the size of this double."

"This one has edging and ruffling, so it will enhance anything I cross it with."

"This one has an interesting magenta color, but the flower itself doesn't open well. Could I keep the color but extend the petals?"

Pat Sayers continues along the pathways of her passion and tries to determine the shape of things to come.

Chores Galore

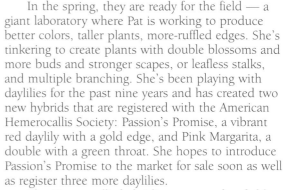

PRUNE a little foliage off tomato plants to let the sunshine in to ripen fruit. But don't overdo it — especially if you haven't been pruning all along. Keep plants watered so tomatoes will grow big and juicy.

PATROL your tomato patch every evening on the lookout for the voracious green hornworm on leaves and fruit. Pick off the plump 4-inch caterpillars and drop them in a pail of soapy water. If they have ricelike grains on their backs, leave them alone; these are cocoons of a beneficial parasitic wasp that will do in the little green monsters.

GIVE scraggly plants a haircut. Coleus, petunias, begonias, impatiens, coreopsis are likely candidates. So are phlox, artemisia and yarrow.

PICK beans and cucumbers every other day so plants keep producing. Harvest zucchini and summer squash before they get too big and lose their taste.

PLANT colchicums (autumn crocuses) as soon as they're available.

FEED roses one last time before Aug. 15, so new growth will have time to harden off before the cold weather.

MULCH deeply in this month of heat and give the garden one inch of water each week.

PULL out onions when their leaves wilt and flop over. Dry them in the sun a few days, then move them to a warm place for a month. Braid them while the stalks are pliable or let the stalks shrivel, cut them off and store the onions in a cool place with good air circulation.

MOUND celery or wrap in brown paper to blanch stalks.

PINCH back houseplants so they'll bush out before you bring them back indoors next month. Repot plants that have outgrown their containers: Loosen the roots and move to pots 1 inch wider at the top.

FOR winter bouquets collect flowers, just as they're starting to bloom, on a dry sunny morning after the dew has evaporated. Hang them upside down by the stems in a warm dark place until they're dry. Try baby's breath, blue salvia, yarrow, tansy, strawflowers, hydrangea, money plant, cockscomb, mullein.

HARVEST herbs before they flower, especially basil, which loses its sweet taste if allowed to go to seed. But let a few dill plants go — they'll produce a flavorful crop next spring.

Those Wicked Weeds

Arthur Bing, an expert horticulturalist, stopped by my place recently, and he was bowled over by what he saw. "Boy-o-boy," he said. "Amazing, just amazing." When my husband showed up a few minutes later, Arthur was even more enthusiastic. "You've got it all," he told my husband. Arthur wasn't talking about our garden. He wasn't even talking about me.

He was rhapsodizing about our weeds.

Arthur is an energetic and bright-eyed fellow to begin with, but he got extra-animated as we toured the front and back yards. He was especially taken by the poison ivy hiding near our neighbor's mailbox and the wild cucumbers scrambling along the Belgian block and the purslane sprawling under the rhododendrons.

Arthur Bing is the Baedecker of weeds. He taught greenhouse management and weed control at Cornell University and the State College of Technology at Farmingdale, a career that spanned almost four decades. He's been retired for more than a decade now — weeding his vegetable patch in a community garden in Greenlawn, traveling, mowing his lawn in South Huntington — but he still knows his shepherd's purse and his sheep sorrel and his smooth bedstraw.

I called on Arthur, because, as an obsessive weeder who can't stop pulling once I step into the garden, I wanted to know just what I'm dealing with. As it turned out, our weeds were literally having a field day. Weeds I didn't even know we had. Smartweed and ragweed and quackgrass and common groundsel, for instance. And pokeweed, which Arthur warned me has poisonous berries, and purslane, which is edible.

"You mean, you can eat weeds?" asked my husband, who loves to make salads with arugula and lettuce from our garden and was probably fantasizing about some exotic new ingredients.

"Some of them," Arthur answered, pulling up a pale green plant with small yellow flowers and heart-shaped cloverlike leaves that he identified as *Oxalis*. "It tastes a little like a pickle," he said, offering us the seed pods. To our surprise, it did — though I wouldn't recommend it as a replacement for a half-sour dill. Arthur watched us chew. "Oh, by the way," he said as he popped one in his own mouth, "it's not poisonous."

Arthur Bing, weed expert. A weed, he says, is "a plant you don't want."

Dandelions, a familiar member of our weed population. Leave a piece of dandelion root when weeding and you'll wind up with more.

He seemed to think the already ubiquitous oxalis might be with us for a long while. "They have little springs that send the seeds flying out 15 to 20 feet. Once that happens you might as well forget it. You'll have oxalis for several years."

Arthur — a pixieish fellow wearing white slacks and a green cap who looks too young to be an octogenarian — is a walking encyclopedia when it comes to weeds, and he was having a good time exploring our yard. Especially when we got to the wilderness we're trying to turn into a shade garden. "Oh forget it," he said, almost happily. "You'll never get rid of all these weeds."

I suspect he's right. But then again, none of us is ever totally weed-free. Generally, Arthur defines a weed as "a plant you don't want." I suppose if you hated roses and peonies and hydrangeas, they'd be the same as weeds. As Ella Wheeler Wilcox wrote at the turn of the century, "A weed is but an unloved flower."

Arthur, for instance, is almost violent about violets, and he hates evening primrose. "You didn't plant this did you?" he asked when he noticed the dark green spade-shaped leaves of English violets

spreading happily under a star magnolia tree. "Some people like it, but I say get rid of it. It's hard though. It's resistant to herbicides."

Which brings up another, sometimes delicate, matter. How do you get rid of your weeds? There have been extreme occasions, I am sorry to say, when I've had to spray weeds — like the mugwort that's trying to swallow my mailbox. But I feel guilty about it. Arthur proclaimed mugwort "the worst weed you could have, because it can take over the whole darn place." He recommends a porous mesh weed cloth or landscape fabric that he says is more effective than black plastic mulch. And of course, the most tried and true method is to get out there and pull them.

Of course, mulching helps when it comes to hand-to-weed combat, since perennial weeds like Canada thistle and field bindweed will root into the loose material, making them easier to pull up. But you have to make sure you get everything. Leave a piece of dandelion root, for instance, and you'll wind up with more dandelions. And try to wipe out annual weeds like comon groundsel and chickweed before they go to seed.

"Look here, you've got yellow nutsedge," he said

as he stooped to examine the yellow-green leaves growing near an ilex. "This is a tough one, because it propagates by seed and by nutlike tubers that can stay dormant in the ground for seven years. Mulch won't keep nutsedge under control."

Everywhere he turned there was something to see. Common groundsel under the azaleas and crabgrass in the lawn and nightshade vines on the woodpile. All of them competing with prettier, more worthy plants for the precious life-sustaining water and nutrients in the soil. Annual weeds and biennial weeds and perennial weeds. Weeds that spread by seeds and weeds that spread by tubers and weeds that spread by creeping stems.

"You've got 'em all," Arthur told us.

And just in case we had any doubts, he pointed out a few more.

"Prostrate spurge," he said, kneeling to pull out the purplish leaves that sprawled near a newly planted Kousa dogwood. "A euphorbia, related to poinsettia."

"Pokeweed," he said, pointing to a leafy stem almost as tall as the white lily towering nearby. "It's a monster — 3-foot-long roots. If you pull it, you'll break your back."

"Devil's walking stick," he said, gesturing toward a skinny green thing poking up among the daylilies. "Oh my, you don't want that around, has thorns like I don't know what. Better wear gloves when you pull it. The wild cucumber, too — it has prickers. It grows a little round thing that doesn't look like a cucumber."

As Arthur conducted his tour, I couldn't help wonder what kind of a world it would be if we could just learn to love our weeds, if we could adjust our vision and see the beauty in dandelions. If we could coexist with our crabgrass and clover and nutsedge. I thought about Morticia Addams clipping the blooms off the roses and making bouquets of thorny stems.

But then Arthur bent to pull a prickly greenbriar vine snaking around a butterfly bush where monarchs and tiger swallowtails stop by for happy hour. "Lousy weed," he mumbled.

"You know it," I said.

Weeds to Watch for

Here is a rogue's gallery of the most unwanted weeds with their MO's, aliases and descriptions.

PIGWEED, a k a green amaranth, *Amaranthus* — Especially dangerous annual because of amazing seed production. Single plants have been known to produce 100,000 black or reddish brown seeds that remain dormant but viable in the soil for 40 years. Some species grow 4 feet tall; others grow low. Be on the lookout for rough hairy stems bearing clusters of tiny greenish flowers.

LAMB'S QUARTERS, a k a *Chenopodium album* — Invades lawns and gardens. Identified by red-streaked stems with clusters of minute green flowers and diamond-shaped leaves that have a silvery underside.

COMMON CHICKWEED, a k a starwort, *Stellaria media* — Hangs out in rich, moist, shaded soil. Presence is a sign of inadequate turf cover. Annual with oval leaves and small starlike white flowers. Needs seeds for reproduction but takes over with slender stems, often a foot or more long, that root at joints.

BARNYARD GRASS, a k a *Echinochloa crusgalli* — Coarse grass with brown prickly spikes and blades 6 to 24 inches long. Frequents moist fertile places.

SMARTWEED, a k a lady's thumb, *Polygonum persicaria* — Member of the infamous buckwheat family. Dark green splotch in the center of the leaf resembles a lady's thumbprint. From a few inches to more than 4 feet tall with pink, rose-colored or white flowers.

CARPETWEED, a k a *Mollugo verticillata* — An invader from the tropics. Grows in patches in poorly nourished lawns and gardens. Produces dainty white flowers and minute kidney-shaped orange-brown seeds.

SMOOTH CRABGRASS, a k a *Digitaria ischaemum* — Large and crablike. Shows up around the time forsythia finishes flowering and hangs around till first frost. Most common summer annual lawn weed, along with its cousin, hairy crabgrass.

YELLOW NUTSEDGE, a k a nutgrass, *Cyperus esculentus* — Grasslike perennial known by its tall yellow-green leaves. Hard to eliminate since its nutlike tubers can hide out in the soil for years.

COMMON DANDELION, a k a *Taraxacum officinale* — Common perennial pest. Any part of the deep fleshy taproot can regenerate a new plant. Seeds are frequent fliers. Can do community service: Young leaves are used as salad greens; flowers make an uncommon wine.

BROADLEAVED PLANTAIN, a k a *Plantago major* — A perennial European visitor easily identified by its wiry spikes. Causes hay fever.

COMMON PURSLANE, a k a *Portulaca oleracea* — An escaped vegetable once used as a salad plant or pot herb. Now an annual sprawling nuisance. Thrives in hot weather. Even when hoed, fleshy stems remain alive a long time. Broken-off bits of stems take root and reproduce.

PROSTRATE SPURGE, a k a *Euphorbia supina* — Small leaved annual. Thrives in well nourished lawns and gardens. Smothers grass. Distinguishing marks include a purple spot on upper surface of dark green leaves. Bleeds a milky juice when stem is torn.

RED SORREL, a k a sheep sorrel, *Rumex acetosella* — Moniker derives from its reddish-brown female flower and the sour taste of its arrow-shaped leaves. Another perennial member of the buckwheat gang. Takes over by sending out slender running rootstocks and triangular brownish seeds. Likes acid soil.

FIELD BINDWEED, a k a creeping Jenny, *Convolvulus arvensis* — Intruder from Eurasia. Roots penetrate to 10 feet with many lateral branches at various depths. Takes years to wipe out. A perennial vine that can pass for morning glory.

August

Tropical Long Island

There I was driving along Route 110 south of the Expressway in Melville on a humid summer day, taking in the sights that define the less than bucolic side of this island of ours. Delis and pizza places and fast-food restaurants. Banks and gas stations and discount wholesale clubs. Office complexes with manicured lawns and landscaped beds. Vacant lots where weeds and wildflowers fight for supremacy.

The landscape and my mood improved when I turned into the main entrance of the state college at Farmingdale and followed the road to the second parking lot on the left. I walked through a towering wrought-iron gate defined by brick pillars and began to feel as if I had slipped through Alice's looking glass. Instead of concrete vistas and tacky signs, I saw a center lawn bordered by a lane of annuals and ornamental grasses.

I passed turf-grass plots and an herb garden and a dwarf-conifer collection and rose beds. "Welcome to Long Island's best-kept horticultural secret," said my guide, Richard Iversen, a professor of horticulture who has a doctorate in herbaceous perennials and — considering that I was unduly late — a master's degree in patience.

I was in the display gardens of the university`s Department of Ornamental Horticulture. Yes, I thought. This is a cleaner, sweeter Long Island. Then a quick left turn and WOW — suddenly we were standing in the middle of what at first scent and sight seemed a totally different island. A tropical island. And with the honk and screech of traffic and the gray monoliths of corporate architecture no longer visible, I thought that it all made wonderful sense.

This was just another side of Long Island. After all, anyone with a car and a bathing suit knows we

have balmy breezes and sandy beaches and ocean breakers and gentle bays. So why can't we, at least in summer, be a tropical island? Bring on the frozen daiquiris with little straw umbrellas. We may not have coconut palms, but we can have Lablab beans and chalice vines and elephant ears and Persian shields.

When tropical gardens are the subject, Richard Iversen is no shrinking hibiscus. He taught at Farmingdale for several years before taking a leave of absence to earn his doctorate at Cornell. Then he got what he calls "an itch for the exotic." So he took a job as director of a botanical garden in Barbados and taught tropical horticulture at the University of the West Indies.

When he came back to Farmingdale as a visiting lecturer a few years ago, he brought the itch with him. So he scratched the earth in a section of the display garden walled by a tall *Taxus* hedge. He got together a handful of horticulture students who took up the sod, prepared the soil with sterilized organic matter to keep down the weeds, added a little 10-6-4 fertilizer and some superphosphate and started planting. That was in early June.

Two months later, Richard was deep in the tropics.

And on a humid August afternoon so was I — smack-dab in the middle of a 35-foot-square, teeming jungle of red-hot cat's tail from Burma and glory bush from Brazil and butterfly ginger from India and velvet plants from Java and cigar flowers from Mexico. There I stood, admiring the fluorescent red-purple foliage of *Amaranthus tricolor*, an edible annual from Indochina also known as Chinese spinach, and the architectural form of towering castor bean plants and the glorious purple and green striped leaves of blood banana.

And I was bowled over by the plants Richard calls "the jewels of this garden" — cultivars of *Colocasia*

esculenta, known in Asia as taro and in the Caribbean as dasheen. Cultivars like Fontanesii and Illustris with giant 3-foot-long, 2-foot-wide, heart-shaped leaves and large swollen tubers that can be eaten like a potato. And that are served beyond Sheepshead Bay as well as the Florida Straits. "You find it in the Caribbean markets in Brooklyn," Richard said.

Not everything in Farmingdale's tropical garden is a stranger. Part of the surprise is that Richard finds garden settings for tropicals that most of us have typecast as houseplants. He uses prayer plants as a ground cover under butterfly ginger, and he positions a spider plant in a large stone urn, then surrounds it with *Dracaena marginata* Tricolor and cascades of variegated Algerian ivy.

It's a matter of going forward into the past. "Tropicals we consider houseplants were used by the Victorians as bedding plants," Richard explained. "Gardeners are always looking for new things — I mean impatiens aren't the only plant — and so we go back to the old ideas and revive interest in them."

He treats purple hearts as annuals, complementing them with the iridescent lilac-colored foliage of Persian shield and the lavender flowers of elfin herb, a native of Mexico and Central America. He turns wandering Jews into ground covers. He plants a mat of chartreuse coleus under the golden-striped foliage of *Canna* Pretoria, then reiterates the theme with waves of mottled *Abutilon* and the curious oyster plant that grows all over the West Indies.

"Most good garden centers carry these plants. It's just that many gardeners aren't aware of how tropicals can be used. This garden can inspire them — especially at this point in the season, when perennials are lagging and limping along. There's no lag here — this garden will keep going until the first hard frost."

I love it. A tropical Long Island into the fall. Bring on the limbo sticks.

Richard Iversen in his tropical garden. "Many gardeners," he says, "aren't aware of how tropicals can be used."

Not In My Garden!

I don't profess to have a garden of Eden, but I do have a serpent hanging out in my yard. It sneaks through the fences along the sides of our property. It slithers about the shade garden. It pops out of the English ivy.

It's poison ivy. I've never succumbed to it but I've seen its victims, and the thought of even brushing against it gives me the creeps. I might touch it with a 10-foot pole, but I wouldn't touch the pole afterwards.

Even saying its name makes me itch. Poison ivy. Yech. I don't care how pretty it looks when it turns scarlet in the fall. I don't care if goats and grouse and mule deer love its leaves or if flickers and mockingbirds and sparrows gobble up its waxy white berries. I don't care if it holds together the dunes at Fire Island. I don't care if it's a native American plant with a genus all its own: *Toxicodendron*.

I don't care if its fossil ancestors predate humans in North America by millions of years or if Capt. John Smith's record of the evil itch was the first description of an allergic reaction in the New World. I don't care if it takes hold everywhere in the United States except Hawaii, Alaska and some regions of Nevada or that you can find it from Canada to Guatemala.

I don't care if your Aunt Tillie says she's immune to it. Get it out of my garden.

Poison ivy can grow as a bush or vine with three shiny leaflets on each stalk. The leaves are green with hairy undersides and can be smooth, lobed or toothed. I agree in the abstract that it's a remarkable plant. I can understand why experts like Vinnie Simeone, assistant director of Planting Fields Arboretum, give it the sort of grudging admiration that Sherlock Holmes gave his venomous archenemy Prof. Moriarty.

"It grows in the sun," Vinnie says. "It grows in the shade. It grows in the swamps and the sandy dunes. Its genetic adaptability is amazing. It has prevailed. It is the cockroach of the plant world."

Terrific. Who wants cockroaches? When it comes to poison ivy, I'm a NIMBY. Let it grow in the swamps. But not in my backyard.

Not unless it's in an area where I'm never going to venture. Vinnie doesn't worry about the poison ivy creeping up the black locusts and white pines in a part of the arboretum where the public doesn't roam. And before we decided to tame the jungle at the edge of our yard, we didn't even know *Toxicodendron radicans* was at large.

But now that we're planting ostrich ferns and columbines and mayapples back there, the poison ivy is a clear and present danger. Still, it holds a certain attraction — like the urge to touch the stove to see if it's really hot. Not long ago at Brooklyn Botanic Garden, poison ivy climbed a trellis in the herb garden, planted for educational reasons. It had the appropriate warning and identification markers, but still, the doubting public trampled through the herbs and got close enough to get poison ivy rash. So it was removed.

Some of the people who got too close at the botanic garden may have been misled by its innocent appearance. There are no thorns or burrs — it doesn't look like it could possess the power to produce the itch from hell.

But it does. The peril stems from an oily resin in the plant's sap called urushiol, which is sticky and colorless and penetrates the skin in a matter of minutes. The stuff oozes from any cut or crushed part of the plant. This doesn't take much — if an insect took a tiny nibble, that would be enough to get the urushiol flowing. And every part of the plant — roots, flowers, berries, stems — are toxic all year round.

Any contact — even indirect — can be hazardous. The toxin can be carried on the fur of your dog or cat or on your clothing, work gloves, garden tools or that 10-foot pole. It's rash to touch anything that's touched poison ivy. "In a cultivated garden, it's a real nuisance," Vinnie says. "I guess you could try a flame thrower." Of course, he's only kidding. You should never burn poison ivy, because the smoke can carry the urushiol and if you inhale, you could swell up or experience other internal reactions.

Basically, the experts agree there are only two ways to get rid of poison ivy. Pull it or spray it.

Some experts recommend spraying it with Glyphosate, the active ingredient in Roundup and Kleenup. But beware — this is a non-selective killer that will do in your groundcover or anything else it touches. If you must use it, remember that the foliage will translocate the chemical to the root via the stem, so use it when the poison ivy is full of moisture — like after a rain.

I'd try pulling — this has its risks, but it's organic as well as more effective. Be vigilant. Wear long pants, a long-sleeved shirt and disposable plastic gloves. Don't get too close, because the eyelids are especially vulnerable — so is the tender skin inside the arm. Grab the plant firmly and pull it up by the roots or dig it out with a shovel. Well-established specimens often have runners as long as 6 feet and as thick as a pencil. Be sure to get it all, since new growth can pop up anywhere.

When you're done, put everything — including your gloves — into a plastic bag and throw it out. Wash your hands and face and rinse your shovel. Toss your clothes into the washing machine immediately.

As for me, I know I'm acting out of fear, but I'm leaving the actual dirty work to Thayer Novak, my neighbor the landscaper, who isn't afraid to touch poison ivy even though he's already had the itch.

Poison ivy. Not in my backyard. And definitely not in my garden.

If You Touch It

WASH ALL EXPOSED skin areas with cold running water as soon as possible. If you wash within 15 minutes, there's a chance you'll escape the evil itch. But even within an hour of exposure, washing will minimize the severity of the outbreak.

A linear rash appears within 48 hours. Redness and swelling are followed by oozing blisters and severe itching. The rash usually heals in about two weeks. Touching will not spread the rash, but repeated scratching may stimulate a systemic spread. New lesions can erupt up to three weeks after exposure, according to Dr. Howard Mofenson, director of the Long Island Regional Poison Control Center at Winthrop University Hospital. To relieve the itch, he suggests calamine lotion, Burrow's solution or Aveeno, an oatmeal bath to soak in or apply as a compress. "Do not use high-potency cortisone creams or local antihistamines or anesthetics on the skin," he cautions.

Cool baths should keep the lesions clean, but if they get infected, you may need antibiotics. If the rash covers 25 percent of your body, consult a physician for oral cortisone treatment.

The Rabbit Wars

"That's not nice," my husband was saying. "Come on, you should know better. Stop it." I knew the tone. Sometimes, it drives me crazy. He was trying to be reasonable. Who was he talking to? I wondered. He was in the garden in our front yard, and his head was the only one I could see above the fence.

Clearly, he wasn't having any effect. Seconds later he was invoking a deity and following with a string of obscenities. "Get out of there! You ————!" I was glad none of the neighbors were around.

By the time I got to the garden, my husband was jumping around inside it like he was doing the chicken dance. He was waving a hoe and yelling loud enough to drown out a wedding band. "Out, out!" More curses. "Get outta here!"

Then I saw who, or more accurately what, he was talking to and I started screaming, too. A rabbit had just finished chomping the romaine lettuce and was disappearing into the flower beds.

I don't know about you, but I have had it with rabbits. And not just adult rabbits. The week before, my adult stepdaughter had been visiting and got to see her father waving a rake at a baby rabbit. "Oh, he's so cute," she said, and I can guarantee she wasn't talking about her father.

Cute, schmoot. The damn thing was eating up our garden. Whatever you do, don't Peter Cottontail me. Bugs Bunny, I can understand. He's a pest. Which is the best thing I can say about the rabbits that seem to be proliferating in my neighborhood. Rabbits are a gardener's natural enemy.

They're much worse than other animal pests. Like squirrels, for instance. Blood meal generally keeps squirrels out of my tulip beds, and I can plant daffodils, which they don't like. I've decided that if the squirrels don't bother me, I don't bother them. We notice each other in passing, but we each go our own way.

It's the same with the snapping turtles that lay

eggs in our garden in the spring — especially where there's newly turned earth. We let them lay. And generally we have no problems with the swans that enjoy the pond behind our house.

Although there was the time we had to hose a swan out of our swimming pool. And there was the day we heard a terrific banging as if something were trying to knock down the house. Bang, boom, smash — it was terrible. When we saw the cause it was even more startling. Two swans were mating against our front door. The door is mostly glass, and we were afraid they'd break through and consumate their relationship in our living room. My husband ran outside with the garden hose. But the swans had uncoupled and one was coming right at him. Old Braveheart wasn't sure of its intentions and took shelter in the garage. We were sweeping white feathers off the walk for a week.

But nothing like that ever happened again. Rabbits are different. I can't get rid of them. It's not that I'm an Elmer Fudd. (I don't believe in guns and I've never eaten rabbit stew.) I try to be organic when it comes to garden pests. But what can you do about a creature that does it like, well, a bunny. The female eastern cottontail can start reproducing at 3 months of age. Under good conditions, she can give birth to three or four litters a year — each with five to six baby bunnies. Experts estimate one pair of rabbits and their offspring could conceivably breed 5 million young in a five-year period.

So call me heartless, but it doesn't upset me to know that, what with disease, predators and traffic, 85 percent of the rabbit population dies each year. Most rabbits usually don't make it past the 15-month mark.

But while they're at large there's a lot of lettuce-eating going on. And the voracious little vegetarians also chow down on peas, beans, beets, Swiss chard, cabbage — and carrots, of course. About the only vegetables they seem to stay away from are corn, squash, cucumbers, tomatoes, potatoes and some peppers. And they eat flowers, too — especially the tender green shoots of tulips — as well as berries and, in winter, the bark of trees and woody plants. There are some supposedly rabbit-proof plants such as agapanthus, catmint, bearded iris, cotoneaster, rosemary and *Fritillaria imperialis*, but I wouldn't put anything past a hungry cottontail.

All I know is that it's a war out there and I'm not alone. Other gardeners have been telling me about bunny brigades attacking their own vegetable patches and flower borders. They're all turning to me for defense strategies. What do I know? I offer the usual list of unscientifically proven repellents, but I make no guarantees. I think that at some point in time some garden columnist somewhere must have said, "Oh, try lion poop" or "Bobcat urine is good," and we've all been perpetuating myths ever since.

The arsenal of most-mentioned deterrents includes lime, sulfur, hot-pepper sauce, garlic, fish emulsion, chili powder, rotten eggs, smelly old shoes, fake snakes, human hair and deodorant soap. As well as used cat litter, wood ashes and fox scent.

My husband and I have tried blood meal with some success to ward off rabbits, but you have to reapply it every time it rains. When the picket fence around the garden was installed, we attached chicken wire 2 feet above ground and 1 foot underground. Actually, chicken wire might be your best bet. But don't be like us. We forgot about the gate.

One of my colleagues came up with a novel idea. For reasons that will soon become clear, this person insisted on anonymity, and I swore that I'd go to jail before I revealed the name of a source. I don't know if he'd heard about bobcat urine, but he staked out his garden in the way male animals have been marking their territory for ages. He said he thought it worked for awhile but that shyness got the better of him. Now he's trying a wind-chime device his wife bought in a garden center. I told him about our unwired gate, and he suggested attaching wire to it at ground level. Barbed wire.

In the meantime, my husband is still out in the garden waving a hoe and yelling his head off. What astounds me is that he seems to believe that somehow he'll actually make the rabbits understand and they'll miraculously hop to. "Get out of there," he says. "It's my lettuce. And stay away from the flowers. Go. Go. Get out of my garden!" But then he starts cursing and doing the chicken dance.

My methods are more subtle. I still believe in blood meal, and I haven't told my husband yet but he has a haircut appointment in a few days. I plan to bring home his shorn locks. I'm hoping that if I sprinkle a little hair in the garden today, the hares will be gone tomorrow.

Besides lettuce, bunnies love your peas, beans, Swiss chard, cabbage and carrots, of course.

Carmela at Tomato

In another time, she was Carmela Castelli, a little girl with shiny black hair growing up in a sea town in Sicily called Porto Empdocle. Her father was a fisherman, but her relatives had a farm in the country where her mother's sister — "I have her name, Carmela" — dried figs and pressed her own olive oil and ground wheat by hand and made jars upon jars of tomato paste.

The farm was only 20 minutes away from the coast but it seemed like a different world. It was a place where Carmela learned to hold the earth in her hands. The effects of World War II were still imprinted on her native island, and life in the town by the sea was hard. But the fruits of the field were plentiful. "It was joy, it was happiness to me," Carmela says of her days on the farm.

Her relatives sold their produce at the market — olives and grapes and cucumbers and figs and almonds and chestnuts and walnuts. "All kinds of fruits and vegetables," Carmela says. And of course, they grew tomatoes. When she visited the farm, the fisherman's daughter would stare with joy at the fields of tomatoes growing in the sunshine. "In Sicily," Carmela says, "I don't know, the sun is different. It is like no other place in the world."

The tomatoes were placed on a great tilted canvas and the juice dripped into containers. The women of the family put on their straw hats and stirred the mixture as it cooked for days in the sun and thickened into the paste that they used as the base for sauce.

When she was 17, Carmela left Sicily to stay with an older married sister in a place called Sheepshead Bay in Brooklyn. She could smell the sea but she didn't speak English when she enrolled in high school, and the floors of her sister's house were made of wood instead of stone and she couldn't get used to the squeaking floorboards. The light wasn't the same, "and the winter was so cold it hurt."

But it helped that there was a strip of yard where her sister had a peach tree and an apricot tree and a few tomato plants. Carmela Castelli stayed in America and prospered.

Now she is Carmela Gardner and she lives in Miller Place on Long Island. She and her husband, Bob, have three sons and two daughters, and the family owns restaurants in Fort Salonga and Long Beach Island, N.J. They have a gracious home and a sky-blue swimming pool and fig and fruit trees and a garden. Each day in the early morning, Carmela comes outside and walks among her tomatoes. "I take my morning coffee out into the garden. I water. I weed. I check to see what's ripe. I look around and say, 'God, this is beautiful.'"

And it is. In the context of where and when, Carmela's garden is as beautiful, perhaps, as the one in Sicily. If the light is different, the spirit is the same. In the yards of suburbia, Sweet 100s and Early Girls and Better Boys and Belgian Giants and Manalucies and Ruffled Yellows and other varieties

> *I look around and say 'God this is beautiful.'*

of tomatoes are as ubiquitous as the impatiens that grow in a window box on Carmela's garden shed.

Carmela grows basil and sage and parsley in pots by the pool, and next to a fence at the side of the backyard, she nurtures a row of fruit trees — peach and apple and plum and cherry and pear. And in a living-room-sized plot alongside the house, she tends strawberries and eggplant and zucchini and fennel and red kidney beans — and tomatoes. Not just one or two tomato plants or even 10 or 12. In Carmela's garden, 70 tomato plants grow in neatly mounded rows. Beefsteaks and Big Boys and plum tomatoes. All of them perfectly staked. All of them thriving. All of them as tall as the petite, vibrant woman with bright hazel eyes whose accent still holds the music of her birthplace.

The tomatoes do not grow by themselves. They

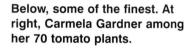

Below, some of the finest. At right, Carmela Gardner among her 70 tomato plants.

Time

are accorded the care and feeding due a cultured fruit of long lineage — the tomato grew wild in Peru centuries ago, traveled to Mexico and was discovered in an Aztec market by Cortez and his conquistadors. Carmela weeds obsessively and holds the earth in her hands. "I can't wear gloves," she says. "I don't like anything between me and the soil."

The fisherman's daughter chops up clamshells and fish heads and vegetable scraps and buries them around the plants. And she has hooked her Brooklyn-born husband — "he grew up on canned vegetables" — on the pleasures of gardening. Bob makes a light-colored tea out of composted sheep manure steeped in water and applies it every two weeks. He also sprays fish emulsion and kelp on the tomatoes every two weeks as an organic fertilizer.

Like the aunt for whom she is named, Carmela makes sauce. Starting at the end of August, she cans the tomatoes. "We're still using the tomatoes we canned last year," Bob says.

Family and the good earth go together at the house in Miller Place where Carmela grows "a little bit of everything I remember from my childhood."

Everything was blooming when her second-oldest son, James, organized a surprise 50th birthday party for Carmela at the house. Seven of her eight siblings and all of her five children were there. There was lots of food and dancing and laughter and joy and lots of babies for uncles and aunts and grandparents to pass around. There were tarantellas and horas and Greek dances in honor of the ethnic diversity of the family. Carmela's brother Jack danced every dance with a small cigar clamped firmly in his mouth, and Bob Gardner lifted his wife of 30 years into the air as if they were still young sweethearts doing the lindy in Brooklyn.

Every now and then guests walked around the yard and admired the fig trees and the other fruit trees and stopped to gaze at the rows of tomatoes with approval and wonder. And Carmela Castelli Gardner smiled and remembered another time on another island where the sun shines as it does nowhere else in the world.

Celebrating St. Fiacre

Some things have happened — or not happened — in my garden over the years that give me pause for wonder. There was, for instance, the time my husband disturbed a nest of yellow jackets in a hose caddy. They swarmed all around him but he didn't get stung. Also, it's amazing the way our yard is a maternity ward for snapping turtles. Every spring, the mothers lumber out of the pond behind our yard and dig holes and deposit their eggs. Even though raccoons are nosing about, the eggs survive. Months later, the babies head for the water.

And let me tell you about the dahlias. A few seasons ago, I simply forgot that my uprooted dahlia tubers were in the garage waiting to be stored for the winter. I dumped them in a cardboard box and never got to it. They should have died. But in the spring, I noticed shoots poking through. I planted them in the garden and, lo and behold, they flourished.

I told people about it with a sense of awe. "It's a miracle," I said.

But then I thought about all the magic moments in our gardens. Moments that we take for granted. Seeds are miraculous, and so is compost. The way plants grow and survive despite wind and drought and frost is remarkable. Just consider the simple symmetry of a maple leaf or the complex beauty of a passion flower. Or the fact that a hyacinth bulb contains its own embryo and the food to feed it.

You have to wonder whether somebody's looking after us gardeners. Maybe somebody is. Miracles happen all the time in our gardens, so you shouldn't be surprised to learn that we have a patron saint.

I didn't know this until recently, although if you'd have asked me, I might have said it was St. Francis of Assisi. He was known for his love of animals and is considered the patron saint of nature. That's why statues of St. Francis include a small bird on his shoulder.

But St. Francis isn't the patron saint of gardeners. That honor goes to an Irish monk named St. Fiacre (pronounced fee-ah-kruh). When it came to the caring of the green, he was an expert. From a distance, statues of St. Fiacre look a little like those of St. Francis. But there are no birds on him, unless of course they're real. St. Fiacre usually has one hand on a shovel and the other on a Bible, a sheaf of flowers or a bunch of onions.

This is the month to toast St. Fiacre — his feast day is Aug. 30. We don't make much of a fuss about him in the United States, but in Europe there are hymns and floats and floral displays in his honor.

As well there should be. As is the case with a lot of gardeners I know, St. Fiacre was an interesting character whose life was tied to the land. He was born in Ireland late in the Sixth Century and could have followed in the footsteps of his father, a tribal chieftain. Instead, he disdained power for peace. He entered a monastery, where he became immersed in an ideal combination — gardening and the classics.

Apparently inspired by a yen for solitude and a place to sow, Fiacre traveled to France where the Bishop of Meaux gave him land for a hermitage. He built a hut and planted vegetables and herbs and flowers. Eventually, he asked the bishop for more land so he could feed the sick and hungry.

As the legend goes, the bishop said Fiacre could have as much land as he could dig up in a single day. The monk prayed for guidance, and the next morning all he had to do was drag his spade across the earth. Trees toppled, bushes were uprooted, trenches appeared and stones fell away. The horticultural monk established a monastery where he grew crops that fed the poor and helped the sick.

There other things about St. Fiacre, who died in 670, that you should know. It saddens me to report that he was said to be a confirmed misogynist. And he is considered the patron saint of Parisian cabbies, because the hackney carriages for hire in the 17th Century plied their trade from the Hotel Saint-Fiacre. They were consequently called fiacres.

While I was digging into garden saints, I came up with a few more names that seem worth mentioning. Consider St. Phocas of Sinope. The buzz on Phocas is that he gardened on the shores of the Black Sea in the Fourth Century and gave his surplus to the poor. He was condemned as a Christian, and soldiers were sent to kill him. Phocas realized the soliders had no idea what he looked like, so he told them he knew the man they wanted and offered to help them search the following day.

While the soldiers slept, Phocas dug his own grave in the garden. The next morning, he revealed all and said that martyrdom would be an honor. They killed him and buried him in his grave. Even in death, Phocas enriched his beloved garden — which sure seems saintly to me.

Other garden patrons include St. Rose of Lima, the first saint of the Americas, who lived in a hut in her garden in Peru around the turn of the 17th Century. She showed her piety through extreme penance. And St. Dorothy, who was executed as a Christian by the Romans in the Fourth Century. On her way to her death, the young gardener was jeered by a lawyer for her refusal to marry or to worship idols. He asked her to send him fruits from paradise. After the execution, a child appeared with three roses and three apples. The attorney was convinced. He became a Christian and was martyred himself.

For the less reverential there are the pagan deities associated with the garden — such as the Greek god Pan, who is said to inspire fertility and sometimes shows up as fountain statuary spouting water into pools. Also the "green man," a primal and mysterious character who goes back as least 2,000 years and is usually depicted as a face partly obscured by leaves or with fruits and vines coming out of his mouth. He is said to represent humankind's harmony with nature.

To each his own. I'm not about to tell you who or what to believe in. All I know is that when it comes to gardening, a little help could be divine.

St. Fiacre standing in the garden. The prayerful monk grew crops that fed the poor and helped the sick.

FALL

September

It is the month when we wave "so long" to summer and make way for fall. The autumnal equinox brings the official farewell, but Labor Day has come to symbolize the people's goodbye. Summer fun is over — it's time for school and the last barbecue.

In the garden, things are not that cut and dried. Especially not in September, when roses bloom and vegetables flourish. Just the other day, we put tuna steaks on the outdoor grill and added eggplants from our own vegetable patch. My chrysanthemums tell me that autumn is here but my cosmos and cleomes show no sign of letting up. My ageratum, a sturdy pilgrim of summer, is keeping the faith in fall.

I like this gradual merging. We make hard and fast boundaries but nature is more gentle. So while you're saving seeds and potting up herbs to bring indoors, make sure you enjoy the roses. And keep on barbecuing.

September

Honey, I Shrunk The Lawn

I walk down a wood-chip path that snakes along borders of spirea and red barberry and rugosa roses. Golden privets snuggle next to blue spruces, and yellow trumpet vines scramble up crimson king maples. Willow oaks and star magnolias and gold-tipped junipers mingle with ribbon grass and purple smokebush and Spanish broom.

As I forge forward I'm surrounded by high-bush blueberries and lemon balm and Montauk daisies. Eastern white pines and blue Leyland cypress screen a wooden fence. Perennial hibiscus with flowers as big as dinner plates glow red, white and pink in the sun. Pastel yarrow blankets the ground. Blue clematis climbs a Korean dogwood. Two redwoods tower over the living bouquet of this yard.

Then the path plunges into the depths of the backyard and suddenly, there it is.

Geoffrey Fennimore's lawn.

Geoffrey stands in the middle of it with a smile on his face and his arms outstretched. "Isn't it beautiful?"

Indeed, it is. Green as an emerald. Plush as a new carpet. And about the size of a beach blanket. Geoffrey can mow it in less than a minute with the push mower he's had since childhood.

"I keep it as a symbol — to remember what it

Kerrin Polaski's Northport home. Beds of shrubs and perennials take the place of a lawn.

In Water Mill, grasses replace the traditional lawn at the home of Joseph and Kate Tyree.

was like when this whole place was lawn," says the suburban lord of the manor, who bought his 110-by-113-foot property about a block from the beach in Blue Point almost a decade ago. "It took me an hour and a half to mow it. Every five, six days — mowing, mowing, mowing. I was getting nowhere fast, using chemicals I didn't want to use, wasting time I didn't have. Now I spend about five minutes a year mowing the lawn. If you like lawns, more power to you. As for me, I don't feel that having a beautiful lawn means I've accomplished something."

What he's accomplished in its place is blooming wildly. Alternative lawns are popping up around Long Island and across America. There's an anti-grass-roots movement afoot in the land, and it covers a lot of ground. To purists it means made-in-America meadows filled with native grasses and wildflowers. To populists, alternative lawns can mean anything that isn't turf — from roses to pachysandra to backyard bird sanctuaries and moss gardens and drought-resistant xeriscapes.

But to purists and populists alike, it means mowing down the lawn. This is something to consider in the month of September when lawn renovations are in full swing across Long Island. When so many homeowners are reseeding and sodding in an eternal effort to have the best lawn on the block.

The fact is, some garden authorities think the green grass of home is a threatened species. "Within the next three generations, there will be a profound change in the cultural aesthetic of the lawn," predicts David Northington, former executive director of the Lady Bird Johnson Wildflower Center in Austin, Texas. "In 50 years, you'll have to go to a museum or botanical garden to see a stretch of rolling, green lawn as we now know it."

This is pretty radical talk in my neck of the woods and, I'm sure, in yours, too. But I'm listening. Almost a century ago, economist Thorstein Veblen cited the lawn as an example of conspicuous consumption. In 1870, Frank J. Scott, author of "The Art of Beautifying Suburban Home Grounds" and no slouch when it came to hyperbole, wrote, "Let your lawn be your home's velvet robe and your flowers not too promiscuous decorations."

Green velvet for the American dream. Our lawns are our public faces. We may have dirty bathrooms and greasy stoves and messy garages, but if our front lawns are green and tidy and manicured, we're perceived as good and proper citizens. So we've clung to them even if we've had to waste water, even if killing chinch bugs with chemicals means annihilating earthworms that aerate the soil, even if we've created junkie lawns that need drugs to look good. Green lawns have become the symbols of status. Which, when you think about it, is a little embarrassing.

"We're all very different as people," says Stevie Daniels, former executive editor of Organic

Gardening magazine and author of "The Wild Lawn Handbook — Alternatives to the Traditional Front Lawn." "So it's hard for me to accept that we all have this green carpet in front of our houses. It takes courage to do something different."

Considering all that, my stroll through Geoffrey Fennimore's yard became the high point of an odyssey. A journey into the evolution of the suburban lawn — and by extension, a journey into my own perspective. A look at the old ways and a search for the new right here on Lawn Island.

I find that the brave exist everywhere. Here are just a few profiles in courage:

In Port Jefferson Station, Sandy Hull took three years to eliminate the Kentucky bluegrass in her backyard, but now she has two koi ponds and a shade garden with columbine and bleeding hearts and groundcovers of periwinkle and ivy. "My grassless backyard has become my haven," Sandy says.

In East Meadow, Marvin Eilenberg's 60-by-100-foot plot has been coming up roses ever since he wiped out his lawn nine years ago. "For some people a green, perfect lawn is their way of saying, 'Hey, I've reached the top,' " says his wife, Lenore. "But ours was never perfect." Now Lenore looks out her window in the morning and smells the roses.

In Centerport, Ruth Case ripped out her lawn not long ago and planted a perennial garden filled with foxgloves and daylilies and delphiniums. She left a ribbon of grass along the above-ground pool and a patch near the driveway that takes all of 15 minutes to cut with her brand new hand mower. "The lawn was ugly and nothing but work," Ruth says. "Believe me, no one in this family misses it."

In Northport, Kerrin Polaski never even bothered with a lawn when she moved into her new house a decade ago. Instead, her yard blooms with blossoms for bees and butterflies and berries for birds. "What kind of wildlife does a lawn attract?" she asks, "Chinch bugs and grubs?"

In Holtsville, Anita Cafferty found the courage to kill her front lawn several years ago with black plastic mulch. She dumped 18 cubic yards of red stones called barnyard chips in its place, and then she smothered the back lawn, too. She put in a flagstone path and a few raised beds and planted everything from dwarf mugho pines and weeping cherry trees to Montauk daisies and baby's breath. "Grass is an exercise in futility," she says. "Now when I see my neighbors mowing and watering and edging and fertilizing, I just laugh and drive away in my convertible."

In Bayport, Lauren Pollack turned her 322-foot-long yard into a series of garden rooms connected by grassy pathways and a few squares of lawn where her two preschoolers can play. Lauren has a vision of a

brave new world. "In my head, I already have their swing set sold and the lawn out of there and a new garden planted. I stay awake at night fantasizing about ripping out every lawn in the neighborhood."

According to the Lawn Institute, a Georgia-based nonprofit organization dedicated to the promulgation of turf, there are 46.5 million acres of the stuff in the United States. About half of that — or 50,000 square miles — are home lawns. This would be like mowing New England. It's not easy being green.

Some experts think the yen for lawns may be genetic — going back to the African savannahs that provided our ancestors with grassland for forage. Others point to the Middle Ages, when the fields around castles deterred sneak attacks and offered food for livestock. Later, English lords surrounded their manors with regal greenswards, and the tradition spread down to the middle class and found its modern incarnation.

Still, if I was drawn to my lawn by some collective unconscious, I never really bonded with it — I never mowed it or raked it or ran barefoot through it. I just liked the idea of it. Until I met a neighbor named Jeanette Stellmann, whose yard is a mosaic of woodland gardens and rock gardens and vegetable gardens and a roadside border of daffodils that gives way to daylilies.

"I know your house," Jeanette said. "You're the one with that big lawn. Why don't you do something useful with that lawn. Why don't you plant — corn. Or something."

Like, a meadow, maybe. Natural lawn people are mad for meadows. I'd love to have a meadow — not a vast one, something in the 50-square-foot range, what Stevie Daniels calls a "pocket meadow." But it's not that simple. A meadow isn't a place where you've let everything go. That's a wilderness. At the least, a meadow requires maintenance. That means you can't dump your lawn mower — a proper meadow needs to be mowed once or twice a year. And sophisticated meadows

Below, Geoffrey Fennimore and the push mower he uses on his tiny relic of a lawn. At left, the gated entrance of his front garden.

In Bayport, Lauren Pollack strolls through her series of garden rooms that occupy the lawn area.

— which include a balance of native grasses and wildflowers — need a little planning.

There are different approaches to meadows. One grows in Kate and Joseph Tyree's 3 1/2 -acre showplace in Water Mill. Kate and Joe's story is like a lesson in Lawn Island history. Once upon a time in suburbia, they lived in a development house on a 100-by-100-foot plot in Massapequa. "Lawns were IT," says Joe. "You mowed twice a week and you practically had to pick the weeds out by hand or you felt guilty — like you weren't a good person or you were somehow letting the neighbors down." But things started to change after Joe built a house in Water Mill and retired. At first, the Tyrees held fast to the familiar — they seeded their two acres with Farmingdale mix and got a ride-on mower. Then they bought an adjacent property — and for the first time as homeowners they stopped to think about their lawn. Enough was enough.

Now they have a sort of laissez-faire meadow defined by grassy paths and a terrace of lawn. The Tyrees take what nature gives them — bayberry, gold-enrod, Queen Anne's lace, milkweed, thistle, chickory, knapweed, oxeye daisies, black-eyed Susans. "I love walking in it," says Kate. " When the wind blows, it's like waves rolling in the ocean."

In the springtime, when the meadow reaches 10 inches high, Joe jumps on his ride-on mower. He shaves his meadow again in late autumn. "I have 10 times as much land as I had in Massapequa, but I don't spend nearly as much time taking care of it," Joe says.

A more restrained approach is that of nursery owner David Seeler, who removed about an acre of turf near his summer home in Amagansett and put in sheep's fescue, a non-native grass that grows in bunches and mingles well with wildflowers. He added coreopsis and wild lupines and oxeye daisies and butterfly weed.

As for me, I didn't know what to say when my neighbor Jeanette asked why I didn't plant something instead of wasting my lawn on grass. But a seed of change started germinating. I doubt that we'll ever look out our front window onto a sea of

116

September

maize. Still, we are making inroads on the grass. Several summers ago, we reduced the front lawn by digging up virtually all of our foundation shrubs and planting them around the periphery of the property. Next, we widened the beds around the house and planted perennials and low-growing evergreens. More recently, we dug out a 2,500-square-foot section of the lawn and replaced it with a vegetable and flower garden.

We're talking evolution here, not revolution.

Most homeowners in our cradle of suburbia still associate lawns with the good life and simple pleasures. As turf grass expert Maria Cinque puts it: "You can't play ball or have a picnic on pachysandra or creeping juniper." Both Maria and Jim Brooks, director of the Lawn Institute, are passionate about the splendors of grass. They maintain that healthy turf actually conserves water and reduces soil erosion and filters pollutants from the air. "The lawn has gotten a bad rap," says Maria, "You don't have to use an arsenal of pesticides to have a green lawn. Certain perennial ryes have a good-guy fungus that renders them resistant to chinch bugs. Some of the tall fescues are drought-resistant."

I'm still taking baby steps. But I am on a journey that comes alive in Geoffrey Fennimore's yard, where carpet bugle spreads a blanket of blue in the spring and arrowwood viburnum blazes orange in autumn and Harry Lauder's walking stick bares its gnarled skeleton in winter — and a small green patch seems like a relic.

Reseeding the Lawn

Old customs die hard and it's difficult to think of our suburbs without front lawns. If you cling to the old ways or are only willing to try alternatives by degrees, you should be doing your best to maintain a healthy lawn. If the green, green grass of home needs a shape-up, get out there now. September is a prime time to renovate your lawn. There's less competition from weeds, and new grass will have almost a year before facing another summer. Here are some tips:

START FROM SCRATCH. Get rid of existing grass. Organic gardeners can use a shovel or rent a sod cutter. Or you can kill the grass with glyphosate, a nonselective herbicide. But be careful — it will kill most other plants it touches.

TEST YOUR SOIL. Its pH should be 6.5 to 6.8.

GIVE the new lawn a little nurturing by rototilling a high-phosphorous fertilizer, lime and about 4 inches of organic matter into the soil.

SMOOTH IT OUT. Rake evenly and take out stones larger than an inch in diameter. Wait a week for the ground to settle or speed up the process with a roller.

SELECT YOUR GRASS. Consider drought-tolerant tall fescues like Falcon, Jaguar or Rebel II, or try varieties of perennial ryegrass like All*Star, Citation II or Commander with an endophytic or "good guy" fungus that makes them resistant to surface-feeding insects such as chinch bugs.

SOW YOUR SEEDS. The best way is to do it with a spreader. Sow half in one direction, half at right angles. Rake so the seeds are covered with soil and roll the lawn-to-be one more time.

WATER. You should moisten the top 5 inches of soil. Then mist several times a day or every other day, depending on local restrictions. You could run your sprinkler about 15 minutes in each section.

LET the grass grow under your feet and when it's about 3 inches tall, get out the mower.

The Most Happy Flower

The botanical name for sunflower is *Helianthus* — helios meaning sun and anthus for flower. Sunflower — the name says it all. I look at a sunflower and my heart warms. I can't help smiling. It's like having the sun itself in your garden. There's a fairy-tale feel to these most happy members of the *Compositae*, or daisy, family that stirs fancies best suited to childhood. Perhaps that's another reason for their attraction. Sometimes I wonder if Jack really climbed a beanstalk to get to the land of fe-fi-fo-fum. I think he might have clambered up a sunflower.

Even the dwarf varieties of *Helianthus annuus* — the common large-flowered annual that most of us grow from seed each summer — seem to stretch up and up and up. Sunflowers of all kinds have been smiling at the sky for centuries.

And it's all been happening in our hemisphere. Long before Van Gogh turned the golden daisies of the sun into an art form, the Incas of Peru decorated temple walls with carvings of sunflowers and used them as a motif for the medallions worn by priestesses. Actually, sunflowers are North American natives — fossil evidence indicates they grew in our southwest as far back as 3000 BC. Experts believe that the Indians cultivated them even before corn — eventually reforming the relatively small-flowered wild varieties into large single-headed sunflowers. They roasted the seeds, then ground them into meal for bread and stews. And in a move modern health-food enthusiasts would applaud, they boiled the roasted hulls for a caffeine-free beverage.

Or to put it another way, sunflowers already had a history when Columbus discovered America. Kansas may be the sunflower state, but Alan Kapuler, who grows thousands of varieties of *Helianthus* as research director for Seeds of Change, an organic seed catalog based in Santa Fe, N.M.,thinks it deserves much wider recognition. "I can't believe that our national flower is the rose," he says. "The sunflower is the *true* American flower." Alan absolutely beams when it comes to sunflowers. "Plant a sunflower," he says, "and grow a happy world."

Still, like a lot of big talents, the sunflower had to leave home to make it as a star. Spanish explorers brought seeds back to the old country with them and the plant took center stage in botanic gardens across Europe. In the late 17th Century, Peter the Great introduced sunflowers to Russia and the peasants literally gobbled them up. The Holy Orthodox Church of Russia banned the consumption of oil-rich foods during Lent but sunflowers were too recent an arrival to make the forbidden list. By the early 1800s, Russian farmers had more than 2 million acres in cultivation.

Now sunflowers shine across the world. They range from foot-high munchkins to 12-foot-tall giants that even Shaquille O'Neal would have to look up at. There are more than 60 species with blossoms that range in size from soup spoons to serving platters. They're not all lollipops with a round flower on a single stem. And they come in almost all the colors of a Fire Island sunset — from the classic sunburst of Ruckman Lite to the deep dark burgundy of Evening Sun to the bronze streaks of Bob's Newest.

Another nice thing about these happy flowers that bloom in our yards from July through September is that they're for gardeners of all ages. The giants make fun clubhouses for children and are terrific at screening compost piles or chain-link fences. The bushy multi-branching varieties are perfect for beds and borders and for hiding the scraggly legs of single-stemmed sunflowers. The dwarf hybrids look great in containers.

When you're choosing sunflowers, you might want to make a distinction between plants known for decorative blooms and plants that produce edible seeds. I was pleased with the pretty sunflowers that reached over pink hollyhocks and red hibiscus in the corners of my fenced-in garden and with orange Mexican sunflowers, or *Tithonia rotundifolia*, that sparkled in my borders.

Some other colorful choices include the Teddy Bear varieties with shaggy double chrysanthemum-like golden flowers or Floristan, a bicolor with rusty red petals and yellow tips that grows 3 feet tall with lots of branches, or Gloriosa with a red bull's-eye and 2-inch-long orange petals blotched by purple. Or Italian White, an heirloom variety with long lemon-custard petals and chocolate centers. And for cut-flower lovers, there's Sunbright, with golden petals and brown disks.

It has a pollenless center, which may be bad news for bees but means it doesn't shed in the vase.

The best-known edible-seed sunflower is probably Mammoth, which was first introduced in the United States in the 1880s. Or you might have a taste for Peredovik, a Russian variety with oil-rich seeds. It's a wise choice for snacking and cooking because the seed shells are thin enough to crack by hand. And you'll enjoy the orange flower that grows 5 to 6 inches across on 6-foot stalks.

In general, sunflowers aren't finicky — they like well-drained soil but they'll tolerate dry conditions. The seeds are big — they're easy to plant and quick to germinate. Just remember though that they're *sun*flowers and make sure they get plenty of it. In the spring after danger of frost is past and night temperatures are above 55 degrees, plant the seeds no more than 1 inch deep. They should germinate in 5 to 10 days. When the sunflowers are about 6 inches tall, thin them to stand about 1 foot apart. Don't overwater or fertilize. Less water encourages better blooms and healthier roots — sunflower roots can reach 6 feet down to find the food they need.

If you're into eating the seeds, wait until the petals around the center disk fall off and the back of the flower head turns brown. Cut off the head and bend the sides back to loosen the seeds. Dry them in a warm shady spot for a few weeks, or pop them in the oven for an instant snack. The National Sunflower Association recommends sprinkling sunflower kernels on everything from ice cream and salad to pasta and hot cereal.

As for me, I'm content just to enjoy my sunflowers. They are the sunshine of my garden.

Sunflowers basking in the sun at Brightwaters Farm in Bay Shore.

119

The Fall Kick-off

There is a tendency in some quarters of the garden world to put down anything that's popular — impatiens for one, Roseum Elegans, better known as mauve rhododendrons, for another. And that goes double for chrysanthemums. There are those who think chrysanthemums are plain common.

At the risk of getting too bold for my blue jeans, I think a certain snobbery is at work here. I wouldn't want impatiens to take over the world, but there's a place for them in my garden. And that goes double for chrysanthemums.

I think of chrysanthemums as the impatiens of autumn — and I mean that as a compliment. Without them, the fall garden would be a paler place. They come in a wide range of shades, they're low-maintenance and they bloom till frost. Besides which, they stand for the season as much as scarecrows and hayrides and Indian corn. Some people hear the word "fall" and they imagine forward passes. I imagine bronze-colored pompons that have nothing to do with cheerleaders.

They're one of those universal transitions — like the way once Labor Day comes, everything is back-to-school and sweaters and long sleeves, and football. In the garden, it's chrysanthemum time. Incidentally, let's call them by their lovely proper name. I hate horticultural diminutives in general — cuke and glad and rhodie. And mum in particular. It's a flower, not an English parent.

Anyway, chrysanthemums kick off the season with instant color. Lots of color. White and gold and lavender and pink and red and bronze. Almost every shade except blue. Their name itself comes from the Greek words for "gold" and "flower."

There was a time not so long ago when 150 species were part of the genus *Chrysanthemum*. But the latest reclassification is a head-spinner. Taxonomists — the botanists who specialize in the identification, classification and nomenclature of plants — have ripped the genus asunder. They've come up with a dozen different names for flowers that were once classified as chrysanthemums. For instance, Shasta daisies are now classified as *Leucanthemum* and marguerites as *Argyranthemum*. And the beautiful florists' chrysanthemums are grouped under the name *Dendranthema*. All that's left in the official genus *Chrysanthemum* is five species of annuals.

This is all pretty technical and I suspect that only the botanical literati are taking the changes to heart. Most garden-variety gardeners as well as true fanciers would agree with Ted Rice of Huntington, who believes that "chrysanthemums are still chrysanthemums." As Ted puts it: "A chrysanthemum by any other name would be easier to spell."

Ted Rice has a garden full of winners. Ted lost his head to chrysanthemums in 1986 when he went to a flower show and ended up joining the Long Island Chrysanthemum Society. He's been growing and propagating and competing ever since.

"There is no such thing as a perfect flower," Ted says, "but chrysanthemums are about as close as you can get. They have it all — beauty, color, many different flower forms. And when just about everything else is getting nipped by frost, garden chrysanthemums keep going. They'll tolerate a little frost, and very few flowers will last as long once they're cut."

On a tour of his garden, Ted gave me a crash course on these Energizer Bunnies of the fall garden.

First of all, chrysanthemums are photoperiodic, which means they flower in response to the length of the day. Like poinsettias and asters, they don't set buds until days grow short and nights long. Which is what makes chrysanthemum-growing on a competitive level such a challenge. Exhibition plants bloom naturally in late October or early November, so serious growers in our part of the country have to provide at least 12 hours of darkness to fool them into flowering early. That's why Ted shades his chrysanthemums with black cloth for three weeks every August.

Luckily, this isn't something most of us have to worry about. Most chrysanthemums you'll see for sale are garden plants with mass appeal — what most of us put in the ground to liven up our yards after the atumnal equinox. Technically, they're perennials, but if you're looking for something that will come back next year, make sure you buy plants labeled "hardy chrysanthemums."

Not that there are any guarantees. "We call them garden hardies, but a lot of them really aren't so hardy," Ted says. "Most people treat chrysanthemums as annuals — they give you a shot of color when and where you need it, and if they die, they die. You've gotten your money's worth." He recommends cushion types or plants that have a short, mounding habit as the most reliable — easy-to-grow cultivars like golden-yellow Sun Dial, bronze-red Remarkable or lavender-pink Debonair.

I like chrysanthemums. Considering the instant color they bring us as the light wanes and winter waits on the horizon, there's nothing common about chrysanthemums.

Left, a Vienna Waltz spider chrysanthemum, in front are Boladeoro. Below, a scene at the New York Botanical Garden.

Hot Plants for Autumn Color

Genus, Species	Common Name	Mature Height**	Fall Characteristics
Small Trees			
Acer palmatum	Japanese Maple	to 25 ft.	Yellow to bronze or purple or vivid red
Acer triflorum	Three-Flower Maple	20-30 ft.	Butterscotch to orange or red foliage
Crataegus	Washington Hawthorn	25-30 ft.	Glossy red fruit and orange, red and purple foliage
Crataegus viridis*	Green Hawthorn	20-35 ft.	Bright red fruits and purple and scarlet foliage
Cornus florida*	Flowering Dogwood	20-40 ft.	Glossy red fruit and red to red purple foliage
Cornus kousa	Korean Dogwood	20-30 ft.	Purple-red foliage
Franklinia alatamaha*	Franklinia	10-20 ft.	Orange-red foliage
Malus floribunda	Japanese Flowering	15-25 ft.	Red and yellow fruit
Malus hybrids	Crab Apple	to 25 ft.	Red or yellow fruit, occasional
Oxydendrum arboreum*	Sourwood	25-30 ft.	Red, yellow and purple foliage
Parrotia persica	Parrot Tree	20-40 ft.	Yellow, orange and scarlet foliage
Stewartia pseudocamellia	Stewartia	30-30 ft.	Yellow to red to dark purple-red foliage
Shrubs			
Amelanchier canadensis*	Shadblow Serviceberry	6-20 ft.	Yellow-gold to orange foliage
Aronia arbutifolia*	Red Chokeberry	6-10 ft.	Red fruit and glowing red foliage
Berberis thunbergii	Japanese Barberry	3-6 ft.	Red fruit, orange, scarlet and red-purple foliage
Callicarpa japonica	Japanese Beautyberry	4-6 ft.	Vivid violet or white fruit
Callicarpa americana*	American Beautyberry	3-8 ft.	Vivid violet to magenta (or white) fruit
Cornus racemosa	Gray Dogwood	to 10 ft.	White fruit and purple maroon foliage
Cotinus coggygria	Smoke bush	10-15 ft.	Red-purple or pink-purple foliage
Euonymous alatus	Winged Euonymous	9-20 ft.	Red foliage
Fothergilla gardenii*	Dwarf Fothergilla	2-3 ft.	Orange to red foliage
Fothergilla major*	Large Fothergilla	6-10 ft.	Orange to red foliage
Hamamelis mollis*	Chinese Witch hazel	10-20 ft.	Yellow foliage
Hydrangea paniculata grandiflora	Pee-Gee Hydrangea	to 25 ft.	Greenish-pink flowerheads with green, yellow and purple-pink foliage
Hydrangea quercifolia*	Oakleaf Hydrangea	4-8 ft.	Red, orange, brown and purple foliage
Ilex verticillata*	Winterberry Holly	6-10 ft.	Bright red fruit, bronze to orange, or red foliage in better varieties like Autumn Glow
Itea virginica*	Virginia Sweetspire	3-5 ft.	Scarlet and crimson foliage
Lindera benzoin*	Spicebush	6-12 ft.	Yellow foliage
Rhododendron arborescens*	Sweet Azalea	8-15 ft.	Glossy dark red foliage
Rhododendron schlippenbachii	Royal Azalea	6-8 ft.	Yellow to orange to crimson foliage
Rhododendron vaseyi*	Pinkshell Azalea	5-10 ft.	Light red foliage
Rhododendron viscosum*	Swamp Azalea	5-10 ft.	Orange to bronze foliage
Rhus typhina Laciniata*	Cutleaf Staghorn Sumac	15-30 ft.	Orange and scarlet foliage
Rhus aromatica	Dwarf Fragrant Sumac	2 ft.	Orange to red to red-purple foliage
Rosa hybrids	Rose	to 15 ft.	Ones with good hips like Inspiration
Rosa rugosa	Rugosa Rose	4 ft.	Purple and bronze foliage, large red hips
Rosa setigera*	Prairie Rose	to 15 ft.	Red hips and bronze foliage
Spiraea prunifolia	Bridalwreath Spirea	4-9 ft.	Glossy yellow orange to bronze foliage
Vaccinium corymbosum*	Highbush Blueberry	6-12 ft.	Combined yellow, orange, bronze and red foliage
Viburnum carlesii	Koreanspice Viburnum	4-8 ft.	Red to wine foliage
Viburnum opulus	European Cranberrybush	8-12 ft.	Red or yellow fruit and red-purple foliage
Viburnum plicatum	Doublefile Viburnum	10 ft.	Red fruit and, in the variety Mariesii, purple-red foliage
Viburnum setigerum Tea Viburnum	Tea Viburnum	8-12 ft.	Bright red fruit and occasional red-purple foliage
Viburnum trilobum*	American Cranberrybush	8-12 ft.	Bright red fruit and red purple foliage

*-Native American plant

**-Ranges reflect many trees are substantially smaller in cultivation than in wild.

Call this "Eggplant — A Love Story." A romance as satisfying as the lavender blooms that show in early summer and as constant as the strong and tender taste of my eggplants' baked, stewed and sauteed flesh. I'm unburdening my heart here. When it comes to home-grown vegetables, I've always had a thing for tomatoes and I'm quite fond of lettuce, especially red leaf and romaine. I'm not fickle — I still care about them. But for the last few seasons, I've been in love with eggplants. The way they look, the way they cook, the whole ratatouille.

I guess the romance began on a winter afternoon when I curled up with seed catalogs in front of the fire. Seed catalogs are full of flowery moments, especially when it comes to vegetables. And eggplants are made for poets. Even the variety names smack of Harlequin romances — Rosa Bianca, Black Beauty, Asian Bride, Purple Blush, Bambino. Just listen to the passion Shepherd's Garden Seeds lavishes on Rosa Bianca: "The rounded, plump teardrop-shaped fruits slowly emerge from their blossom casings forming heavy globes in delicate shades of rosy lavender and soft white . . . Best of all their pretty flesh is delicious." Or catch this paean to Italian Pink Bi-Color in Seeds of Change: "Skin is a creamy, purple-lavender, overlaid with rose-pink vertical stripes. Flesh is sweet and tender."

Couldn't you just swoon?

I couldn't resist. I ordered several varieties of the vegetable that belongs to the nightshade family, which also includes tomatoes, and is more formally known as *Solanum melongena*: Agora, a vigorous hybrid, and Rosa Bianca, an Italian heirloom, and Black Beauty, a widely grown standard.

But love came late that fledging season and was confined to a single variety. My then new garden was not ready for planting until the beginning of July, and when the seedlings I had started indoors withered on their spindly stalks, I bought a few from my friendly neighborhood nursery. They were all Black Beauty, which is actually dark purple and has the sheen of good satin. As the Seeds of Change catalog describes it, "purplish-black glossy fruits have great flavor and hold up well after being picked."

Black Beauty, incidentally, is very well bred — it has historic standing as the first American variety to be put on the market. That wasn't until 1902. Actually, eggplants have been around for ages — Sanskrit writings indicate they originated in India. They spread into China and the Near East, and then into the fields and kitchens of Spain and Italy. Americans were a little backward about eggplants.

Since that first year — Black Beauty lived up to its press clippings — I haven't been the least bit backward about eggplants. Any true romance is a two-way street — you have to give something to get something back — and I give a lot to my eggplants. I plant my seedlings with a plethora of caring and even more compost in a sunny spot that gets plenty of water from a sprinkler system.

Purple Passion

Plump, luscious eggplants like this one delight the senses and satisfy the soul.

Chores Galore

BRING houseplants inside. Check first for insects and disease. Cut back leggy plants, repot if necessary.

TAKE 4- to 6-inch cuttings of annual geraniums, coleus, wax begonias, impatiens, zinnias, lantana, marigolds and petunias and overwinter them indoors. Pinch off flower buds and root the cuttings in moist vermiculite. Cover with a clear plastic bag and keep them out of direct sun for a few days. Then place them in a sunny spot. Feed and water and watch for blooms in 6 to 8 weeks.

DIVIDE peonies if they need it. Leave several eyes — the little pink pointed buds on the root — per division. Replant in rich, well-drained soil with the eyes no more than 2 inches below the surface. Remember, peonies like sun.

KEEP picking pole beans and squash. The more you pick, the more the plants will produce.

SALAD days aren't over. Sow a final crop of lettuce, spinach and radishes.

PLANT pansies. They'll bloom till frost, and they may even brighten winter before they put on a grand show in the spring. Remember to mulch after the ground has frozen.

STOP deadheading roses. The plant will develop rose hips and know its time to prepare for dormancy. Cut back diseased or damaged canes but save major pruning for spring.

PLANT lilies. You can never have enough.

PUT in spring-flowering shrubs such as lilacs, buddleias and forsythias. It's best to plant in the morning or late afternoon on an overcast day.

SAVE seeds of heirloom tomatoes such as Brandywine or Old Striped German. Cut overripe tomatoes in half, squeeze the seed-laden pulp into a clean container and discard the skins. Add one tablespoon of water, stir, cover the container with cheesecloth and place in a warm location, indoors or out, to ferment. Soak seeds for about three days or until froth forms on surface and liquid is clear. Good seeds sink to the bottom, infertile ones rise to the top. Dump the good seeds in a strainer and rinse. Dry the washed seeds in a single layer on a fine-mesh screen for about 48 hours. Store in an airtight jar in a cool place. You'll have viable seeds for 3 to 5 years.

TRANSPLANT or plant evergreens. Cooler temperatures encourage root growth. Remember to loosen the roots of containerized plants, and be sure to mulch and water thoroughly.

HARVEST potatoes when the tops fall over.

REPLACE tired annuals with ornamental cabbage and kale.

PICK herbs for drying. Collect them in the morning when their oils are at their peak. Hang small bunches upside down in a dry room out of direct sunlight.

Now my eggplant love is a many-splendored thing. It is September and there are five varieties flourishing in my garden. Each has its own virtues and attractions. I couldn't help but bring back Black Beauty, and I also planted another dark purple passion called Dusky that my husband picked up in a nursery. And I have very tender feelings about Neon, which I started from seed. The catalogs describe it as dark pink but I think it verges on lavender. I love this description in a Johnny's Selected Seeds catalog: "Neon is a productive, edible work of art."

My Neon eggplants stand out in their gently curving glory as if there are lights shining inside them. I walk into the garden and the minute I see Neons' blushing lavender, I can't wait to get my hands on them so I can hustle them into the kitchen. Their taste is mild but excellent without the slightest hint of bitterness.

My other varieties — one is a white hybrid known as Ghostbuster and another is an Oriental eggplant called Ichiban — are equally enticing. The white eggplant is softly pale and pure, slightly oval and sweet to the taste. The Asian eggplant is dark purple but slim and shaped like a curved zucchini. As the eggplants of my experience go, it is a little different — with 12-inch narrow fruit and a small seed cavity — but we're talking romance here so vive la différence.

And my Black Beauties are tall, dark and handsome. Eggplants are easily as voluptuous as Bartlett pears and butternut squash. And they not only delight the senses, but like same-day corn and just-picked strawberries, they satisfy the soul. Perhaps they don't offer much in the way of nutrition, but they don't make you fat, either.

I'm very happy when I grill eggplants or bake them or even puree them or add them to my tomato sauce. This summer, I found a lovely recipe for eggplant and chick-pea stew and another for a baked casserole of tomato, eggplants, low-fat mozzarella and turkey sausage. And I just tried a recipe for baked ratatouille that got four stars from my husband and five from me. What could make you happier than that?

Nothing except going into the garden on a morning made for thoughts of love with butterflies for company and the sun beaming down. And then filling my green harvest basket with ripe red tomatoes and green bell peppers and dark purple and deep pink and pure white eggplants. Oh yes, I read that you can freeze eggplants, and I'm trying that so I don't have to spend the winter in longing. In the garden of my mind, eggplants are forever.

A Dancer's Dream

Carol Mercer in her East Hampton garden.

If gardening in its highest sense is an art and art imitates life, then it follows that we plant where we've been and where we're going. And what and who we are. We cultivate the shapes and textures and rhythms and colors of our own experience. It is like that for Carol Mercer, who has had five careers — Broadway dancer, actress, photographer's rep, flower arranger, garden designer. And who likes to say she's had "three husbands, three lives."

Carol Mercer looks back and perhaps forward at her life when she looks across the nooks and crannies and borders and beds of her garden. A garden that verges on magic with thousands of perennials and vines and ferns and ornamental grasses around and about four acres in East Hampton. A garden that stretches to the sandy dunes and the sea beyond.

"Gardens should be about the gut of a person," says Carol, a chatty woman in a gray sweatsuit. Behind her in the driveway, the license plate on her station wagon testifies to her own passion — FLEUR. In front of her, a late summer border runs along the length of her swimming pool and amplifies the point. The border speaks to the heart of someone who explores color and texture and the contrast between light and dark

Above, an old willow stands gracefully near a fenced-in flower garden. Top, dahlias are pretty in pink in the cutting garden. Right, *Artemisia* Powis Castle shines against a backdrop of *Euonymous alatus*.

and who grows plume poppies not for the flower but "for the silver underleaf that shimmers in the wind."

She looks at the plum-purple leaves of *Rosa glauca* and the white daisylike flowers of feverfew against a backdrop of black mondo-grass — and sees herself. "I love the unexpected," she says.

"My first perennial garden was all reds and yellows. Every flower was round. *Heleniums. Helianthemums. Helianthus.* The hellies. I planted everything in threes and fives and sevens like they tell you in garden books. What I planted on one end, I repeated on the other. Maybe it had something to do with my background in flower arranging, which is a more structured way of seeing things. Then I started going to gardens in England, and I realized I didn't have to be so structured. I fell in love with the silvers. *Artemisia. Helichrysum.* My palette became softer and a new garden was born. It's like a big blowsy lady now."

The big blowsy lady dances in the breeze for its small vibrant choreographer. The dancer's sense of movement and the actress' flair for drama flow through the perennial border and the series of gardens touched not only by Carol Mercer's talents but

by the aura of the faraway places where the men she has known have taken her to live.

Her life has been a series of husbands, careers, adventures. She was an Agnes DeMille dancer and performed in the original production of "Oklahoma!" Her first husband was actor William Windom. "We lived in the city. We acted together in stock. It was wonderful to be young and in show business." They were married in 1947 and divorced seven years later. In 1957, she married Bob McElfresh, an automobile executive who worked in Switzerland and Germany. "I was an executive's wife. I put on fashion shows for the American Women's Club."

They were back in the States when the marriage ended. Carol became a photographer's rep for clients like Irving Penn and got into flower arranging. She did the flowers for balls honoring Nancy Reagan and Barbara Bush and created floral arrangements that filled Catherine Deneuve's hotel suite every time the actress came to New York.

Almost 30 years ago, she married Norman Mercer, who was in the import-export business in the Far East. They moved to a sprawling modern house in East Hampton, and that's when the garden that

had been germinating in Carol's life was born. The garden blossomed into a fifth career. She and a partner, Lisa Verderosa, operate The Secret Garden, creating living art in other people's landscapes.

Just as her life has been a chain of adventures, Carol Mercer's garden is a series of gardens. The perennial garden, the blue and yellow garden, the rose garden. The experimental garden — where Carol and Lisa nurture seeds snitched from places like Wave Hill in the Bronx and the Edinburgh Botanical Garden in Scotland — that unfolds beneath a giant weeping willow. The cutting garden, where sunflowers stretch for the light and more than 30 varieties of salvia grow — cherry reds and baby blues and startling *Salvia leucantha* with fuzzy chenillelike purple blooms and a variety called Tula, which is gorgeous in its transition from chartreuse buds to blue flowers.

And the water garden that marches around the great green-velvet lawn. Tall Phragmites sway in the distance. *Gaura lindheimeri* undulates in the front row. "It's like a dancing plant," the ex-dancer says. Ironweed rises 8 feet high and gunnera unfurls its leaves 8 feet wide. Huge hostas and black-stemmed baptisia and the bronze foliage and scarlet flowers of *Lobelia* Queen Victoria.

Even in her garden, Carol Mercer is still dancing. She plants in a rhythm. "There's a basic movement in the way plants are placed. It's something you feel."

Much of the rhythm is achieved by planting in masses. Her garden sways with masses of fountain

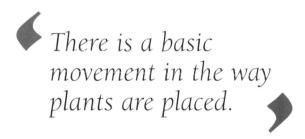

There is a basic movement in the way plants are placed.

grasses such as *Pennisetum alopecuroides* Hamlen and Moudry and *P. setaceum* Burgundy Giant. Drifts of *Aster tataricus* dance nearby.

Carol Mercer's garden is rhythmic and confident and grand in scale. The gardener who plants it grew up in Great Neck, where her mother was a flower arranger. "When I was a kid, if my mother had flowers to work with, the house could fall apart. She was always noticing color. 'Look at the blue of that sky. See the red in that salad.'

"Color is what gets me charged up in the garden," says the woman who isn't afraid of new beginnings. "But change is what it's all about, and I have a lot left to do."

Adventures await. So does the garden.

Loving a Day of Labor

I t is one of those days when the sunshine pours down like silent rain, drenching earth, plants and gardeners with late summer heat. I keep a water bottle alongside me in the flower beds and vow to take a break at noon, or at least take shelter in the shade. It is late August and I'm a few days early, but in the garden every day is Labor Day.

I can hear birds going about their business outside the fence — chirping, calling, commenting about the day. Talking perhaps about returning south now that summer is winding down. Or chattering about the silly humans laboring in the dirt. But in the garden, everything is quiet as if sound itself is muted by the heat.

Bees forage among the cone flowers — maybe they're onto the virtues of *Echinacea*. Butterflies explore the blue salvia. I spot a black swallowtail

and a pearly crescent, but no monarchs. The air is heavy and the movement of the bees and the butterflies has a dreamlike quality. For the most part, the garden is still. The garden waits for my labor. Such honest labor. The tomatoes need staking, the weeds are beyond the pale, the spent blooms of the lilies are ready to be removed.

I love such days.

In the heat and stillness, the world beyond the green picket fence and the arbors and the gates melts away. For the moment, family frustrations and office tensions fade. Perhaps that is the Zen of gardening — you become one with the plants, lost in the rhythm of the tasks at hand. Snip, tie, dig, pull. Actions become synchronized. The minutes tick away.

My husband ties the tomato vines to the bamboo stakes and cuts off fruitless side shoots. The vines are turning into tangles — he is trying to set

vinyl-coated metal Y-stakes and sink the stakes into the ground to prop up the cleome and purple cone flowers. It is time to shear off the spent spikes of lavender that are no longer the color purple but have turned a dusty pale shade of silvery blue. Waves of perfume reward me as I bend to them.

I cut a bouquet of white lilies and purple cone flowers and yellow snapdragons and pink cosmos for a galvanized-steel French bucket I bought at the Philadelphia Flower Show. It is almost 1 o'clock before we remember to take our break. On the way into the house, I spot a dead leaf on a taro plant in our small fish pond and go into automatic deadheading mode. But I reach too far forward and in a splash, I'm knee-deep in the pond. Actually, it's refreshing. After lunch we return to the fenced-in world of the flower-vegetable garden.

We share the stillness. In the garden, tranquility is my reality. I love the look of weeded beds and the sense of virtue they engender in me. They are like freshly dusted rooms and newly cleaned garages. But work begets work. One of my favorite quotes — the source is anonymous — goes "A garden is a thing of beauty and a job forever."

It's hard to be perfect in a world beset by bugs and disease, a world that's at the mercy of the weather. A garden, it seems to me, is a perpetual work in progress. But perfectionism is different here than in the office. Tension fades. Tranquility beckons. The garden offers satisfactions hard to come by in the workaday world. We make mental lists of things to do — put new pine bark mulch on the paths, get weatherproof tags, prune the climbing roses.

The heat fades with the dying afternoon. I am still at peace but more aware of the life in my garden. I once walked through Old Westbury Gardens with Sir David Attenborough and he told me about the secret life of plants — the stealing and cheating and sexual goings-on. I know such things are happening in my garden, and flora as well as fauna are involved. I reach beneath a weathered cedar bench to yank out a weed and find a sun-bleached rabbit skull.

Minutes later, my husband hollers as he tries to dig out the lovage threatening the passion flower vine. He has uncovered a nest filled with baby rabbits. Confused, they stumble out on the path. One of them tries to get back into the nest. My husband bends down, and for a moment I'm frightened. He smiles and very gently nudges the baby rabbit back home with a trowel.

Soon, dusk falls and the moon flowers appear like white saucers against the dark green fence. Their fragrance blends with the scent of the lilies. We gather up our tools and water bottles and close the garden gate.

things straight. Throughout the spring and summer in the garden, sun and earth and water performed their magic. Suddenly, seeds grew into plants, buds became flowers. But nature runs wild. In what seems like an instant, the neatly planted garden of spring verges on becoming a jungle. Gardeners keep order — or at least a semblance of it.

And so my husband maintains a modicum of discipline among the tomatoes, and weeds the vegetable beds and enjoys the fruits of his labors. He harvests the string beans and Swiss chard for tonight's supper and delights at the discovery of green peppers and ripening eggplants.

The browning heads of *Dianthus* and marigolds fall to my faithful Felco pruners, and I prop up the lilies that have grown as high as my shoulders. I pull purslane and quackgrass and errant tomato seedlings out of the paths. I adjust the arms of

The neatly planted garden of spring verges on becoming a jungle.

October

October is the flagship of fall. The earth cools and we turn our clocks back. In the fading afternoons, the world is like a perfectly appointed movie set as the sun slips into the pond behind my house. The gold and amber hues of the sunset are reflected in my garden — the great green leaves of the hostas fade to yellow, the Japanese maple glows in soft, maroon raiment. My beloved Sedum Autumn Joy glories in its change from rosy pink to burnished mahogany, and the feathery, rust-colored plumes of the fountain grass flutter in the wind. Life goes on in the still-sweet earth with salvias and scabiosa and asters and Japanese anemones and callicarpa and crape myrtle. I walk around the yard in the waning russet light and open the garden gate. I touch the cottony blooms of the fall clematis and stare at the colorful stalks of the still-lusty Swiss chard. I smile ruefully at the last tomatoes that cling forlornly to a browning vine. And my heart sings the bittersweet anthem of autumn.

Tulips: diamonds of the bulb world.

The Miracle Of the Bulbs

I look at the wizened bulbs as I press them into the hardening earth of fall and imagine the flowers of spring. The blue scilla by the mailbox and the lavender crocuses along the front walk and the drifts of daffodils in the beds and borders. And I wonder at the miracle of it all.

When I was a child I didn't think beyond the blooms themselves. Even on Easter, when fragrant white flowers bordered the pulpit where the minister in a black robe spoke of renewal and rebirth and life after death. All I saw were the trumpet-shaped petals of the Easter lily. It was the same with the red tulips and purple hyacinths we gave to my aunts later that day at dinner. I saw flowers, not symbolism.

But now that I have discovered the sweet mysteries of gardening, I stand spellbound at the miracle of the bulbs. The miracle takes place everywhere on

Long Island, where estimates are that as many as 15 million bulbs flower in spring. They bloom in back-yards and front yards and relieve the concrete land-scapes of shopping centers and corporate headquar-ters and traffic triangles and gas stations. They chase away memories of winter in parks and public gardens.

It's even more amazing when you realize that each bulb contains its own story and the story of genera-tions to come. If you slice a hyacinth bulb in half, you see the perfectly formed embryonic flower surrounded by the fleshy tissue that nourishes it. True bulbs like daffodils and hyacinths and tulips come fully packed, not only with the whole plant inside but with enough sugar, starch and protein to sustain it as it grows.

A bulb planted in autumn puts down roots with-in a few weeks and remains dormant through the cold months. The flowers push through in the spring. When the flower dies and the leaves wither, the roots draw nutrients from the soil and the fading foliage provides food for the bulb through photosyn-thesis — the process in which chlorophyll in the leaves uses the sun's energy to convert carbon diox-ide and water into carbohydrates and oxygen. This builds up strength in the bulb for the next year's blooms. And it nurtures new bulblets that form at the sides of the parent bulb — the tender beginnings of a new generation of flowers. That's why you can cut the stem off when the blossom wilts, but you shouldn't cut back the dying leaves.

The more I learn about bulbs, the more I'm amazed. A bulb is a plant that learned to survive by going underground during adverse seasons and stor-ing food until it could grow again. All the plants that are loosely called bulbs have this ability to nourish themselves. But only true bulbs contain complete miniatures of themselves inside the fleshy scales that are modified leaves. A true bulb like an Easter lily or a tulip was a leaf millions of years ago.

There are several bulb wannabes. A corm is the base of a stem that becomes swollen with nutrients. It has a bottom plate from which roots grow, and a dry-leaf covering but no fleshy scales. A tuberous root is exactly that, a real root that stores its food in root tissue rather than in stems or leaves. A tuber is a stem that has no covering and no basal plate. Roots and buds grow from its surface. A rhizome is a thick-ened stem that grows horizontally and sends shoots above ground. Technically speaking, crocuses are corms, dahlias are tuberous roots, anemones are tubers and cannas are rhizomes.

But for most of us, what's in a name? Bulbs by any other name grow as sweetly and profusely.

I realized just how profusely a few years ago when I traveled to Holland to get a close look at the miracle of the bulbs. Cold winds blew in from the

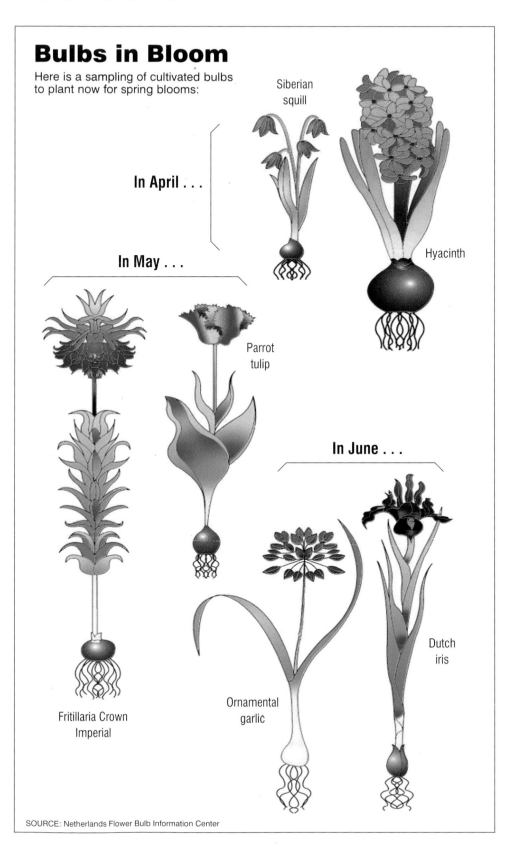

Bulbs in Bloom

Here is a sampling of cultivated bulbs to plant now for spring blooms:

In April . . .

Siberian squill

Hyacinth

In May . . .

Parrot tulip

In June . . .

Fritillaria Crown Imperial

Ornamental garlic

Dutch iris

SOURCE: Netherlands Flower Bulb Information Center

ocean and blustered across April. Spring was late and tulips were just beginning to run in rivers of red and gold and purple and orange.

I could only imagine what it would be like weeks later when the rivers of tulips overflowed the fields. But I was not unhappy. There was so much more to see. And not just yellow fields of early daffodils. Scented streams of pink hyacinths and rows of purple crocuses streaked the roadsides. Pots of *Anemone blanda* and mats of *Muscari* and *Scilla* colored the streets and homes of towns and villages in blue and white and pink and purple.

And in a park called Keukenhof — known as the spring garden of Europe — where 7 million bulbs are planted by hand every year, I saw more bulbs in flower than I had ever dreamed of. In the greenhouse, I saw the darker-than-dark purple tulip known as Queen of the Night and I marveled at tulips that looked like windmills and tulips that looked like lilies. But outdoors, the parklands of that slow spring belonged to other bulbs. Crocuses and daffodils ruled. Purple and pink hyacinths

crowded giant planters, blue and yellow crocuses and pink and blue and white *Chionodoxa* — also known as glory of the snow — speckled the sweeping lawns. The imposing *Fritillaria* Crown Imperial, which grows 3 to 4 feet tall, held court on a hillside with orange and yellow blooms.

That fall I planted a Crown Imperial in a pot outside my front door. And it came up — quite regally, I might add. I impressed myself. Pale blue *Camassia* — a late-spring bloomer that unlike most bulbs likes damp areas — flowered by the pool. And bright yellow *Erythronium*, a k a dog's-tooth-violet or trout lily, grew in a bed near the fritillaria, while *Iris bucharica* showed its dainty yellow petals by the koi pond. And tiny *Tulipa tarda* — which doesn't look like a tulip at all — crept along the front walk. It's actually a wild tulip from Turkestan with star-shaped yellow and white flowers that open so wide they almost form a carpet.

Tulips and daffodils remain the diamonds of the bulb world, and crocuses and hyacinths gleam alongside them. I love them all. I'm a confessed daffodilophile. I melt at the sight of crocuses poking through the snow, and I think we should all stop to smell the hyacinths. But there are a lot of other gems that can glitter in your garden. And you should try them — that's part of the adventure of gardening.

If you plant bulbs — with the pointy part facing up, of course — they should appear on schedule. "You could be an idiot and plant a bulb, and it'll grow," says my friend Debbie Van Bourgondien, director of retail sales for Long Island's bulb giant, Van Bourgondien's in Babylon. The firm is a clearinghouse that brings in bulbs from Holland, Japan, India, Israel and South Africa and sells them through its catalog to everyone from your next-door neighbor to the gardeners at the White House. Between August and November they bring in more than 100 million spring-flowering bulbs, making them the second largest importer in the country. Debbie, whose license

The Other Bulbs of Spring

Think spring and the gardener's thoughts turn first to daffodils and tulips. But a host of other bulbs – generally smaller but no less endearing – make the picture complete. Here is a sampling of what are referred to as the minor bulbs, which are also planted in the fall. All are well adapted to Long Island and can be found at most garden stores or from mail-order catalogs.

Botanical Name	Bloom Time	Height	Color	Planting Depth	Spacing
Allium giganteum	June	40-48"	lavender	6"	6"
Anemone blanda	April	4-6	white, pink, blue	2-3	4
Camassia	May	18-36	blue, white	5-6	6-8
Chionodoxa	March-April	3-6	white-lavender, white	3-4	2-3
Endymion hispanicus	May-June	10-15	blue, pink, white	4	5-6
Eranthis	February-March	4	yellow	2	3
Erythronium	March-April	6-12	violet, pink	3	3
Fritillaria	April-May	24-36	orange, red, yellow	6-8	8-12
Fritillaria meleagris	April-May	9	white, purple, red-brown	3	3-4
Galanthus	February-March	4-6	white	3	3
Iris Danfordiae	March	4-6	yellow	3-4	2-4
Iris reticulata	March	4-6	purple, blue	3-4	2-4
Leucojum aestivum	April-May	12-15	white	3	3
Muscari	March-April	6-10	blue, white	3	3
Pushkinia	April	6	blue	3	3
Scilla	March-April	4-6	blue, white	3	3

plate puts her in context as BULBLADY, grows 53,000 bulbs at her own house. "In the spring," she says, "you're never disappointed."

She's not just talking about tiptoeing through the tulips. "There's a bulb for every letter of the alphabet from A to Z — except X and Y," she says. And she has the list to prove it — everything from *Allium* to *Zantedeschia*. *Alliums* are ornamental onions that range from little yellow asterisks to towering purple globes as much as 10 inches in diameter. I carried white *Zantedeschia* at my wedding. They're more commonly known as calla lilies and show up in late spring and early summer in pink and yellow as well as white.

Fanciers call all these other bulbs "special bulbs," and they certainly are. Special bulbs that have added to my enjoyment of spring include *Muscari armeniacum*, or grape hyacinth, and *Scilla siberica*, a hardy azure bloom that I mix among my daffodils. And *Leucojum aestivum*, known as the summer snowflake even though it blooms as early as April. It chimes in my spring garden with white bell-shaped flowers edged in green that dangle from long stems.

Debbie Van Bourgondien and my other bulb buddy, Sally Ferguson of the Netherlands Flower Bulb Information Center, suggest a bevy of special bulbs you might want to give a chance. Both Debbie and Sally oohed and aahed about chionodoxa, which impressed me so at the Keukenhof I'm dying to try it along a section of my lawn between a bed of rhododendrons and the curb. *Eranthis*, or winter aconite, also looks grand. Sally describes them as "itty-bitty buttercups with green hula skirts." The only caveat is that they should be planted no later than September if you want good flowers the first year.

Think about fritillarias, not just Crown Imperial, but it's smaller cousins, *F. meleagris* — the so-called snake's head fritillaria with 10-inch stems and white checkered pink or purple flowers — and *F. persica*, which has deep purple fragrant blooms on 30-inch stems. *Fritillaria* has another attribute, one that is very appealing to me. As Debbie points out, it's a natural rodent repellent — a deterrent for those furry freeloaders called squirrels who crave crocuses, harvest hyacinths and terrorize tulips.

I, for one, am also interested in *Ipheion uniflorum*, a member of the lily family — in case you didn't know, lilies are bulbs, too — which has funnel-shaped white and icy blue flowers on 18-inch stems. Not to confuse the issue, but it also goes by the names *Triteleia* and *Brodiaea*, but its simplest moniker is spring star flower. By any name, it should be mulched over the winter.

And who isn't warmed by the sight of those early harbingers of spring — snowdrops, or to give

them their botanical name, *Galanthus nivalis*. You can expect them in February when they mingle with real snow drops.

In any case, when you're planting bulbs and by the way, plant them in clusters rather than singly — think beyond the obvious.

The bulbs that we plant in fall will bloom in spring and pay homage to renewal and rebirth and life itself. Winter melts away in the warmth and vibrance of their colors. And our own gardens, no matter how small, become cathedrals — where we celebrate the miracle of the bulbs.

Bulb Basics

IN THE GROUND:

To judge your bulb, give it a good squeeze. It should be firm. If it's a softie, dump it.

And reject bulbs with deep scars or cuts. If the papery covering, called the tunic, is torn or missing, don't worry about it. If you want the color combinations to work, remember that you can't tell a red tulip from a yellow tulip by the bulb, so don't open the packages until it's time to plant.

If you can dig a hole, you can plant a bulb. First check your site. Bulbs love to be watered but don't like wet feet, so avoid low areas where puddles collect. Soggy soil can cause bulbs to rot. Don't worry about sun or shade — trees won't be decked out in summer greenery when the bulbs bloom. Plant in bunches or drifts. Create visual bouquets by massing bulbs in groups of 15 or more.

As a general rule, smaller bulbs, such as crocuses and snowdrops, are planted 5 inches deep. Larger bulbs like tulips and daffodils are planted 8 inches deep. Be sure the bottom of the hole has a couple of inches of loose dirt. Bulbs are always planted with the pointed end up.

Work composted cow manure into the soil or sprinkle in a controlled-release bulb food. And give them a good watering.

Once the bulbs are in the ground, make sure they stay there. Squirrels detest daffodils and alliums and fritillarias, but they dig almost everything else. I've had a lot of success with dried bloodmeal, but you can also try sprinkling crushed hot pepper, human hair or perfumed soap over the beds. Or lay wire mesh or an old screen over the ground and anchor it with stones. Don't use bone meal. Eau de bone meal drives squirrels crazy. It smells yummy.

IN CONTAINERS:

There's a cornucopia of containers available as bulb planters — everything from wooden casks and whiskey barrels and window boxes to wheelbarrows and wagons and old truck tires. I've also recruited a discarded gas grill and a broken-down dinghy.

If you use clay or terra-cotta pots, store them in an unheated porch or garage, because they can crack in severe cold. You can keep containers made of other materials outside as long as you put them in a protected place out of the wind. Make sure your choice has a drainage hole to prevent root rot. Containers should be at least 14 inches in diameter.

Don't be afraid of crowding — a finger's width between each bulb is the general rule of thumb. Touching is allowed as long as the bulbs aren't up against the sides of the container. This prevents frost damage. And for real fun in large containers, use the double-decker technique. Plant a layer of tall-growing bulbs like tulips and daffodils 6 to 8 inches deep and cover with 3 inches of soil. Then add a layer of low-growers like crocuses or muscari and cover with 5 inches of soil. Add an inch of mulch — and water.

Or go wild. Fill an old whiskey barrel with layers of bulbs. Plant a layer of lily-flowered tulips in white, yellow and pink — White Triumphator, West Point, China Pink. Sandwich in a layer of midseason blooms like the white and canary-yellow-cupped narcissus Ice Follies and the deep pink Triumph tulip Don Quichotte. Top it off with a layer of bright pink and yellow hyacinths — Anne Marie and City of Haarlem — and the 4-inch tall *Anemone blanda* White Splendour. Then wait for spring, and enjoy.

A Planting Primer

Generally, for planting most bulbs, dig a hole three times as deep as the bulb's height. Here is how deep and how far apart various bulbs should be.

1"	Persian buttercup *(4 inches apart)*
2"	

Tuberous begonia *(10 inches apart)*

Poppy anemone *(3 inches apart)*

Jacobean lily *(10-12 inches apart)*

Fall cyclamen *(4-6 inches apart)*

3"
4" — Ethiopian gladiolus *(5 inches apart)*

Gladiolus *(6 inches apart)*

5"
6"
7" — Summer hyacinth *(6-8 inches apart)*

Canna lily *(16 inches apart)*

Calla lily *(10-12 inches apart)*

8" — Dahlia *(16 inches apart)*

In a historic sense, you could trace Bill Allgeier's roots back to Montezuma. His dahlia roots. "Some people say that I'm dotty for dahlias," said Bill, a past president of the Mid-Island Dahlia Society, who has 120 dahlias growing along the side of his house in Hicksville.

None of Bill's ancestors were Aztecs, but his flower fetish is firmly rooted in the ancient Mexican civilization. When the Spanish conquistadors showed up in 1519, Montezuma's palaces were surrounded by dahlia gardens and his nobles wore dahlia symbols on their helmets and shields. Aztec poetry compares the dahlia's scarlet petals falling in the morning breeze to drops of blood shed by warriors in battle. And dahlia blooms were sprinkled over victims sacrificed to the sun.

It's hard for me to believe that when the Spanish conquistadors first spotted dahlias in Mexico — they grow wild at altitudes of up to 10,000 feet in Central and South America — they were more interested in the tubers, which look a little like potatoes, than the blossoms. But the dahlia was a dud as a spud — one early critic described its taste as repulsive and peppery. It took the French to finally realize that if the dahlia was a disaster in the kitchen, it was la crème de la crème in the garden.

And when Marie Antoinette took a fancy to dahlias, their prices skyrocketed to the point where a single tuber was said to have been swapped for a diamond. But then a Polish prince who was courting the queen got into her dahlia bed and stole more than a kiss. He made off with some of her prize cultivars and the market crashed.

Nowadays, you don't have to be royalty to enjoy dahlias. And there are so many to choose from. The American Dahlia Society recognizes 17 dahlia classifications, which are based on the flower forms. There are dahlias that look like daisies and orchids and water lilies and dahlias shaped like anemones and peonies and cacti. Flowers can be big blowsy stars more than a foot across or petite ingenues less than two inches in diameter. Plants themselves range from 6-inch dwarfs to 10-foot giants. And then there are the colors, 15 different categories of colors and blends of colors that appear in late June and linger through autumn until frost. Red, yellow, purple, pink, bronze, lavender every shade under the sun except blue, even though a prize of £1,000 was offered for a blue dahlia in 1826.

Bill's in the garden through the season — putting his time and energy into the care and feeding of his favorite flowers. His obsession began more than 30 years ago when his wife Mary Lou came home with a package of dahlia tubers. Bill had never

Dahlias: Divas Of the Garden

really gardened before, but he put the tubers in the ground and waited. When the flowers blossomed he couldn't believe his eyes.

"It was like magic. I was stunned at how big they were — and how gorgeous. I was thrilled that I could grow something like that."

The following season he planted a half-dozen more dahlias — this time named varieties — and when he saw an ad for a dahlia show with a novice category, he cut a dark red bloom called Juanita and entered. His dahlia won second place, and Bill

Dahlia blossoms become brighter as the nights become cooler.

137

Putting Dahlias To Bed

Like most divas, dahlias need a beauty rest. And you have to put them to bed for the winter properly.

Most growers wait until the first hard frost blackens the blooms. You can dig them out before then as long as they've had 150 days of growing. But you shouldn't wait much longer than one week after the frost.

Some fanciers actually wax their dahlia tubers with paraffin before storing them, but it's

not necessary. And it's okay to wait till spring to divide the root clumps: With a sharp knife or pruning shears cut the tubers so that each division has at least one shoot or budding eye.

HERE'S SOME ADVICE FOR DIGGING AND STORING DAHLIAS:

1. Cut tops off the plants to within 12 inches of the ground and label each clump. Don't put the

---

Allgeier was on his way down the garden path.

Bill's showstoppers grow in raised beds in a 10-by-70-foot border — all of it irrigated by his own watering system, which includes tiny plastic spigots that send jets of water in low arcs across the bed. He protects his darling dahlias as if they were daughters. He grows them under tobacco cloth attached to 11-foot-high poles to keep off beetles and borers and to filter the sunlight so his big winners have to stretch even higher for the sun. When rain threatens, Bill brings out umbrellas and tapes them to the wooden stakes that support the tall hollow stalks. "I put up 10, 15 umbrellas. It's quite a sight."

Indeed. Bill doesn't dillydally with his dahlias. When he isn't running his electronics sales firm, he's likely to be out there with his plants. He's introduced three new varieties to the American Dahlia Society — a big yellow cactus dahlia, named Mary Lou after his wife, and others named after two grandchildren, Katlin and Christopher. He grows jewels like Long Island Lil and Irene's Pride and Miss America. And of course Juanita — as well as a child of Juanita's named Nita. Bill wins ribbons in dahlia shows all over the East Coast. "Juanita still wins big for me," he said.

On Long Island every plant from azaleas to zinnias seems to have its own fan club, and dahlias are no exception. The Mid-Island Dahlia Society, which has 300 members, is one of the largest dahlia societies in the country. Besides working in his own yard, Bill keeps tabs on the group's display garden and on the Eastern Trial Garden of the American Dahlia Society, which dazzle alongside each other in a little patch of land behind the Administration

Building in Eisenhower Park. He's director of the trial garden, where growers from around the world send dahlia tubers to be evaluated.

Throughout the summer and fall Bill and other dahlia diehards come to the trial garden on Sunday mornings with tape measures and scoring sheets. They measure the length of stems and the depth and diameter of blooms and examine foliage for firmness and thickness and smoothness. They compare the shade of petals against a color chart and note each plant's susceptibility to mildew and insects. And they're always on the lookout for the perfect 45-degree angle of the bloom. "You want that dahlia to look right at the judge," Bill said.

I'm glad I'm not a judge. I don't think I could be objective about dahlias, because they're all so drop-dead gorgeous. I faced this on a visit to the Paul Callahan Memorial Dahlia Garden at Planting Fields Aboretum in Oyster Bay, where Bill and other members of the Mid-Island Dahlia Society also volunteer their services. There are 17 beds in the 100-by-100-foot garden, which is named after the late chiropractor and Planting Fields volunteer who helped establish the original dahlia plot that once bloomed nearby.

At a time of year when most gardens snooze, this garden was wide awake. That's the wonder of dahlias — they can be big and brassy but they're no here-today-gone-tomorrow hussies. Although they may be flashy, they're not frivolous. They are the divas of the fall garden — their blooms become brighter as the nights become cooler. And they keep on flowering until that sad day when the first hard frost turns them black and they stop dead in their tracks.

Don't hold me to it, but with the help of Bill

4. Pack tubers upside down in cardboard boxes filled with newspaper, vermiculite or pearlite. Pack tightly. Don't use peat moss; it pulls water from roots. Cover with sheets of newspaper and close box, leaving hand holes at each end for ventilation.

Store in a cool place between 35 and 50 degrees — 45 is ideal. If it's too cold, tubers turn to mush. If it's too hot, they dry up.

When tubers are stored, fork compost into dahlia beds.

cut stalks in the compost, because slugs and borers may lurk in the hollow stems.

Dig around each clump, about a foot from the plant and gently pry out the root mass. Don't pull out the plant by the stalk. Shake off excess soil.

2. Cut stems to about 2 inches.

3. Wash or hose off the clumps, then dry them in a frost-free area for half a day.

and Steve Nowotarski, his successor as Mid-Island president, I think I saw representatives of all the official classifications. When it comes to flowers, dahlias have it all except for one thing — fragrance. "Dahlias have no scent — yet," said Steve. Some dahlia growers get ideas when they see visitors sticking their noses into the blooms at juried shows. "If you're at a show and you come across a dahlia with a scent, it just means that the grower squirted some of his cologne in the blooms," Steve explained with a grin. "It's been known to happen."

It seems that most growers of exhibition dahlias are men, and I have to wonder if there isn't a testosterone thing going on here. I've seen Bill at the annual dahlia show at Planting Fields, and when it comes to his entries, I can tell you he's no shrinking violet.

"The shows are fiercely competitive," Steve said. "There's a guy from Connecticut who calls me every year and dares me to beat him."

As for me, I gave my sense of smell a rest at the Paul Callahan garden and delighted in the sights. There are more than 300 plants featuring 250 named varieties — all of them perfectly staked as they should be. I admired deep red Juanita, Bill's prizewinner with blooms that are reminiscent of cactus flowers. And orange Hamilton Lillian, which Steve called "one of the most perfect dahlias in the world. It's difficult to grow to perfection, because it has a recessive yellow gene that wants to come forward. But it's won more higher awards than any other dahlia."

I was taken by Ellen Huston, a saucy little number with foliage that is unusually dark for a dahlia. It looked resplendent in red massed at the corners of a low tumbling border of *Verbena* Homestead Purple. I dallied near a dahlia called Fidalgo Kay, a spidery flower in blends of yellow and peach. I was struck by Ferncliff Flamingo, a hot pink bloom bigger than a baseball. I couldn't help noticing Shrimp Louis, which has a purple bud that opens into an orange blossom. And I was dazzled by yellow Bo-De-O, as big and brilliant as the sun itself.

Clearly, it was an inspirational visit. Dahlias are dangerous for people like me who want to grow everything they see. Dahlias are at their best in fall, but you can't plant them until the earth warms in spring. So I took a lot of notes — especially when Bill and Steve suggested dahlias for those of us who are content with growing them for our own enjoyment instead of blue ribbons. I liked what Steve said about Magic Moment, a white semi-cactuslike flower with a flush of lavender. "It grows like a weed. It's the one I give to friends who've never grown dahlias."

And there's Long Island Lil with brilliant orange blooms 4 to 6 inches in diameter and Brookside Snowball with moderate-size pure white flowers. I was intrigued by Honka, which resembles a yellow orchid and looks great in bouquets. And I marked my notebook the minute my guides mentioned Zorro. I don't know if it's as much of a turn-on as Antonio Banderas, but it sounds exciting and has stunning dark red flowers.

I don't know if I'd swap a diamond for a tuber or trade in my husband for Zorro, but like Bill Allgeier and Steve Nowotarski, I'd go a long way for a dahlia.

139

My Autumn Gallery

Nature paints a still life of rose hips.

bronze beyond the bedroom windows. Tall white Japanese anemones nod gracefully outside the kitchen panes, and their pink cousins are wonderfully framed by a long, narrow window off the den. Every time I pass the pink anemones, I stop and stare at them through the glass. The pink blossoms curve across the window and a golden pond glints behind them. It is like walking through an art museum and happening upon a painting you want to treasure forever in your mind.

If this were a museum, I would wish ruefully that I could touch the blossoms. The nicest part about the scenes framed by my windows is that I can go outside and make them come alive. I can crane upwards to smell the roses or reach out to touch the anemones, and I become part of the paintings.

It is important to note that this blooming gallery is a visiting exhibition — one that will not come again for another year as nature changes its palettes. Like most good art shows, this one has a theme. If I were to give it a title, I would choose "Transitions." I am thinking of my writing-coach husband's belief that transitions are the key to long compositions. How we go from paragraph to paragraph determines the shape of longer passages and ultimately of the whole work. I suspect it is like that in our own lives as we go from stage to stage and place to place. Certainly, transitions are elemental to the cycle of life and death in the garden.

In fall, the passage from season to season is at its most graceful and gradual. It is a time when we are putting the garden to bed and planting cover crops to nourish the soil. But the flowers of fall come into their own. Rose hips and fiery pyracantha and the red berries of Kousa dogwoods and cotoneaster make their debut. And yet at the same time the blooms of summer linger.

Through the guest room windows, I watch white and pink dahlias dance in the borders of the garden and cleome reach for the sky. Monarch butterflies float past orange gomphrena, and blue salvia keeps blooming along the picket fence. Some of the tithonia are still dressed in bright orange while others have dropped their petals. Passion flowers dangle from the arbor like tiny Tiffany lamps. A giant red hibiscus appears unexpectedly. And a flush of thistle and lavender makes an encore.

As I look out my windows, I like to think that

I t is October and all my windows are picture frames. The picture window in the front of our house that used to be veiled by giant rhododendrons has lived up to its name ever since we uprooted our overgrown foundation plantings and moved them around the periphery of the yard. Now the window offers a landscape of groundcover and lawn leading to the gate and arbor of a flower-vegetable garden. In the deepening light of fall, a single pink rose glows softly atop the arbor. It is the first bloom on the climbing bush that was planted two years ago, and in my view it makes the scene through the picture window a masterpiece.

But the loveliest gallery of all runs across the back of our house. *Sedum* Autumn Joy blossoms in

Chores Galore

WORK COMPOST into cleaned-out beds. The more, the better.

PLANT cover crops such as winter rye or hairy vetch to enrich and lighten garden soil for next spring.

PLANT PERENNIALS by the end of the month so roots have time to make themselves at home before the ground freezes.

GIVE YOUR amaryllis a rest. Put the potted bulb in a cool dry dark place — on its side in a basement closet is ideal — and stop watering until Thanksgiving. When you take it out of hiding, cut off the foliage, water well once and watch for signs of life. If it doesn't respond, let it rest 2 more weeks, then water again.

BRING your poinsettia out of the closet — at least during the day. Give it full sunlight, but make sure it's back safely in the dark between 5 p.m. and 8 a.m.

DIG gladiolus before a hard freeze. Trim all but an inch of foliage and comfort the corms by letting them dry for several weeks in a warm place. Twist off the withered foliage, then hang them in mesh bags in the dark in 40 to 45 degrees temperatures.

GET A START on next season's garden by collecting the seeds of non-hybrid flowers such as hollyhocks and cleomes. They should be thoroughly dry before you store them in Ziploc bags or Mason jars in the fridge. They'll be ready to plant in the spring.

HARVEST pumpkins and winter squash before the first frost to make the most of their taste and texture. Use pruning shears and leave a few inches of stem to prevent rotting.

LET POTATOES that haven't been harvested yet stay where they are. They'll be fine for digging as needed till at least Thanksgiving, even Christmas barring repeated hard freezes.

TRIM OFF the central growing tips of Brussels sprouts so the smaller, uppermost sprouts will develop. Don't eat them yet —their taste improves with cold weather. Harvest as needed into winter.

CONTINUE PICKING the tasty leaves of collards, kale and Swiss chard, but don't disturb the central bud, which is responsible for the production of new leaves.

LEAVE Jerusalem artichokes, leeks, carrots and parsnips in the ground all winter. They grow sweeter after frost. Mulch with straw or leaves before the ground freezes.

DIVIDE rhubarb plants that are 4 or 5 years old. Dig up the entire plant and use a sharp knife to divide it into clumps of five or six stalks. Trim the stalks to about 4 inches above the crown before replanting.

TAKE another soil test to make sure your pH is still in the healthy zone. Adjust with lime as needed.

DON'T stop watering — especially those newly planted perennials. Remember moist soil retains heat.

CARRY chives indoors in deep pots for the winter. They'll do best in a sunny, cool spot. Make cuttings of rosemary, dip in rooting hormone and plant in small pots.

PLANT or transplant deciduous trees and shrubs once their leaves have fallen. Mulch and water thoroughly.

KEEP weeding. Get the roots out. Life will be easier in the spring.

in small ways I have been a patron of nature's arts. In past years, for instance, I had grown impatient with invasive and unruly Montauk daisies that threatened to take over my borders. But we pulled some out, and this year's survivors prove the benefits of understatement. Through the sliding glass door of the kitchen, they are neater and more sharply delineated than I have ever seen them before — they have never suited the autumn light so perfectly. And they accent the blanket of gaillardia that warms the season in orange and bronze.

The hydrangeas are part of the view and they speak to the theme of change. Some of them continue to show off in summer's pink and blue. Others have donned their fall colors of maroon and bronze and brown. That is why I don't like to cut my hydrangeas — I enjoy watching the transition. And in the crispness of fall, the morning glories put forth their truest blue.

This is no mere illusion. As the earth cools and the light wanes, flowers achieve their most vibrant colors. The world becomes an art gallery.

John

John Youngs' heritage grows in his fields. Youngs' Beauty and Youngs' Pride. They go back to John's father and his father's father and generations before that. Large and orange and wonderfully round. Big is not enough for John Youngs. Most of all, he believes a pumpkin should be round. John is standing in his barn, a newly renovated structure more than two centuries old. "My grandfather would have given me what-for if I'd let this barn collapse," he says as the autumn sunshine pours through the open door. John is surrounded by the pumpkins that are his beauty and his pride. He is a plain-spoken man in his 70s wearing a blue sweater and blue cap, and there is a sweetness about him, almost a fragility. He is not given to hyperbole or rhapsodic expression, and yet a poetry of sorts runs through his story. The poetry of rich earth and ripening crops and sprouting seeds.

The seeds are heirlooms — the birthright of Youngses to come. Their story is one of people cultivating the land. It began in the 1600s when members of the Youngs family first planted crops in that portion of the New World that would become Suffolk County. They cultivated squash and carrots and corn — and pumpkins, too. There are still Youngses on the East End, but in the mid-1800s John's great-grandfather ventured across the county line and planted new roots in Muttontown. He was only 42 when he died, but his widow kept to the land. And when her son — John Youngs' grandfather — married in 1892, she made sure the tradition endured by buying him and his bride their own 120-acre farm in Old Brookville.

John points to the white two-story house just down a gently sloping hill from the old barn. "My father was born right there in that house. Me, too. My wife Vivian and I moved into a house across the street in '51. My daughter Jo Hana and her family live there now."

It was on an autumn day in the 1940s on the land John Youngs still tends that he and his father discovered something special in the 6-acre field they devoted to sugar pumpkins — a heavy round giant that dwarfed its peers. Charlie Brown would have loved it. And John and his father gave the great pumpkin the respect it deserved: They saved its seeds and propagated the new variety successfully over the

Youngs' Pumpkins

succeeding seasons. "After four years we had our own strain of pumpkin," John says. "It was very exciting."

The fame of the great pumpkins in the Youngs' field grew far beyond Old Brookville. The owner of Harris Seed Co. came down from Rochester to check out the long-stemmed orange beauties. "He was amazed and wanted to buy the seed rights," John recalls, "but we just gave him a half-dozen pumpkins. They sold Youngs' Beauty through their catalog for 20, 25 years."

But according to John, the good seed didn't get the TLC it had received from the Youngs family. "The seed went down in quality and eventually was taken out of the catalog." Meanwhile, back in Old Brookville, the family never stopped growing Youngs' Beauty. More than that, they were constantly improving the breed — saving and planting the seeds from their largest pumpkins each year. Youngs' Beauty got bigger and better and rounder and more ribbed until it transcended itself. It became Youngs' Pride.

"Now I have the biggest pumpkins around," John says. "I don't think anyone's beat me with a bigger pumpkin in I don't know how many years — and I've been showing at the Long Island Fair for 59 years."

Youngs' Pride has tipped the scales at 94 pounds, which is not just a lot of pie but all pumpkin. And that's no squash. "Those things that weigh in at 700 pounds in the giant pumpkin contests aren't pumpkins," John says. "What we have here is a misnomer. They're squash. It's just that pumpkin sounds better than squash."

John — who has been president of the Agricultural Society of Nassau, Suffolk and Queens for more than a quarter of a century — is pretty definite on what makes a pumpkin. He has a rule of thumb, or possibly forefinger, about this. "If you can press your fingernail into the stem, it's a squash. A butternut squash is a pumpkin, so is an acorn squash. I'm not dreaming this up. I've made a study of it. I went up to Cornell and asked them. It's just that somewhere along the line someone makes a mistake, and after a while it's accepted — even if it's not true."

There's no argument about the fact that John Youngs' beauties are gorgeous. He's spent the morning harvesting them, because he's afraid of the weather and doesn't want any frost on his pumpkins. A truck outside the barn is filled with Youngs' Beauties

and a few "cheese" pumpkins that make the best pies. Inside the barn, Prides hold the floor.

John's daughters — Jo Hana Gooth and Paula Weir — sell Youngs' Beauties at the family farm stand and bakeshop in front of their field. And as a matter of good economics, they supplement their inventory with pumpkins they get from a wholesaler. "We're down to 12 acres now, so it's not feasible to grow tons of pumpkins like we used to." But John keeps the Prides off the market. He grows them for competition. And he protects their purity. There are no bad seeds in his pumpkin patch.

Even in the field, the Pumpkin King of Long Island keeps the two Youngs varieties as far apart as possible to avoid cross-pollination. And every three years he produces a "plant self." He isolates a female bloom and hand pollinates it with a male flower from the same vine. He covers it with plastic to avoid contamination by wind or insects. The result is a perfect seed, which produces a perfect pumpkin called Youngs' Pride.

John dries his seeds on newspapers in his basement — where he builds model airplanes when he's not in the field — and keeps them in mayonnaise jars with vented lids until he's ready to plant at the end of May. And he doesn't take any chances with the future; he saves seeds for eight years in case of crop failure.

He looks respectfully at the 79-pounder in the barn where his father and grandfather stored pumpkins before him. "Now, that's what a pumpkin should look like. It's a terrific pumpkin, but it's not good enough to show." John had already picked his entry for the Long Island Fair — an 84-pound pumpkin that is as round as a truck tire and as orange as a setting sun. And that brought home another blue ribbon for Youngs' Pride.

"We've never sold the seed rights to Youngs' Pride, and we never will," John Youngs says. "The seeds will stay in the family. They're our heirlooms. Youngs' Pride is our family treasure."

For John Youngs, when it comes to pumpkins, what grows 'round, comes 'round.

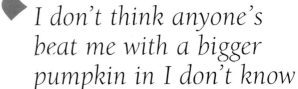

I don't think anyone's beat me with a bigger pumpkin in I don't know how many years.

Halloween Ghost Garden

Silver and gray and blue foliage create a haunting effect in Richard Iversen's ghost garden.

The last eve of October is when goblins walk the Earth — or at least trick-or-treaters — and spirits go bump in the night. But if you're looking for a little ghostliness in the garden, you don't have to wait for Halloween. If you'd like to have a favorite haunt in your yard, you can do it without spells or incantations — although if you know any good ones, I don't suppose they'd hurt. All you need are the sorts of manifestations that materialize with soil and sunshine and tender loving care. Plants whose shade and shape convey the mood.

Specters with silver and gray and blue foliage. Apparitions like Russian sage and santolina and woolly thyme and lamb's ears. Try plants that glisten in the sunshine and shimmer in the moonlight, and you may not have Casper flitting about the yard, but you will have what's known as a ghost garden. Or more prosaically, what some people call a gray garden.

In the early years of the 20th Century, Gertrude Jekyll, whose trowels may well have been magic wands, wrote about her gray garden, a luminous vision of silver-toned plants such as lavender and nepeta and stachys and *Cineraria maritima*. A few years later Alice Martineau, another British gardener, waxed poetic over ghost gardens in the former colonies. "In America, ghost gardens are rather the fashion. Here everything is dim and subdued." She talked about the misty effects of masses of silver thistles and gray mulleins and carpets of sage and salvia.

For a finishing touch, Martineau added: "A small marble basin with water lilies growing in it is sunk in the cool green turf, the water reflecting the early moonbeams; for no one walks in the ghost garden except at evening."

I like that. I find the idea, well, haunting. But gently so. Ghost gardens are not in-your-face "BOO!"

My friend Richard Iversen, who teaches horticulture at the State College of Technology at Farmingdale, conjured up an ideal ghost garden for the fall flower show at Planting Fields Arboretum in Oyster Bay back in the early 1980s. He still has slides to bring it alive. He devised a sepulchral theme by letting gray and silver plantings float among old tombstones. It was no place for Beetlejuice, but Casper would have loved it.

According to Richard, ghost gardens are at their best from summer into early fall. The horticultural display at the Farmingdale campus includes a ghost garden of lavender and rue and lamb's ears and globe thistle and *Gypsophila paniculata* and *Nepeta mussini* — a catmint that flowers in June. The plantings make up a 40-foot-long double border divided by a bluestone walkway and surrounded on three sides by a hedge of American beech that once grew at the 1939 World's Fair. Actually, the walkway and the hedge were there first. "They inspired me to plant a ghost garden," Richard says.

The hedge adds to the atmosphere. In late fall it loses most of its outer foliage, revealing its silvery bark. At the same time, the gold and brown inner leaves that remain rustle eerily in the wind throughout winter.

"There's a lot of subtlety in this garden," Richard says. "It won't bowl you over. Its beauty comes from the contrasts in the size and shape and texture of the plants." He places green sage next to evergreen rue and underplants slender Russian sage with fuzzy lamb's ears for a ghostly contrast. And he takes advantage of the season itself. "The rue and the nepeta look beautiful with a touch of frost on them."

Richard's ghosts are invariably enchanting. In their season, clouds of gray-white Gypsophila and drifts of gray-purple Echinops gentle the borders. The corners of each border are strengthened with the same types of yuccas Gertrude Jekyll used in her gray garden — *recurva* and *filamentosa*, which go well with silver-leaved plants. But it is the *Artemisia absinthium* Huntington that Richard calls "the jewel of the garden." "It stands upright 4 to 5 feet tall with fabulous silver foliage."

You can start planning your own ghost garden now. Or at least imagining it. The time to plant is in spring. And remember, most plants with silver foliage prefer full sun and well-drained alkaline soil.

Once your garden grows, wait for a night when the moonbeams shimmer on the lamb's ears and the Russian sage waves its spectral arms in the wind. Even if it's All Hallows Eve, don't be afraid. The ghosts are friendly.

The fuzzy, gray-green foliage of lamb's ears, *Stachys byzantina*, glistens by day and shimmers in the moonlight.

November

We tend to associate November with crunchy apples and cauliflower and cranberries. But it's almost Thanksgiving and I sliced a couple of tomatoes for sandwiches. They were so red and tasty. If they weren't fresh from the vine, they were as close as you can get this time of year. I picked them green a few weeks ago to beat the frost and wrapped them carefully in newspaper and stored them in a box in the garage. They ripened quickly. Outside, I thought, I'm putting the garden to bed. Inside, I'm still tasting summer. That speaks to the month. The growing season is over, but November leaves us plenty of reminders — from crinkling hosta leaves to lingering Gaillardia and the final bows of Verbena bonairensis. They're reminders that the garden will be back next year. And that gardening is a continuum and rebirth carries through the seasons. All that musing stirred by a red tomato wrapped in newspaper. Perhaps that's because no matter what the season, we are never far from our gardens.

Little Acorns, Tall Oaks

An oak tree at Planting Fields Arboretum. Oaks can endure for centuries.

Acorns are ubitquious. I've been crunching them underfoot all fall. They scurry into the corners of the yard and congregate among the browning leaves. Sometimes they even sneak into the house. We take them for granted — signs of autumn like the billowing waves of fountain grass and the orange patches of ripening pumpkins and the russet glow of the countryside. Even in childhood — when so many commonplace things seem like miracles — I never thought much about acorns. Or, for that matter, about oak trees.

There were only maple trees on the street where I grew up in Bridgeport, Conn. But on the walk to school I picked up pinecones and chestnuts and acorns and put them in the pocket of my brown corduroy jacket as if they were lucky charms. I shined them up with a dust rag and placed them in a glass bowl on my dresser.

I guess I never really considered acorns and their place in the universe until I moved into my house and acquired an oak tree of my own. Or perhaps it would be more accurate to say until I had an oak tree living near me. I don't think you can own a tree anymore than you can possess the breeze that rustles through its leaves. It's in your safekeeping — like your children — but you don't really own it.

I picked up an acorn the other day and pondered its potential. And I gazed up at the black oak it had fallen from. Oaks belong to the beech family, and there are hundreds of species of them in the world — blackjack oak and bear oak and turkey oak and poison oak and silk oak, to name just a few. About a dozen species are found on Long Island, especially red, black, white and pin oaks. You can identify an oak by its acorns as well as its bark and its leaves, which can have rounded or pointy lobes. For instance, black-oak acorns are about 3/4 inch long and half enclosed in cups that look like toy tops with rust-brown hairy scales. White-oak acorns are as long as 1 1/4 inches with shallow cups covered by warty scales.

I stood in my yard and looked from acorn to oak and back again and thought about the sheer wonder of the old saying that comes from an anonymous Latin source: *Parvis e glandibus quercus*. Tall oaks from little acorns grow.

It doesn't happen overnight. It takes at least 20 to 30 years before an oak tree is mature enough to produce acorns. And even though a single *quercus* can produce millions of acorns during its lifetime, very few of them survive into treehood.

There's no sure climb to success for an acorn. Nature gives us all obstacles to overcome. While it's still clinging to the mother tree, an acorn can be attacked by weevils and moth caterpillars, and devoured or socked away for future meals by squirrels. Which is ironic when you think about it, because oak trees offer shelter to squirrels.

Things don't necessarily get any better once an acorn hits the ground. Now it's not only snack food for squirrels, it's also sustenance for deer and rodents. And if an acorn happens to live in Europe, it runs the risk of being eaten by wild boars. If an acorn anywhere makes it to winter, it still has to worry about a fungus that can turn it into a mummified black stone.

It's hard to say which comes first — the acorn or the oak. Like most productions of this sort, it all starts in spring. An accommodating breeze carries the pollen of the male flowers of the tree to the female flowers. And an acorn is born. The baby acorn contains up to six seeds, but only one of them develops. The ring of overlapping scales around the base of the female flower grows around the acorn and becomes the cup, or if you turn the acorn upside down, the part that looks like a Scottish tam.

If the acorn survives denizens of the woods and disease, it ripens and turns brown in autumn and falls to the ground. You may not think trees know what they're doing, but there's a good reason why the oak sheds its acorns before it loses its leaves. The leaves cover the acorns and offer protection from frost and foragers. And in places like ours, bluejays become unwitting helpers by burying acorns and forgetting where they're hidden.

If everything's in sync, the acorn germinates. Its hard brown shell is cracked by the emerging root, or radicle, which burrows downward. Some acorns stay dormant until spring, but the majority are at work during the winter and greet the new season with taproots 4 to 8 inches long. And a seedling is on the way. But the way is fraught with danger; the seedling is vulnerable to feeding deer and falling caterpillars. Even mature oaks have their problems: Caterpillars defoliate them, beetle larvae chomp on their roots and wood, storms topple them and humans chop them down.

The survivors are among the monarchs of the woods — in ancient days they were considered sacred and connected to such gods as Zeus and Thor. *Quercus* is quite literally a tree for the ages — oaks can endure for centuries. It's common for them to live as long as 200 years, and in one rare instance the rings of an oak in Switzerland showed it to be 930 years old.

They are magnificent as well as venerable. Red oaks can reach 80 feet into the sky and spread their leafy arms to a width of 50 feet, while white oaks, which grow equally tall, reach twice as far.

And all this grace and majesty starts with an acorn measured in mere inches. I stood in my yard on a rain-scented autumn morning. Oak leaves crinkled beneath my feet, and I looked in wonder at the acorn in my hand and the tree in front of me.

I pressed the acorn beneath the leaves and muttered an ancient incantation. *Parvis e glandibus quercus.*

Growing Up   How an acorn grows into a tree:

1. After pollination in late spring, each acorn may contain up to six seeds, but usually only one of these develops.

2. By autumn, the acorns are fully grown and are turning brown.

3. An oak sheds the acorns before it sheds its leaves. This sequence buries the acorns under the leaves and gives them some protection. Some acorns germinate immediately – others are delayed.

4. By the end of winter, most acorns have a 4- to 8-inch-long taproot. By late spring, a shoot appears above ground.

5. By midsummer, the shoot will have five to six leaves and will develop a terminal bud at its top.

6. By the end of its second year, the sapling will have its first side branches.

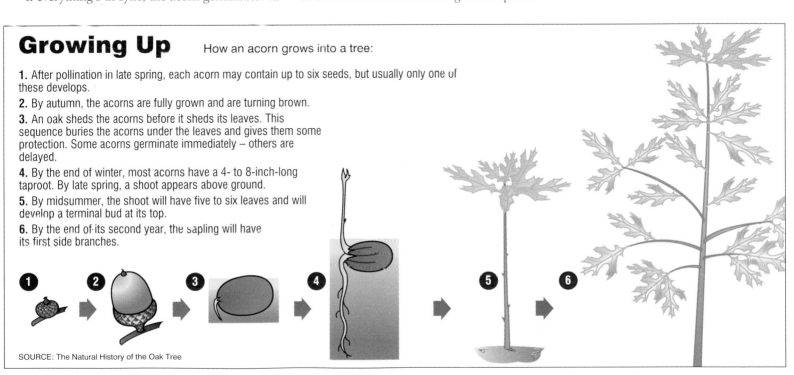

SOURCE: The Natural History of the Oak Tree

A Good Year in the Garden

O n a bright November morning, I labor in my tucked-in garden. Downy autumn clematis garlands the fence and fading roses defy the chill of the new day. Still-lusty Swiss chard grows in the corners of the recently cleaned-out vegetable beds where I am working compost into the soil.

I love the way the beds look as I rake them — newly brown with the rich earth I created from eggshells and teabags and the peelings of raw vegeta-

bles. There is a sense of completion to the garden as it is being put to bed. In the soft glow of autumn, I think about the season that has gone before.

November is a good time for assessing the triumphs and tragedies of the blooming season. It's another metaphor for the greater landscape. In the garden, as in life, knowing where you've been and where you are helps you go forward.

Next spring, for instance, we won't make this year's mistake and plant sugar peas on the fence so they can become tangled up in the clematis. And when we planted our bulbs a few weeks ago, we steered clear of the vegetable garden. Last season, we put Blushing Beauty tulips in the vegetable beds and they were tall and exquisite. But the squirrels appreciated them even more than we did, and the blooms that survived bent badly after a stiff rain. They absolutely sprawled. The slugs loved it. Worst of all, the tulips slowed our veggie planting schedule.

Still, we wound up with a soul-satisfying harvest. The Swiss chard my husband disliked as a child but has learned to love in his maturity was as prolific as ever. And I tried a new variety properly named Bright Lights that I will surely repeat next year. It is still as ornamental as it was edible, with large, graceful leaves and white and red and orange and pink stalks. The eggplants were pure romance and I'll keep planting them happily ever after. I'll also reprise the bush beans we tried instead of runner beans. They saved us climbing space for morning glories and passion flowers and sweet peas and provided several weeks of crunchy beans that we could eat right off the bush. We cooked them al dente.

Tomatoes are suburbia's crop and we were as proud of ours as the next guy — I'm sure real farmers laugh at us. But I have to tell you that even for us, this season was an absolute tomato surprise. We've taken a vow to plant fewer next year. The tomatoes all started ripening at the same time and it was hard to give them away, because everybody else grew them.

On a single day we picked 45 pounds of tomatoes. I know because we weighed them on the bathroom scale. Half of the poundage consisted of plum tomatoes that — I am proud to say — are canned and waiting for winter. The rest found their way into sauce and our daily tomato and grilled eggplant sandwiches and several new dishes. Although our Sweet 100s lacked their usual panache, we discovered a new variety — an heirloom called Old Striped German — to put on the table with our Brandywines. Old Striped German is a huge tomato with a pinkish crown that runs through its orange body. And the taste is sweet and non-acidic.

I think all our beds — both flower and vegetable — proved the value of composting and mulching. And we tried something new and nurturing around the tomato vines in mid-season: a compost tea brewed from llama dung. I got the dung from my friend, Joe Kusick, the garlic king of St. James. Only gardeners are lucky enough to be able to sprinkle their small talk with throwaway lines like "Oh yeah, I used llama-dung tea on my Old Striped Germans."

My balance sheet shows generally good marks for flowers. My gently brave and lonely witch hazel graced the end of winter, and daffodils — the bulbs squirrels don't like — danced splendidly through

At left, edible – and ornamental – Swiss chard. Above, the colorful kale.

spring. They stopped traffic. The *Echinacea* was a revelation. Just looking at the purple coneflowers made me feel good — I didn't have to brew them into tea.

It's November and I work the bare earth and grin at the memory of summer. There were so many satisfactions. I repotted my clivia and placed it on the patio, where it finally bloomed in elegant orange. I suspect it liked the dappled sunlight it got under the cherry tree. Of course, my night-blooming cereus also summered on the patio, but it never flowered. I think it has a sex problem.

The bright-orange *Tithonia*, or Mexican sunflowers, I tried in the garden borders were a pleasure. So were the plate-sized hibiscus and the passion flowers. I wish I had the foresight to put more morning glory vines on the arbor that leads into the garden. And I've learned to be careful with cleomes. They rise up with slender majesty in white and pink and purple — but they reseed like crazy.

Our crape myrtle tree gets lovelier each year. The Kousa dogwood we planted a year ago shone with creamy white blossoms in June and was adorned with bright red berries later on. And I'm so glad I put a hot pink mandevilla in a cedar planter by the pool.

My herb garden got a little out of control, and as summer ended I saw traces of lace bugs on the azaleas. I don't know what's attacking the mazus that makes such an attractive ground cover by the foundation plantings. And we've got to find a way to deal with the rabbits. But as I stand in my garden in November and enjoy the scent of newly worked earth, I think that, all things considered, it's been a very good year.

Joe Kusick,

It's not that I won't waste my breath on garlic, but I have a real problem. My husband is allergic to the pungent little bulb, *Allium sativum*, which is a member of the lily family. If I hadn't seen his reflection in the mirror and if I didn't know he loved the sun, I'd wonder if there was any vampire in him. In any case, for the seven years of our marriage I've been living a garlic-free life. Not only do I not cook with the herb, which was so revered by the ancient Egyptians that the pharaohs were buried with it, but I even gave up ordering garlic dishes in restaurants. After all, we do nibble off each other's plates now and then. Besides it's a matter of love — though I do wince when he tells waiters he'll get violently ill right there at the table if he eats the slightest bit. In Provence I cringed at the smirks of waiters when he explained in bad French that he couldn't eat *ail* and they looked at us like we were barbarians. Garlic, of course, is "the truffle of Provence."

And so it was with a certain trepidation that I headed off to visit Joseph Kusick at Nissequogue Farm on the day he was planting 40 pounds of garlic.

Actually, garlic planting starts in October — folklore has it that Columbus Day is a good time to sow. But Joe says there's nothing wrong with planting it now in early November. And he should know. Joe Kusick is to garlic what George Balanchine is to ballet.

Joe is a retired biology teacher with a master's degree in botany who bought 5 acres on Route 25A in St. James back in 1980. The land once belonged to the Smiths of Smithtown, and if the place seems caught in a time warp, so does Joe. He's a softspoken man with a white beard who likes to go down to Stony Brook Harbor with his dog, Gabby, and dig up a few oysters to saute for lunch. His farm is the kind of place where people tuck thank-you notes in flowerpots and drop off surplus cinnamon ferns in a Nordstrom shopping bag with the promise "more to come." Nothing goes to waste at Nissequogue Farm. Joe is a scavenger and a recycler and a barterer — and if he doesn't have an immediate use for that rusted fan, well, it might come in handy next week.

He collects carpet remnants that he puts between rows of vegetables and perennials to hold down weeds. And he gets manure from a nearby horse farm and leaves from the town and builds a 10-foot high compost heap along an outer wall of the greenhouse put up by a couple of shop teacher buddies. As the compost cooks at temperatures up to 150 degrees, all that CO_2 and ammonia get vented into the greenhouse through plastic sewer pipes.

I've learned all these things and more about Joe Kusick and his farm. It's time to get down to business.

"My husband's allergic," I say as Joe separates cloves of garlic piled by variety in plastic flats.

He looks puzzled as if I'd announced "It's raining scrambled eggs" or "A pterodactyl just landed on your head."

"To what?" he asks.

"To garlic."

Joe pulls out his pocket knife, peels a clove and pops it in his mouth. "I never heard of such a thing."

Joe Kusick is up there with big-time garlic eaters like Aristophanes, Hippocrates, Virgil, Gandhi, Henry IV and Eleanor Roosevelt. Roman soldiers chewed garlic to fortify themselves for battle. Hippocrates prescribed garlic for intestinal problems — which is what it gives my husband. Today, garlic is believed to lower cholesterol, prevent atherosclerosis and combat cancer and heart disease.

Joe's been eating garlic ever since he was a kid in Pennsylvania and his mother gave it to him raw as a cure for the common cold. "We'd sit around the coal stove in the middle of the room and chew garlic." Now, he enlarges his garlic patch every year. I talked to Joe for the first time when he called last month to tell me about his annual garlic festival. That's when I invited myself over to lend a hand on planting day.

"You want to plant the biggest cloves," Joe says. "Each clove produces a head, and the bigger the clove the bigger the head. One pound of cloves will give you 10 pounds of garlic. We're putting in about 40 pounds today."

And that's not just the garlic you buy in Waldbaum's — which, by the way, is part of the subspecies *sativum*, also called softneck garlic. Softnecks compensate for their inability to sprout flower stalks by producing more cloves — anywhere from eight to 40 — that can be stored for

Garlic King

> *You want to plant the biggest cloves. The bigger the clove, the bigger the head.*

up to 12 months and still stay pungent.

But it's the hardneck varieties of the sub-species *ophioscorodon* that are the gourmet garlics. Hardnecks produce a woody flower stalk with a circle of four to 14 cloves that are larger, easier to peel and more flavorful than softnecks. Joe hands me a peeled clove of Spanish Roja, a hardneck described in a catalog as "the most piquant garlic in the world."

"Here," he says, "taste it."

I shudder and take a nibble.

"Don't be afraid." Joe pops a clove in his mouth.

I close my eyes and do the same. Wow-za.

Joe smiles. "Now it's time to plant."

The soil in the 125-foot-long bed is rich and black. "Garlic needs a sunny place and well-drained soil," Joe says. He picks up a homemade contraption with 2-inch-long wooden pegs that are 4 inches apart — just the right depth and space for garlic — and sinks it into the damp earth. I place plump cloves of Spanish Roja, scar end down, in each hole, then cover them with about 2 inches of soil. We're still on the first row when the rains come.

When I leave, Joe hands me bags filled with garlic for eating and garlic for planting. My grown stepson gobbles some up for dinner. Raw. My husband sniffs at the bulbs on the kitchen counter. Then he sniffs at me. "You smell like a blast furnace," he says.

I chew on a sprig of parsley, which is supposed to be a cure for garlic breath. But it doesn't help.

I put the garlic bulbs in the garage to plant this weekend. I have until mid-July to find an antidote for my husband's allergy — that's when my own crop will come up. And that's when I'll head back to help Joe Kusick harvest his 400 pounds of garlic.

Chores Galore

PRUNE weak wood from trees and shrubs to hold down the damage from nasty winds.

SCATTER seeds of larkspur and nigella and other annuals and biennials. They like to chill out before they get up and growing in spring.

MAKE a compost pile just for leaves. They'll provide the perfect mulch for next year's beds and borders.

PLEASE next spring's peas. Till a bed now so you'll be able to sow the seeds around St. Patrick's Day.

POT up chilled paperwhite narcissus and amaryllis bulbs to force into bloom indoors.

MAKE a future home now for your live balled and burlaped Christmas tree. The trick is to dig a hole about twice the width of the root ball. Store the soil in a wheelbarrow in the garage so it isn't frozen when you're ready to backfill around the root ball. Fill the hole with mulch or leaves to keep the spot warm till planting time after the holidays.

CUT asaparagus foliage to soil level. Top-dress beds with 2 to 3 inches of aged manure so it can leach into the soil and nurture next year's crop.

CREATE a temporary cold frame. All you have to do is arrange several bales of hay in a rectangle and cover it with an old storm window weighed down with bricks. Then sprinkle leftover spinach seeds, a few varieties of lettuce, some parsley and arugula seeds inside. They'll have a jump start on spring.

PROTECT the queen of flowers. Mound soil 10 inches high around the base of your rose bushes to insulate the tender bud unions. If you want to provide more protection for your rose plants, don't hesitate — surround them with chicken wire and fill the cylinder with leaves or a light mulch.

HARVEST Jerusalem artichokes when the stalks are completely dried. Lift the potato-sized tubers out of the ground and cut off the foliage.

SHAPE up your tools for storage over the winter. Clean rakes, shovels, trowels and the rest of your gardener's helpers before putting them away. Brush off soil, rub metal surfaces with motor oil and work linseed oil into wooden handles. Sharpen edges with a file.

A Farm Family's

O n the last Thursday of November, families from sea to shining sea give thanks for the bounty of the land and the blessings we manage to find in our lives. For a farm family, there is an even deeper appreciation of Thanksgiving — one that stems from an intimate relationship with the cycles of the seasons, with rain and drought and feast and famine.

If you're a member of the Schmitt family of Melville, your roots grow deep and so does your understanding. When Teresa Schmitt and her sons Ferdie Jr. and Bill and her daughters Margaret and Marianne and their spouses and children say grace over their Thanksgiving meal, they're not just celebrating the abundance of their table. More than most of us, they are acutely aware of the blessings of the bounty.

"We know what it takes to put every vegetable on the table —from seed," says Bill Schmitt. "We know how many days it takes to grow those vegetables, what it's like to plant and irrigate and worry. When we sit down to eat, it's with real thanksgiving."

For the past 38 years since Teresa took over Thanksgiving from her own mother, the Schmitt family has gathered in the kitchen of her two-story green house with a white barn out back. As the family grew, a kitchen wall was knocked out to enlarge the room so everyone could fit around the table. Now there's a kids' table right by the window —Teresa has 12 grandchildren who range in age from 5 months to 21 years. And there's another grandchild she holds in her heart. Margaret and her husband,

Kirk, lost an 8-month-old son, Matthew, to sudden infant death syndrome a few months before last Thanksgiving. "We have an angel up there but a very heavy heart," Teresa says. "But then God gave Margaret a little girl she named Hope Mary."

And so joy and bittersweet remembrance merge in Teresa Schmitt's thoughts as she looks out the kitchen window onto Pinelawn Road, a four-lane thoroughfare lined with corporate headquarters and glass buildings and parking lots. A framed needlepoint of the farmhouse hangs above the microwave. It took Teresa five winters to complete and shows the lawn that existed before the road was widened — now the front door literally opens within inches of speeding traffic. "We always use the back door."

Later, her son Bill will go out the back door into the fields where the brown earth of the 22 acres they own and the 60 acres they rent is relieved by the green of a cover crop of oats. Where they grow arugula and romaine and red- and green-leaf lettuce and tomatoes and turnips and sweet corn and yellow squash and bell peppers and basil and rhubarb and cauliflower and broccoli and, of course, Long Island potatoes. A few years ago, they built an addition to their greenhouses, where they sell vegetables and flowers retail. And the family leases another 50 acres bordered by the Long Island Expressway, where they mark the seasons with pick-your-own strawberries and pumpkins.

On this windy autumn day, Bill picks turnips, which are served mashed with a little sugar on Thanksgiving. The Schmitt Thanksgiving also is abundant with their own broccoli and yams and cau-

Thanksgiving

liflower and celery and acorn squash. Carrots picked a few weeks before are in cold storage in the garage, and there are Hudson Valley apples for fresh applesauce. A week before the holiday, Teresa drives out to the East End for a fresh 20-pound turkey and an 8-pound turkey breast, "since most like white meat."

Desserts are generous. "My daughter-in-law Mary bakes the delicious crumb cake and a vanilla sheet cake decorated with fall colors," Teresa says. "My daughter-in-law Alice makes the apple pies and pumpkin pies from our own cheese pumpkins." Cheese pumpkins, or *Cucurbita moschata*, heirloom vegetables that go back to the 1500s, are round and flat like a wheel of cheese and the color of butternut squash. "They make the best pie, with a darker filling and better flavor," Teresa explains.

A few years back, Bill and Ferdie Jr. grew red potatoes for the pick-your-own crowd, but the demand wasn't there. Their father grew potatoes on this land, and their mother remembers when her father grew potatoes on his farm in Hicksville.

"That was before mechanization," Teresa explains. "I'd get down on my knees to plant them and I'd cultivate them with the tractor, but mostly I was into digging. You did that on your knees too. I'd dig eight rows of potatoes, shaking them off the dead vines, grading them by hand according to size. I'd put the big ones in burlap bags that held 100 pounds."

Teresa Rottkamp was a farmer's daughter who married Ferdie Schmitt, the son of the farmer next door on Carman Avenue in Hicksville. They dreamed of a farm of their own and found it in

1951 — 11 perfectly flat acres on a country road in Melville. Ferdie Sr. and his father dug into the land, and the father turned to the son. "The soil is good," he said. "You won't have to irrigate much here. This will be a good farm."

It was. The land and the years were good to them. Teresa and Ferdie Sr. had four children in five years. And the family was part of a farming community. "There were 10, 12 families farming along Pinelawn Road in those days," Teresa says. "Even National Cemetery was a farm. It was all farms until the 1960s. We're the last survivor."

"We're the fourth generation of our family farming on Long Island," says Ferdie Jr., whose father died in 1986.

Will there be a fifth?

"As for the future," Teresa says, "I have three grandchildren attending local colleges, sort of part-time. And my grandchildren still all work at the farm in the summer — the girls in the farmstands and the boys in the fields and on tractors. So only time will tell."

"We want to stay here farming," Ferdie Jr. says, "but the question is, can we?" Houses are going up on the site of a sod farm next door. Ferdie's not sure how the new neighbors will take to the sound of tractors in the early morning and to dust blowing across the flat land on a dry summer day.

But the family's roots go deep into the good earth and there will always be Thanksgiving. And with a little luck the Schmitts will continue their intimate relationship with the cycles of the season, with rain and drought and feast and famine.

Teresa Schmitt on Thanksgiving Day at the family farm in Melville.

WINTER

December

*O*n the twelfth day of Christmas my true love sent to me

Twelve baskets hanging

Eleven edgers edging

Ten cans a watering

Nine sprinklers sprinkling

Eight rakes a raking

Seven hoes a hoeing

Six weeders weeding

Five gold trowels

Four yards of mulch

Three pruning shears

Two wheelbarrows

And a poinsettia in a pear tree.

Seeing Red

Just before the holidays last December, I fled from the northern cold to Charleston, S.C. The sun warmed my flagging spirit and so did the scenery. I strolled along The Battery and looked out at the sparkling bay. I imagined older times in the antebellum houses and smiled at the pastel stuccoed brick facades of Rainbow Row. I got my first look at Spanish moss hanging from live oaks and took a dozen photos of a fat old wisteria vine winding through a wrought-iron fence. And most of all, I stared in happy amazement at the poinsettias that spread cheer all over the historic district. They were growing in stone pots. They were thriving in window boxes. Outdoors. In December.

It was hard to compute, at first. Sure, I'm used to poinsettias around Christmastime. But as seasonal houseplants. I expect to see them in nurseries. In living rooms. Inside. But the red and pink and white marvels that adorned Charleston were outside, and they were glowing. And then as I took off my sweater in the springlike warmth and spotted camellias blooming in front yards, I realized there was nothing to be amazed at. It was warm, it was sunny. I was the visitor. The poinsettias were at home. And I asked myself the sort of question one has time for on vacation.

How did a nice tropical wildflower from Mexico become synonomous with December — a Christmas classic in the cold, cold north?

The question seemed worth researching and I thought you might be interested in what I discovered. The rise of the poinsettia — if you say poyn-SEHT-ee-uh and I say poyn-SEHT-uh, we're both correct — is one of the big success stories in the horticultural world. Less than 200 years ago, botanists tended to write off this member of the *Euphorbiaceae* family as a weed. Today, about 150 million potted poinsettias are sold annually throughout the world.

The leggy wild plant that grows as much as 12 feet high has been cultivated down to the pot sizes we buy at Christmas and even to bonsai dimensions. There are 30 cultivars of *Euphorbia pulcherrima*, and they range beyond the traditional red to pinks and salmons and whites and lemons and apricots. All this and marbled and speckled combinations, and a pink- and peach-tinged cream beauty that has the feel of an impressionist painting and is appropriately named Monet.

The real dirt on poinsettias is that they originated in Mexico, where the Aztecs incorporated the plants into religious ceremonies, used the sap for medicinal purposes and made red dye from the brachts. These are not petals but modified leaves at the base of the plant's flowers. Look at a poinsettia closely and you'll spot the flowers. They're the unobtrusive little yellow or green clusters called cyathia that the bright-colored brachts surround. The same thing goes for dogwoods and bromeliads.

But back to the narrative. It picks up in 1828 in the person of an amateur horticulturist named Joel Robert Poinsett, who also happened to be a skilled politician and diplomat and the first U.S. ambassador to Mexico. On a trip to Taxco in the month of — you guessed it — December, he spotted a wild shrub with red blooms and stopped to snip. Poinsett sent the cuttings back to his plantation in South Carolina — everything sort of fit into place for me when I learned that he was born in Charleston — and the poinsettia had found a new field to conquer.

Fame is often fleeting but plants live on. Poinsett was a congressman, a secretary of war and a founder of a museum that would become the Smithsonian Institution. But he's best known for the shrub that bears his name.

A year after Poinsett's discovery, the fiery blooms were a smash hit at the Pennsylvania Horticultural Society's 1829 exposition. Soon afterwards, a Philadelphia nursery owner named Robert Buist realized the potential of a green-leafed shrub that blazed red at Christmas. And a tradition was born. It got a boost in December, 1906, when a Southern California nurseryman named Paul Ecke spotted the red blooms on a hillside and picked some for his family's Sunset Boulevard stand. Today, the Ecke family maintains 35 acres of greenhouses in California and Denmark.

On its climb to the top of the Christmas bloom list, the poinsettia has spawned various legends. One is that the brachts turned red in memory of a maiden who died of a broken heart when she was separated from her lover on Christmas Eve. Another is that the leaves were turned to the color of flame by the Star of Bethlehem as it burst through the night. The one I like best is about a poor little Mexican girl who couldn't afford to buy the Baby Jesus a gift on Christmas Eve. An angel appeared and told her that a gift offered in love would be just as good and that she should take some of the weeds growing along the road. As the child bent to pick the green leaves, her tears fell on them and they burst into beautiful red blooms. In Mexico, poinsettias are known as Flores de Noche Buena or Flowers of the Holy Night.

It's nice to think about a child's tears turning to joy. So in this cold month, I take pleasure in warming the inside of my house with poinsettias. If you feel the same way, there are a couple of things to remember when you buy these cheery euphorbias. Nursery poinsettias sometimes come covered with a plastic or protective sleeve. But if the plant has been under wraps for more than a few days, the foliage may be damaged. Select poinsettias with stiff stems and tight cyathia, with dense foliage all the way down the stem and fully-colored brachts. And get your poinsettias in the house as soon as possible — cold weather makes them wilt.

And take good care of them. Poinsettias do best in 60 to 70-degree temperatures and need about six hours of indirect, natural sunlight. Avoid drafts and don't put them near fireplaces or heating ducts or against windows. They like moist — not soggy — soil, so give them a sip of tepid water when the surface of the soil is dry. Misting them every other day helps too.

You can keep this season's poinsettias alive for next year. When they drop their leaves, move them to a window that gets partial shade and water sparingly. Around the end of March, cut back the stems to 8 inches. When summer comes, repot in fresh soil and give the plant a sunny spot — indoors or out — and fertilize periodically. They should be inside by Labor Day. Poinsettias, like chrysanthemums, are photoperiodic — they need long nights to bloom. So from Oct. 1 on, keep them in the dark from 5 p.m. to 8 a.m.

If all goes well, you should be happily seeing red by December.

Or if you can afford it, go to Charleston for the holidays.

Birthday Gifts From the Garden

When you become a gardener, it happens in your heart as well as in your yard. Even in December, when the days grow cold, you think of the earth and what it nurtures. The lessons I've learned from my garden are lessons for life — I think of them as gifts — and today is a good day to remind myself of them. It's Dec. 1, my birthday.

I realized how far I've come as a gardener when my husband asked me what I wanted. "I want to get you something really nice," he said. He mentioned a weekend in London or a night at the opera or a shearling coat. Who would have thought I'd tell him I wanted a $325 pot made out of a tree root? Sure it's teak, but it's something you put plants in. Or there's the potting bench I lusted after for an entire season — the one with a roomy bottom shelf and a galvanized steel lid that opens to a compartment with enough space to hide away work gloves and plant labels and pruning shears. It's in our house now. The Irene Virag of not so many years ago would have thought I'd lost my mind.

Birthdays tend to make you reflect on where you've been and where you're heading. It's time to take stock — to reiterate your priorities and make adjustments. More than anyplace, my husband and I are in the garden. We're there even in winter, when we plan for spring and make garden books and magazines an important part of our reading, and start seeds indoors. When the first slender shoots of the nasturtiums and tomatoes and eggplants come up, we feel as if a miracle has occurred in our upstairs office. And when we transfer them to the garden, I think that maybe it has.

That's one of the lessons I've learned from gardens. Joy doesn't have to be complicated. It's time to light the wood stove, to throw an extra blanket on the bed, to get out the woolen sweaters and scarves. But flocks of geese wheel in a slate sky, and the long gray arms of beech trees fan out like delicate traceries. A lone rose fades on a trellis — reminding me that beauty doesn't have to be a bouquet. It can be a single flower.

There are other lessons. At 43, I've come to understand the importance of maintenance. Of vigilance. Of tidying up. Of not putting things off. If you turn your back for too long, the weeds take command. If you don't stake the tomatoes, they'll fall over and rot on the ground. If you forget to hack back the butterfly bush in March, it will grow up spindly and ragged, with just a few flowers.

It's that way at work. If I let down my guard, a stack of mail spills onto the floor. There are suddenly 15 saved messages piled up on my voice mail. At home, unread magazines become chores to accomplish instead of pleasures to contemplate. I'm weeding and pruning my life so I can grow.

Like people, gardens need good foundations. You have to work the soil, establish beds, add compost. We're making our own compost, recycling detritus into brown gold. We're giving our flowers and our vegetables something to grow on. There are metaphors in the garden for careers and for marriage. You can sift out what doesn't work and recycle what does. If you pay attention to the basics, you'll keep love alive. If you establish a foundation, you'll have what gardeners call good bones — a framework of evergreens, a bedrock of perennials — and then you can embellish with fluffy but fleeting annuals.

There has to be discipline, balance and structure in the garden. Even nature has a grand plan. There's always a design. And above all, you have to tend it. You have to weed and prune and cut back and water and fertilize. But in proper degrees and amounts. Too much water can drown a plant. Too much indulgence can be destructive. Just because a little fertilizer may be good doesn't mean a lot will be better. Plants, like people, are not all the same. You have to get to know them.

I'm 43 and I want to nurture and to be nurtured. I know the importance of nurturing — I'm a breast cancer survivor. I want to grow, to realize my potential. I want my life to be in order. I'm very glad I'm a gardener. My husband and I never promised each other a rose garden, but we've planted one. And so I'm wishing for a pot made out of a tree root. I've learned that I can be content with a fading rose when cold trembles in the wind. That's a nice thing to know about yourself as you go forward into your 40s. I think I'll have a happy birthday.

At left, a planter made from a teak root—a present from the author's husband.

A Master's Winter Garden

J. Barry Ferguson among the evergreens he planted "with an eye toward cutting."

The trim, white-bearded man in the blue-plaid flannel jacket clips a branch from the Harry Lauder's walking stick in his garden and plucks its fading leaves. "Look at that." He holds up the wonderfully gnarled branch. "It's absorbingly interesting, isn't it?"

His absorption continues as he turns the branch this way and that. "This, all by itself, is a flower arrangement."

He should know. J. Barry Ferguson, who sums up his personal equation in the title of his book "Living With Flowers," is famous for his floral arrangements, which take advantage of everything from evergreens to anemones. He's a horticulturist and floral designer whose garden is with him all year long. He brings it in for the winter.

Barry's barn-style home on Nassau's North Shore is a portrait of the artist — from the giant evergreen wreath on the front of the house to the dried hydrangeas arranged in massive urns set on pedestals in the living and dining rooms. In his studio, a walk-in refrigerator is filled with huge arrangements of flowers imported from his native New Zealand — pink peonies and yellow calla lilies for a social function in Manhattan. "The peonies should cause a stir at this time of year," he says.

Not that he has to rely on imported flowers to cause a stir. Take a walk with him in his winter garden, and he'll find objects of floral art for the home just about everywhere. His property is situated in a valley, and he has filled the hillsides with a cutting garden for all seasons.

"When I came here, the woods were overwhelming. There were bloody great trees here. They hung down to the house and covered the cupola. It was an intimidating situation." Barry did some selective tree removal and replanted with his craft in mind. "I plant with an eye toward cutting."

He makes the point by snipping some blue spruce to combine with a bow and pinecones for door sprays. Then he stops at an imposing *Magnolia grandiflora*, a glossy, broad-leafed evergreen with big, orange-red seedpods. "The branches are perfect for big vases and to spread across your fireplace mantel or for a church decoration," he says, his passion for his art beginning to color his voice. "The foliage is incredible, and there's a brown texture to the underside of the leaves, and the bonus is the seedpods. These pods are sexy — all the fertility is there, the hope of the next season."

He moves on to a *Taxus* and eyes the big yew judiciously. "Why not make a few swags and wreaths? It's so fresh, it's classic."

Barry — a frequent traveler who has gone on horticultural expeditions to such places as Guatemala, the Galapagos, South Africa and Sikkim in the Himalayas — stops at a blue Chinese fir with prickly needles that he propagated from one he saw 12 years ago during a trip to China. "The color is wonderful. You can use it in table decorations with gold fruit and ribbons."

He bends to examine the snakelike stems of the euphorbias growing at the foot of the tree. "I'd use these in candle cups. They hang down like a medusa.

Just add some red grapes, a few red roses."

It is as if his yard is filled with art forms. "You walk around, and there's a hell of a lot of stuff out here to use." He singles out Scotch thistle, variegated English holly, the luminous green and gold foliage of the euonymous, the pinkish berries of mountain andromeda, the lustrous leaves of *Skimmia japonica*, a group of hollies and junipers that lines a hillside. "I planted them to hold the bank, but they give me a bonus." Barry clips off holly branches for a door swag and holds up variegated juniper called Nellie R. Stevens. "Look at that. Perfect for a table centerpiece. Or on top of your Christmas pudding."

For the artist, who believes that flower-arranging doesn't have to be stiff and serious, it's a matter of imagination. Of seeing something growing in his garden and transforming it indoors for a winter of content. "The raw materials are all in the garden," he says. "You just have to have the wit to go out there and find these things."

Barry's discoveries include a few twigs of winter-blooming heather that he arranges in a vase on the bedside table. He also finds places for leaves of wild geraniums coupled with a few roses. The elegant foliage of heavenly bamboo are accented with pomegranates in a low wooden bowl. And he does magic by combining the blue-green branches of *Mahonia bealei* with a few sprigs of holly, some *Magnolia grandiflora* and a couple of golden pears. And he decorates the mantel with trails of ivy.

Barry snips a little of this, a little of that, takes it all into his workroom and comes out 10 minutes later with an elegant arrangement set in a wooden bowl with an orange-colored ribbon. He used the seed-laden magnolia, the Harry Lauder's walking stick, *Ilex* Blue Boy and Blue Girl, variegated English holly, golden juniper and silver and green euonymous. "It's a long-lasting arrangement that's easily managed. You could even add some red anemones or tulips or roses. And to make it last longer, it could go in a mudroom or a garage where it's cooler or it could be spritzed every now and then. It's really just a handful of little bits and pieces from the garden."

J. Barry Ferguson smiles. "So what can you cut from your garden to bring indoors, my dear?" he asks. "There's no end."

A Wreath From Your Own Forest

If you're into Christmas wreaths, it might make you merry to know that you don't have to go out and buy one. You can make your own with materials from your backyard. Here, flower arranger J. Barry Ferguson shows how.

1. Barry's choices include *Ilex* Nellie R. Stevens, American boxwood, blue spruce, juniper, variegated English holly, *Cumminghamia lanceolata*, or China fir, and the hips of *Rosa foliolosa*. You can use any combination of evergreens you might have on hand. Cut 7- to 8-inch lengths with enough of a stem to catch onto the frame. You also need a 3-foot double-ring wire frame, a spool of grade-21 wire, sharp pruners and gloves. Here, Barry starts the wiring of the greens.

2. A handful of the blue-berried juniper forms the base of the wreath. Barry adds sprigs of spruce, holly, fir and boxwood, then wires the bouquet to the frame. "Tug tightly," he advises.

"Weave the wire through the frame and double back."

3. A second bouquet is layered on top of the first one and wired in. Rose hips add a touch of red.

4. Work layer by layer around the frame. Here the wreath is three-quarters completed as Barry adds variegated holly to provide a contrast of texture and color.

5. The finished wreath lends a holiday touch to the wall of Barry's studio.

How To

A Vote for

I know this is the time of year when the lights are going on again all over the world, and I don't mean to put a damper on things, but I'm not electrified by outdoor illumination. Or illuminated by outdoor electrics. I just don't see the point — or to be more accurate, considering the multicolored multitude of holiday decorations sparkling in our suburbs, the points of it.

Don't get me wrong. I'm not the grinch who wants to short-circuit Christmas. Basically my philosophy is one of live and let light. In fact, I was very impressed by a wooden obelisk I spotted in a garden catalog that was decorated with evergreen roping and tiny white lights. I thought that next year if my budget permits, I'll try that on the cedar obelisk in my own garden and along the picket fence that surrounds it. But that's as far as I'll go.

My motto for outdoor decorations is that less is better and moderation matters. I'm puzzled by people who put all that money and effort into front-yard Christmas metropolises and plastic St. Nicks and prancing Prancers. And it's up for such a short time. It's like a gardener trying to pack summer into a few days.

Like I said, I'm not trying to black out the holidays. I have no trouble getting into the spirit that goes along with the season. I love singing Christmas carols and hanging up stockings even if I'm the one who fills them. And my husband is Jewish and I look forward to getting a present every night for the eight nights of Chanukah. Just because we don't have any lit-up Santas or Donners and Blitzens on the roof or electric menorahs blinking in the picture window doesn't mean we're living in a bleak house.

We certainly shine on the inside. In line with the mixed culture of our household, we put up a live Christmas tree with a big red bow on top and we light candles in a menorah during Chanukah. Actually we collect menorahs and dreidels and nutcrackers, too. And this year we bought a Christopher Radko dreidel ornament for our tree. We know that Christmas and Chanukah are not synonymous holidays, but for us, the dreidel on the tree says something about love.

As for the outside, well, I decorate with wreaths and roping and holly and pinecones. I wish I were artsy-craftsy and could make my own fantastic creations right out of my garden. I know people who can turn a few twigs and a sprig of holly into something that would be worth a week's wages for one of Santa's elves. But it's all magic to me.

Restraint

At left, a twig chair trimmed with a holiday wreath, Above, an evergreen swag graces the mailbox.

What I'm terrific at is picking out ready-made wreaths. Not the jazzed-up kind that jingle and jangle with bells and balls but simple sweet-smelling evergreen wreaths modestly decorated with pinecones and berries and occasionally with pretty red or green bows. We put wreaths on the front door, the backyard shed and the stone swan planter that reigns near our pool.

This year, we're also dressing up the mailbox with an evergreen crescent of pine and juniper and decking the gate of our front-yard garden with boughs of holly. And if we can't afford a thousand points of light on the picket fence, we might just string roping along it and put a red-and-gold bow at each corner.

That's more than enough for me. The best decorations of all grow around me. That's why I don't cut back my *Sedum* Autumn Joy. I'm touched by the solemn beauty of the brown seed heads, especially when they're dusted by snow.

I like watching the silvery skeletons of the Russian sage dance in the winter wind. The buds of next spring's rhododendrons seem like precious jewels when they're encased in ice. I think there's grace and stark elegance in the naked brown canes of the roses that ramble up the arbors of our garden. The orange berries of heavenly bamboo and the red of cotoneaster perk up the landscape. The parsley is still green in the barren vegetable beds and so is the Swiss chard. And there's poetry in the subtle green shading of two Hinoki cypresses that stand out in the thin light of winter.

Like snow itself or the ice that sometimes covers the pond behind our house and turns it into an animated Currier and Ives print, these things are true season's greetings. They're nature's way of lighting up the world. And you don't have to plug them in.

Chores Galore

SPRAY broadleaf evergreens with an antidesiccant and remember to treat the undersides of leaves. This is the time when they and newly planted conifers lose water through their foliage.

TAKE a peek at your stored dahlias and gladioli to make sure there are no signs of decay.

DON'T use de-icing salts to melt snow on walkways. It can damage or kill plants. Use sand, sawdust, urea fertilizer or clean kitty litter instead.

HELP holly boughs keep their cool. Move cut holly to an unheated porch or garage at night and mist the foliage several times a day.

QUENCH thirsty Christmas trees. They need plenty of water.

WAIT till the ground freezes before you mulch perennial and bulb beds. Winter cover isn't intended to keep plants warm, but to protect them from heaving out of the ground during alternate periods of freezes and thaws. Keep them in place with 2 to 3 inches of loose mulch like pine needles or salt hay. After the holidays, lay boughs from Christmas trees and holiday wreaths over tender shrubs and perennials.

PLANT magnolia seeds from this year's fruit.

MULCH strawberries with clean straw.

MISTLETOE may be romantic but it's also poisonous. Don't hang it where it can tempt children or pets or fall into food.

SOW seeds of larkspur, stock and sweet peas in the greenhouse for April blooms, and tuberous begonias and gloxinia for May flowers.

GET more out of deciduous shrubs like honeysuckles, hydrangeas, mock oranges, privets, viburnums, spireas, forsythias, deutzias. Propagate by taking 6- to 9-inch cuttings of the past season's growth, label them and tie in bundles. Bury in 6 inches of sand outdoors or in a cold frame. In spring, dig them up and plant, with just the tips above the ground.

DIG up clumps of lily-of-the-valley for forcing before the ground freezes. Put them in soil-less mix and keep in a cold protected place for 10 days. Move pots indoors to a cool dark room for another 10 days then to a warm sunny window until they bloom.

KEEP cyclamens happy. Give them bright indirect sunlight and chilly night temperatures — low 50s is ideal. Don't overwater — the crown should be dry — and be sure to remove lower leaves as they yellow. Fertilize every two to four weeks. When they stop blooming around April reduce watering and put them in a semi-shaded spot.

CREATE a ring of ivy using small-leafed cultivars of *Hedera*. Cut a length of galvanized wire and secure each end in a container of potting soil. Using two plants, place one at each end of the ring. Train the growth up the wire and secure it loosely with a plant twist'em. Continue doing this to create a lush ring of green.

ASK Santa for gardening tools.

January

*O*n a night in January, when stars glittered diamond-bright in the blue vel-

vet sky, I looked out onto the patio and saw a red fox standing in the snow.

An instant later, only its paw prints remained. January is a gray-white

month when color comes in flashes. Blue jays dart across the sky. Red berries

drip from hollies and viburnums, orange bittersweet winds along fences.

Fireplaces and woodstoves crackle and gray smoke spirals out of chimneys

into the sky. For gardeners, there is comfort amid the cold. It is a time to

force paperwhites and arrange dried flowers and lavish attention on

houseplants. To read all the garden books and magazines that piled up

during the growing season. And to wander through a seed catalog into

dreams of gardens to come.

Catalog Moments

I've got my treadmill set up so I can listen to Edna Kelly of "Midnight in the Garden of Good and Evil" fame on my CD player and look out the window at the front yard. That way I don't need a television set in the room while I imitate a hamster. The vista is terrific.

I see snap peas climbing up the picket fence around our flower-vegetable garden and Costoluto

January

Genovese tomatoes ripening in red fluted splendor on sturdy wooden stakes. I see butterhead and romaine and red-leaf lettuce growing in unblemished splendor. I see purple eggplants bursting with goodness and beauty the way their ancestors did many years ago in Italy. I see beets and beans and squash and spinach and — maybe, just maybe — the beginnings of what will someday be asparagus.

OK, I know none of this is actually there yet, but I can still imagine it. Sweet dreams to tread by. I'm placing the plants in my mind's eye as I look out the window. It's the best kind of daydream because unlike winning the lottery or spinning gold, I can make it come true. I have hope, desire, a bin full of compost ready to be worked into the soil, and I'm ready to think about ordering the seeds.

Meanwhile, I can wallow at will in descriptions of some of my favorite veggies and some flowers, too. French Vanilla marigolds and Peach Melba nasturtiums and Little Sweetheart sweet peas and the scarlet-orange Mexican sunflowers that were such a success last season. On winter nights especially, seed catalogs are as absorbing as Ruth Rendell mysteries or junk TV. I admit that I couldn't wrench myself away from the adventures of my role model, "Xena," the warrior princess who lets out this terrific war whoop, somersaults into the air and knocks six men sprawling at the same time. But there was one night when I gave up "Star Trek: Voyager" to read about fragrant melons that taste like butterscotch and giant daikon radishes that look like they could take over the world.

I have last year to lean on — I did well both with indoor and outdoor starters. My nasturtiums spilled over the corners of the vegetable beds and we harvested early peas through the spring. Tomatoes, bush beans and eggplants overflowed my harvest basket. This year, I'm being even more ambitious. I'm looking at seeds from six catalogs — Johnny's, Shepherd's, Burpee Heirlooms, Burpee Seeds & Plants, The Cook's Garden and Seeds of Change.

Each catalog has its own virtues. Johnny's and Seeds of Change have lots of full-color photos, and the Seeds of Change seeds are organically grown. Cook's includes bright drawings, and Burpee's Heirlooms has paintings from nature. Burpee's Seeds & Plants has wonderful photos of

Building a Cold Frame

A cold frame turns gardening into an all-season affair. It's a springtime way station for tender vegetable seedlings that need hardening off and the perfect summer place to pamper young perennials and biennials. In fall, it coddles your late crop of leafy greens, and in winter it's a chilling-out space for daffodils and crocuses that are destined to be forced into bloom.

Place your cold frame in a sunny spot with the slanted glass top facing south. Don't forget to water plants – even in winter, and pay attention to light and heat. You may have to use a shade cloth in summer and the lid should be propped open when the interior temperature reaches 70 degrees.

Now is a good time to build a cold frame. Here are a few tips to keep in mind. Use galvanized nails and rot-resistant wood such as cedar or redwood; never use pressure-treated wood. The cover determines the dimensions of the cold frame. Select a lid that is about 2 1/2 to 3 feet wide and at least 4 feet – an old storm window works well. The frame should slope from at least 18 inches high in back to 12 inches in front. Attach the cover to the back of the frame with galvanized steel hinges and apply weather stripping around the edges.

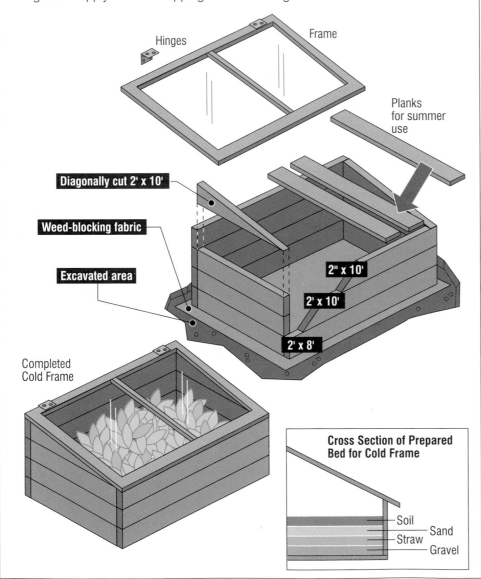

Hinges

Frame

Planks for summer use

Diagonally cut 2' x 10'

Weed-blocking fabric

Excavated area

2" x 10'

2' x 10'

2' x 8'

Completed Cold Frame

Cross Section of Prepared Bed for Cold Frame

Soil
Sand
Straw
Gravel

flowers and vegetables. Shepherd's doesn't get into color photos but charms the reader with graceful sketches and appetizing descriptions that don't spare any adjectives. Of course, almost all garden catalogs make good reading.

Just try the blurb from Shepherd's for its Ronde de Nice squash. After rhaposidizing about the "fine, light green skins" of "these tasty, little round zucchinis," the copy adds, "This lovely old variety produces a good supply of custardy-smooth, rich-tasting round fruits ... Serve the petite globes steamed, sautéed whole or stuffed as an elegant entrée."

You guessed it. I'm getting Ronde de Nice from Shepherd's, and I'm thinking about Rouge d'Etampes Cinderella pumpkin, which the catalog claims "is the original model for Cinderella's fairy-tale coach — we found it described in an antique French seed list ... if a fairy godmother happens to appear, so much the better."

And the Seeds of Change description of its Half-Runner bean made my mouth water: "Originally cultivated by the Anasazi, the 'ancients' of the Southwest. The large, plump beans make a hearty, thick soup." Cook's stirred my appetite with it's come-on for Red Verona radicchio: "Produces bright red heads the size of a baseball with prominent white veins. Intriguingly bitter flavor."

I suspect I'll order something from every catalog. I look for taste and color and disease resistance. I'm interested in the Cinderella pumpkin and the intriguingly bitter radicchio and a sweet Yellow Fame pepper I spotted in Johnny's. And my eggplant varieties usually include the Black Beauty heirloom that Burpee introduced nearly 100 years ago.

It takes me hours to narrow down my list and I always wind up with more than I need, but that's part of the fun. I'm a sucker for catalogs. The folks at L.L. Bean, Land's End, Crate & Barrel and Williams Sonoma know me well. Maybe that's why my past orders have included a mini-food processor from Shepherd's — after all, why grow vegetables if you don't eat them? — thorn-proof gloves from Burpee and a great garden tool called a Hori-Hori from Seeds of Change that can be used for digging out weeds and planting bulbs and has a saw-toothed blade for cutting through roots.

Even after I send in my orders, I still enjoy the catalogs. They may not have much in the way of character, action and dialogue but I sure eat them up. Seed catalogs offer winter reading you can sink your imagination into — and eventually your teeth, too.

What's in a Name?

When it comes to flowers, I've always been charmed by names like love-in-a-mist and bridal wreath and lady's mantle. Especially love-in-a-mist, which oozes with romance — it stirs visions of courtly cavaliers bowing to fair damsels in glades by soft flowing streams as a fine mist films the morning.

As it turns out, the origin of the name love-in-a-mist may have more to do with sex than affairs of

A flower by any name has a story — including orchids, previous page; morning glories, at right; lupines, below; and balloon flowers, following page.

the heart. Instead of describing the lavender blooms, the name refers more anatomically to the delicate hairlike leaves that encircle them. Bridal wreath is an eminently proper name — stemming from the small white flowers reminiscent of weddings. But lady's mantle is no goody-goody. The moniker derives from its leaves, which resemble not just a soft green cloak but one whose precincts invite a lover's intrusion.

In old, old times, such earthy associations were common. By the 1700s, the allusions had been softened, but it was popular practice to describe women in terms of flowers. And at the heart of all the flowery language, sex was still an operative word. Carl Linnaeus, the Swedish scientist who developed the botanical classification of plants according to genus and species, offered a cogent perspective. He said the sexual attributes "of plants we regard with delight, of animals with abomination, of ourselves with strange thoughts."

Linnaeus, who used a trumpet and French horn band to call his students together at outdoor lectures, stirred controversy by describing stamens as "husbands," pistils as "wives" and petals as "bridal beds which the Creator has so gloriously arranged, adorned with such noble bed-curtains and perfumed with so many sweet scents that the bridegroom may celebrate his nuptials with his bride with all the greater solemnity." Personally, I think the man had problems.

The flowers we enjoy are part of our lives, and so it's nice to know about their roots. Looking into the origin of their names is a pleasant pastime for a winter's eve. It's also instructive. Not just for gardeners but for everybody with a healthy curiosity who responds to the scent of a rose or the sight of an orchid or the splash of daffodils on a spring day. When the subject is flowers, what's in a name is just about everything under the sun — love and lust, myths and magic, people and places.

I'm talking, of course, about common names — garden Latin is another matter. Some common names of flowers are clearly descriptive. Balloon flower and morning glory, for a couple of examples, and bleeding heart, too. Bleeding heart is also known as "lady in the bath" because that's what it looks like when you turn the bloom upside down and pull it slightly open. Impatiens describes the flower's nature. In Latin it means impatient. It refers to the way the plant's seeds explode from the pod — as if it can't wait to get rid of them.

The nomenclature of dogwood is a little more complex. Legend has it that the Trojan horse was built of Cornelian cherry, a variety of dogwood, and that its berries were gobbled up by Odysseus' troops after Circe turned them into pigs. John Parkinson, a 17th-Century London herbalist, called English dogwood "the Doggeberry tree, because the berries are not fit to be eaten, or to be given to a dogge." Other authorities credit its name to a concoction made from the tree's leaves that was used to rid dogs of fleas.

The name lupine also has an animal background. It comes from the Latin *lupinus,* for wolves, because the ancients thought mistakenly that the flowers ravaged the land. And the name delphinium derives from the Latin *delphus* for dolphin because of the flower's form.

camellia was named for Camille, the famous French courtesan better known as the Lady of the Camellias because she always carried a bouquet of the flowers. I'm not sure what message she was trying to send, but on 25 days of the month they were white and the other five days they were red. Anyway, it's more likely that Camille took her name from the flower rather than the other way around. Linnaeus named the camellia in honor of Georg Josef Kamel, a Jesuit pharmacist from Moravia, who may never even have seen one. By the way, Linnaeus changed the "K" in Kamel to a "C" in order to conform to the Latin alphabet.

And then there's the orchid. It comes from the Greek orchis, which means testicle and alludes to the plant's tubers. For that reason, it's long been considered an aphrodisiac. I'll leave it at that.

The legends behind many flower names are lovely. Forget-me-nots are true blue on Valentine cards and D.H. Lawrence placed some of them in a delicate area that Lady Chatterly would be sure to remember. But the name forget-me-not actually comes from a German expression, which means just that. Legend holds that a knight was picking a bouquet for his fair lady on a riverbank, lost his footing and fell in the water. Before he drowned, he tossed the flowers to his sweetheart and cried out "Vergiss mein nicht." Forget me not.

Another love story is the tale of Narcissus, the young Greek hunk who went ga-ga over his reflection in a pool. He pined away for the unattainable image and died, turning into the flower that bears his name and demonstrates that narcissistic behavior can be fatal.

Some flowers are named after interesting people. Forsythia's namesake was William Forsyth, superintendent of the Royal Gardens of Kensington Palace in the late 1700s. I'm intrigued by Forsyth, who shook up his fellow horticulturists by huckstering something called "Forsyth's Plaister." He claimed the concoction could heal wounds in growing trees and even bring back oak trees "where nothing remained but the bark." The "plaister" was eventually discredited. It was composed of cow dung, lime, wood ashes and sand mixed into a paste with soap suds and urine.

Bougainvillea was named after an explorer, Louis Antoine de Bougainville, who sailed around the world from 1767 to 1769. It was discovered in Tahiti by his botanist friend, Philibert Commerson, whom Bougainville invited on the trip to help soothe Commerson's grief over the death of his wife.

If you're like me, you probably thought the

Chores Galore

BATHE your houseplants. Wash them with soapy water and a clean cloth to get rid of pests like mealy bugs and spider mites. If there's real trouble, they may need a shot of insecticidal soap. While you're at it, rotate plants 180 degrees each time you water so they'll grow evenly.

THINK Irish. Start shamrock seeds for St. Patrick's Day.

VENTILATE cold frames and greenhouses on sunny days.

BEGIN pruning of dormant apple and pear trees and finish before April.

DUMP paperwhite narcissi that have bloomed — they're not meant to be forced again next year. Amaryllis is a different story. Cut back the finished flower stalk and let the plant grow in good light through fall. Then it will need to rest awhile in a dark place before it flowers again.

PLACE fuschias on a cool window sill for fragrant winter blooms.

CURL up by the fire and make your seed order. You can save wood ashes for spring. They help neutralize soil and add potash, calcium and potassium. But beware — wood ashes also can throw your pH out of whack. Do a soil test before spreading ashes in the garden. In any case, use them sparingly.

PLAN your garden. Do it on paper. When designing the vegetable patch and annual beds, make sure you're not growing the same plants or their relatives in the same place every year. Crop rotation helps prevent diseases. For instance, don't plant cucumbers in last year's melon patch. Here's a quick checklist of plant families:

Beet family - beets, Swiss chard

Cabbage family - Brussels sprouts, cabbage, cauliflower, kale, radish, sweet alyssum

Carrot family - carrots, celery, dill, parsley

Daisy family - lettuce, marigolds, cosmos, ageratum

Onion family - chive, garlic, onion

Pea family - beans, peas, sweet peas

Squash family - cucumber, melon, squash

Tomato family - eggplant, pepper, petunia, potato, tomato

Paradise in the Attic

Above, Lee Calchman comes in from the cold to enjoy the garden in her attic greenhouse.

I've never been good with houseplants. Maybe it goes back to childhood. My mother wasn't much for outdoor gardening, but she had a knack for houseplants. She grew African violets and the house was fragrant with her favorite gardenias. Every Saturday, it was my job to carry all the plants to the kitchen table and give them a good soaking. Once a month I had to shine the leaves of the philodendrons and ivies with a plant polish that brushed on white and dried to a bright sheen. My mother liked everything to sparkle.

To this day, my track record with houseplants is notorious. My college roommate never forgave me for doing in her coleus our freshman year. We were seniors before she stopped calling me Killer. I've killed spider plants and zebra plants and jade plants. I've killed cacti and peace lilies and prayer plants. I've killed ferns and

ficus and peperomia. I've even killed a snake plant, a plant the guy in the garden shop assured me was "tough and easy to grow — you can't kill this plant." He didn't know he was talking to the Dillinger of Diffenbachia.

Lately, I've been giving houseplants another try. But the hibiscus that bloomed all summer wasn't happy in the den. I moved it to the front hall, which is warmer and lighter, but it's still turning yellow and dropping leaves. And then my cyclamen keeled over. My schefflera succumbed. And my gloxinia died.

So I searched for someone who could inspire me. Someone who has a way with houseplants. I found Lee Calchman. Lee is an indoor-outdoor, 365-days-a-year gardener. In her 60-by-30-foot backyard in Westbury, she has a center island garden devoted to miniature rhododendrons and lilacs and Japanese maples. She

176

has a perennial border and a vegetable garden and a step-table for her bonsai.

But when winter comes, Lee isn't content to sit inside and dream of spring. Even the few months between putting the perennial border to bed and starting herb and vegetable seeds indoors are too long for her to go without dirt under her fingernails. Her house is filled with plants, from the fan-palm in the dining room to the fuchsia in the foyer. But that's only the beginning. "I put plants everywhere," Lee says.

She's not kidding. Lee Calchman has a greenhouse in the attic.

The horticulture in the 16-by-14-foot attic started soon after the retired executive secretary and her optician husband Warren moved into their Levitt ranch 20 years ago. She joined the Long Island Horticultural Society and the Greater New York Orchid Society and the Gloxinia and Gesneriad Society. She joined the Long Island chapter of the North American Rock Garden Society and the Hobby Greenhouse Association.

"You can't live in an environment like that and not become an addict," she says. "Every plant society has an annual sale. My husband would just shake his head and say, 'Honey those are very nice, but where are you going to put them?'"

"I need a greenhouse," Lee replied. A greenhouse she could get to in any kind of weather. One that wouldn't take away outdoor garden space. She looked up instead of out — and saw the attic. They hired a carpenter to install cedar planks and two skylights. Those plus an existing window provided light from the east and south. Plumbing was installed. Warren built plant tables. "When we started the project, I thought, 'Oh, God, it's so big,'" she recalls. "But it was filled before it was even finished."

I wouldn't show my attic to anyone. But Lee is all smiles as she leads the way up to hers. She opens the door — and forget snow. Forget ice. Forget blizzards and windchill factors. Enter Lee Calchman's attic and you're in a tropical jungle.

A pale pink *Vanda* orchid blooms by one skylight. There's a variegated hibiscus that has small orange flowers when it's in bloom. And gloxinias, more properly known as *Sinningia speciosa,* and a terrestrial orchid, *Ludisia discolor*, which sends out a spike with many tiny white flowers. A yellow *Primula* and a *Clerodendrum* with pink bell-like flowers. Mexican heathers and a succulent called *Rhipsalis*. And *Aeschynanthus* with a seedpod that looks like an anorexic string bean.

Lee snips and clips and pinches and prunes. Her scissors are an extension of her hands. "But I can't cut a bud," she says. "That's like throwing away one of your children."

She sprays the plants with a mister attached to a

yellow hose with an on-off valve that was installed a while back after she left the faucet running and a leaf clogged the drain and water leaked down into the kitchen and living room.

"I do best with gesneriads. We're a good match, I guess; they like me, so I like them. The best advice I could give anyone who gardens is not to listen to anyone who tells you, 'You'll never be able to grow that.' Try it anyway. If you don't know you can't grow it, maybe you will."

Lee's plants prove her positivism. There's an evergreen amaryllis that blooms earlier than its cousins. Bougainvilleas, even a bonsai bougainvillea. *Phyllanthus angustifolia,* a New Zealand shrub with minuscule red flowers that bloom on each serration of the stalklike foliage. *Hatiora salicornioides*, or drunkard's dream, which blooms bright orange. *Codonanthe crassifolia* Paula with hairy leaves and white blooms that give way to orange berries. And a calamondin orange tree that produces tiny tart fruit that makes excellent marmalade.

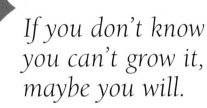

If you don't know you can't grow it, maybe you will.

Her collection runs into the hundreds. "I don't keep count, and I've reduced the number over the years. I used to keep records — I had an index file with the label of every plant I killed. Now I just keep a list of the things I'd like to try again."

She spends at least two hours a day in her attic, where four fans provide ventilation and fluorescent lights are on 14 hours a day in cloudy weather and the nighttime temperature doesn't drop below 62 degrees, and even on a gloomy winter afternoon it climbs into the 80s.

In another month or so, Lee will start seeds in the greenhouse. Lettuce and tomatoes and basil and parsley. And by mid-May all the plants will be outside — soaking up the sun in a lathe house Warren built or on the wooden table that surrounds a pin oak tree in the backyard.

"The only thing I have to worry about is bugs. I don't use chemicals. Before I bring the plants back into the greenhouse at the end of summer, I hose them off and dip everything in a messy, soapy, liquid goo and wash down the greenhouse. Bringing the plants in and up is torture. But it doesn't lessen the joy of having the greenhouse."

The joy of seeing flowers bloom when your garden is buried under snow. What could be better than spending a few hours on a dreary winter day in your very own tropical paradise?

I'm going to try harder with indoor plants. I don't have a basement in my house, but I do have an attic.

New Year's Resolutions

I thought about my New Year's resolutions during a much needed winter vacation — my husband and I spent three weeks driving to the Grand Canyon with lots of verdant stops along the way. I admired camellias in Charleston and Spanish moss in Savannah. I visited the pecan tree outside the apartment in Austin where I once lived. I marveled at the *Saguaro* cacti in Tucson's Sabino

Canyon and gaped at the red-rock glory of Sedona. I wept with wonder when I saw the Grand Canyon.

The beauty of America made me realize how much I have come to appreciate the natural world. I thought of my garden and the metaphor it has become for my life. I had time for the garden magazines I brought along and time to thumb through my treasured volume of Celia Thaxter's "An Island Garden." When people asked Celia for the secret of her glorious garden, she had a ready answer. "Love."

For the poet-gardener of the late 1800s, that single word covered all the sweat and labor of trial and error in the flower beds, and as she put it, "the patience that endures continual trial, the constancy that makes perseverance possible, the power of forgoing ease of mind and body to minister to the necessities of the thing beloved."

Clearly, I thought, Celia was telling us that gardening is a higher love. A love that calls for discipline and dedication. A love that demands true resolution.

And so in the spirit of love and gardens and the new year, I'm making my resolutions. Whether they will grow into reality only the coming months can tell.

Before I even get to the outside, I'm going to do better with houseplants. That is my first resolution. My pair of Christmas cacti have stayed alive — one of them just barely — and I'm raising a philodendron and an aglaonema and begonias and a Norfolk Island pine and a sansevieria. I have a bromeliad in bloom and my clivia flowered for the first time this past summer. But some of my houseplants are looking ragged this winter. I have to be more conscientious about watering and feeding. I also have to be more attuned to each plant's particular needs. I want my night-blooming cereus to bloom. And I'd like to try orchids.

Spring will be here sooner than we think, and I've promised myself that I'm not going to buy every plant I see. I walk into a nursery and I'm immediately transformed into that cliche of consumerism — the kid in the candy store. I grab for the hisbiscus in the corner and then I spot the tall willowy pampas grass that captured my fancy at a flower show. I'm entranced by the green-blue foliage of the dianthus and the muted grace of the heaths and heathers. I reach for blue salvia, I pick up another rosebush. I want, I want, I want. "Do you know where you're going to plant that?" my husband asks. "Yeah, yeah," I say, and I think that maybe I should go plant shopping by myself. But then I come home and plop the plants on the patio wall where they wait for days until I find the perfect place.

I've resolved to be more industrious when it comes to labeling my plants. I'm going to buy sturdy markers, or I might even have someone make engraved labels for

me. I simply can't seem to settle on the right look for my labels. I want tags that blend naturally with the garden — I don't want it to look like a botanical garden. But I also want something that's easy to read and holds up through all kinds of weather. Maybe I'm a snob but I don't want plastic. I might just try the copper markers I see in catalogs. For me, the importance of plant tags is that they help me remember variety names.

I'm going to do better at spreading the word about the very real danger of invader species such as purple loosestrife and kudzu, which take over like wildfire and threaten our natural world.

I vow to find the time to get my garden photos into shape — or at least into albums. I have seasons upon seasons of photos to catch up on. And I'm going to plunge into cyberspace. Up until now, I've done little more than tiptoe into the World Wide Web. I've been told there's a virtual garden out there.

There are a few shrubs I'd love to have in my own yard, and this year I resolve to plant them. The first is *Callicarpa*, which has stunningly vibrant pur-

ple berries in the fall. And double-file viburnum, which is a beautiful multi-season shrub. And a Harry Lauder's walking stick, with it's wonderfully contorted branches.

And I'll expand my composting operation. I'm going to build an open bin exclusively for composting leaves, which are super-abundant in my yard. My compost bin was a big success last year, but there's no reason why I can't do more. This is not necessarily a resolution, but I'd love to use little red wigglers in a worm composter in the kitchen. I just have to convince my husband.

Above all, in the garden, as in life, I'll try to come to terms with my need to be perfect. By it's very nature, gardening defies perfection. There's always another weed to pull. There's always a plant that withers no matter what you do or where you put it. There's always another flower to fit in. There are no perfect gardens. Or gardeners.

All we can do is our best. That's why we make resolutions.

Above and at left, a "higher love" of gardening blooms in a recreation of Celia Thaxter's garden on an island off the Maine coast.

February

There are intimations of spring. In February, the garden comes to life in hops and skips — if not in leaps and bounds. Winter aconite dances into yellow bloom and the crepe-papery flowers of witch hazel follow suit. When I see the witch hazel, I look for hellebores — for the flowers of the Christmas and Lenten roses. And the earliest of bulbs that have been gathering strength through the winter are coming up out of the cold. Snowdrops appear and suddenly, before the season of ice and snow is over, there are crocuses. For me, the sight of a crocus in the snow is heartbreakingly beautiful. The world looks to the groundhog as a prophet of spring, but truth blooms with the crocus.

Winter's Wonderful Witch

182

A s a child, the only witch hazel I knew about was found in the medicine chest. I had no idea that the clear liquid we used for cuts and bug bites came from the twigs of a deciduous shrub. Or that the plant's beauty itself was an astringent for souls wounded by the dark and cold season known as winter.

Which it is, of course. But I had to have a garden of my own before I realized this. Witch hazel — which gets its name from the fact that its forked twigs were sometimes used as divining rods — is an absolutely magic tonic for winter doldrums. "The witch hazel's blooming," I announced at breakfast on the first day of February, and my husband smiled even though it was a workday and he was running late.

If you care about spring and warmth and all those nice things, you have to like witch hazel, or *Hamamelis*, as the genus is called. Even when snow and ice cover the landscape, this free spirit goes its own way and perks up the season. The Japanese have a word for witch hazel. They call it mansaku, or "first flowering." There are five or six species in North America and Asia — plus a good number of hybrids and cultivars — and each has its own time for making a debut. *H. virginiana*, our native northeastern witch hazel and the source of the astringent, blooms in the fall. *H. vernalis*, a native of the south-central states, shows off in late winter or early spring, as does *H. mollis*, a sweet Chinese species.

And what a lovely debut. Witch hazel has spiderlike flowers — other descriptions range from dish mops to pinwheels to shredded coconut or crepe paper. They range from a half inch to 2 inches in diameter and come in different colors — everything from bright yellow Arnold Promise to red Diane and coppery Jelena and orange-yellow Vesna. All of these varieties, incidentally, are more formally known as *Hamamelis x intermedia*, crosses between the two Asian species, the Chinese *mollis* and the Japanese *japonica*.

And there's more to witch hazel than meets the eye now. Although the winter performance is what it's known for, there's another show of sorts in the fall when the foliage takes center stage. Not a single leaf appears until all the flowers are gone. The leaves stay green through summer and then join the fall revue — turning colors that range from gold and bronze and orange to maroon and scarlet and tangerine.

The witch hazel in my own front yard is Pallida, a *mollis* cultivar. I'm always bowled over by its arrival. I can see it from the window of my potting room, beneath the white branches of a birch tree, not far from a couple of rhododendrons and just beyond a covey of purple and white pansies. Pallida has a delicate scent, and the sulphur-yellow flowers weave their spidery charm for weeks.

Despite its delicate appearance, witch hazel is a hardy shrub. It should be planted in the fall in slightly acidic, nutrient-rich soil. It can grow as high as 15 to 20 feet and is not a demanding plant — it does its thing in both full sun and dappled shade and needs virtually no pruning except to remove dead wood. It shows off well against a dark backdrop of rhododendrons or conifers.

Some people are so uplifted by the blooming of the witch hazel that they hold celebrations to mark its arrival. James Shuart, the president of Hofstra University, is famous in our neck of the woods as a tree-lover who turned his college campus into an arboretum. What is not as well known is that he's practically a party animal when it comes to witch hazel. There are at least 11 varieties of the plant, including Pallida, on the school grounds, and Shuart holds a party for friends, colleagues and students each year at the first blooming, which he can see from his office window. It's a 15-minute coffee break, and the bagels and muffins are on him.

"February is a tough month for all of us," he says. "I'm very appreciative of this splash of yellow that pops out and spreads sunshine during winter's gray steely days."

At the last party, the celebrants cut twigs from about eight varieties and brought them inside. "When you bring them in," explained Fred Soviero, Hofstra's director of grounds and landscaping, "they puff up like a grouse and a wonderful fragrance is released."

I'm wary about cutting my witch hazel because I just have the one bush and it's still young. I don't have blossoms to spare. And it seems to me that its main purpose is to brighten up the outside and perfume the winter. One of the best things about witch hazel is that it's no here-today-gone-tomorrow bloom. The flowers open to the sun, then close if the temperature dips. When the sun warms things up again, they reopen. And, as I said, this can go on for weeks.

Besides, they're heralds of more beauty and vibrance to come. When you see the witch hazel, you know that winter aconite and snowdrops and all those wonderful crocuses are sure to follow. That's something to celebrate.

Far left, witch hazel blossoms on the grounds of Hofstra University. Left, the plant blooms under a cover of snow.

The Winter Rose

Hellebore: the early flowering plant that whispers of spring.

For the past few years, hellebores have been high on my wish list. So when we carved out a shade garden under the locust and sassafras trees in the front yard, I made sure I put in several of the plants popularly known as the Christmas rose. Of course, *Helleborus niger* isn't a rose and it doesn't bloom at Christmas. At least not in these parts. One thing it could use is a good PR person to help it get past its name. Hellebore comes from the Greek hellein, to kill, and bora for food. The ancient Greeks claimed it either caused or cured insanity, and the Irish smeared it on their weapons as a poison. The plant is indeed poisonous if ingested, and if you crush the leaves of some

species, you may wind up with a rash. When I first heard the name hellebore, I couldn't help but think: hell of a bore.

Actually, hellebores are rather heavenly. And they certainly aren't boring.

Before we leave the name issue, the *niger* in *H. niger* is Latin for black, but that refers only to the plant's roots. The flowers of *H. niger* are white with pink flushes and have greenish centers and bright yellow stamens. They resemble old-fashioned single roses or even camellias. Like witch hazel and winter jasmine, they whisper of spring. I'm excited because mine should bloom any day now.

And then they'll be joined by their more popular

cousin, *Helleborus orientalis*, the Lenten rose, which is probably the easiest hellebore to grow. Just writing about them cheers me up. These dainty blooms show up in warm luminous shades like pale yellow and soft pink and also in deep purple. Although the Christmas rose looks straight ahead, the cup-shaped flowers of the Lenten rose droop at a 45-degree angle. But orientalis isn't nodding out of shyness or lack of energy — it's a survival mechanism to protect the flower against pollen-killing snow, sleet and rain.

Hellebores are all the rage now, and I can understand why. With their evergreen foliage and flowers that pop up long before tried and true early-bird perennials like pulmonarias and bleeding hearts, they do wonders for winter.

And they have other attributes. They're easy to establish and the blooms last for weeks — the Lenten rose flowers well into May. They're also relatively disease-free and pest-resistant, not to mention drought-tolerant. They self-seed and hybridize with each other, leading to unexpected color combinations and speckles and spots and splotches. Of course, you have to be patient — it takes two to four years before the first blooms arrive.

Generally, hellebores enjoy shade and make a nice evergreen carpet for hillsides. They're happy beneath rhododendrons and azaleas and *Pieris*, and complement purple-leaved groundcovers like bergenia and ajuga. Orientalis hybrids look great with delicate bulbs like galanthus and muscari and scilla. When the bulbs fade, fill in the gaps with pastel primroses or yellow *Corydalis*. And hellebores are right at home in woodland gardens, where they mingle happily with ferns and epimediums and Solomon's seal. Bees love them and so why shouldn't we?

Hellebores are part of the buttercup family, or *Ranunculaceae*, which claims peonies, clematis, globe flowers and meadow rue. The Christmas rose and the Lenten rose are the best known hellebores, but the genus includes 15 species. For instance, you might want to try *H. foetidus*, better known as the stinking hellebore. Actually, it sounds worse than it smells. Its lacy leaves, which almost look like palm fronds, do give off a faint eau de skunk if they're bruised, so don't hurt them. What's more important is that the flowers are a very pretty chartreuse in March and will tolerate some sun. Heavenly hellebores include *H. argutifolius*, known as the Corsican hellebore because it is native to that island. This hellebore isn't as hardy as some of its cousins but offers a striking appearance with leathery spiny-toothed leaves and pale green flowers.

The big thing is that hellebores are a cold-weather tonic. I go through the winter wishing for warmth. So you can understand why I think hellebores are hot. They give me hope — hellebores are a wish come true.

Chores Galore

KEEP things underground. Alternating intervals of freezing and thawing may cause bulbs and perennials to pop out of the ground. Tuck them back in, then cover with mulch.

SHAKE snow from evergreens so limbs don't break. But let ice melt naturally or branches may split.

GET a glimpse of spring by forcing branches of early-flowering trees and shrubs into bloom. Forsythia, pussy willow, quince, dogwood, witch hazel and crab apple are good choices. On a mild day, collect 1- to 3-foot-long branches with nice fat buds. Cut on an angle with sharp pruners right above the leaf node. Split stem bottoms or smash them with a hammer and place in a deep bucket of warm water. Mist a few times a day as buds start to open.

TRIM summer-blooming clematis to within 24 inches of the ground. Remove half of last year's growth on autumn-flowering varieties. But don't prune spring bloomers until a month after they've done their thing. Hack back *Buddleia davidii*, better known as butterfly bush. And I mean hack. Cutting buddleias almost to the ground gives young shoots a chance to develop since they bloom on new wood that will grow this summer.

ORDER seeds. Savor the past with heirloom varieties like Brandywine tomatoes or Tom Thumb lettuce or Sweet Banana peppers or Southport Red Globe onions.

GIVE last season's seeds the viability test. Spread 20 seeds of each variety on moistened paper towels. Cover with clear plastic wrap and keep the seeds moist at room temperature for 2 weeks. If half the seeds germinate, the packet is still worth planting, but sow them a bit thicker than the directions suggest. If less than half germinate, toss out the whole batch.

SOAK all pots, flats and seed-starting supplies in a 10 percent bleach solution before cleaning. This will help prevent damping off, a fungal disease that kills indoor seedlings.

GIVE houseplants an extra drink and a light helping of fertilizer. Root cuttings of houseplants such as Swedish ivy, wandering Jew, grape ivy and lipstick plant.

START tuberous begonias indoors. Place tubers, round side down, in trays of moist vermiculite. Move to a bright warm spot — 70 degrees is ideal — and in a month or so transplant them into 6-inch containers. After the last spring frost give them a home in the garden.

SOW delphiniums and lupines in peat pots now and they should reward you this summer. Do the same with perennial rudbeckia and you'll have flowers for cutting by fall.

THINK veggies. Start seeds of beets, celery, chives, leeks and onions indoors.

Taming the Lilac Beast

Richard Weir, pruning expert, at work with the author, on her giant lilac.

Richard Weir, Prince of Pruners, showed up at my house equipped with a Swedish bow saw, a pair of pruners, heavy-duty lopping shears and a folding saw. Then he looked up at my lilac bush. "Do you have a chain saw?" he asked. Richard is the program manager for the Cornell Cooperative Extension of Nassau County, and pruning is his game. Especially rejuvenative pruning. Cutting things down to make them grow back healthier and happier.

I'd asked him to help me practice what he preached when he lectured on pruning at my master gardener course. It's one thing to learn in class and another to lop in the field. And it didn't hurt that I have this behemoth of a lilac that blocks out the western world.

But when Richard and I made our appointment, how could we know that the afternoon we settled on would turn out to be one of those days when winter was making noise. It was snowing — wet smushy glop that soaked through collars and crept into shoes and socks.

And I guess I hadn't given Richard a sufficiently realistic picture of what he'd be going up against. He thought we'd be dealing with some sweety-sweet lilac bush, not with the linebacker of all *Syringia vulgaris*. Certainly not with a lilac bigger than some trees — about 20 feet high with canes the size of Evander Holyfield's neck.

"It's a monster," Richard said as he gazed skyward.

The lilac standing alongside my driveway was indeed imposing. It was planted more than 30 years ago in an ideal location — one that offers plenty of air circulation and sunlight. The bush was vigorous, Richard said, but its future was chancy. It was getting too big for its own good. "It's unusual to see a lilac that big and old still be so productive," he said. "Its main limbs are productive, but the younger canes are dying back because they're not getting enough light."

Also, for the last few springs, most of the bush's flowers bloomed at the unreachable top. It looked nice from a distance, but without a ladder you couldn't get a bouquet out of it.

"It's a fine candidate for rejuvenative pruning," Richard said.

Rejuvenative pruning is far more drastic than maintenance pruning, which calls for the selective removal of a few branches now and then. Primarily, there are three methods for deciduous shrubs.

Method No. 1 is when you cut back the entire bush to within 6 to 10 inches of the ground. Method No. 2 is when you remove about half of the oldest, innermost unproductive branches at the base of the plant all at one time. Method No. 3 calls for taking away a third of the oldest stems each year for three years.

Besides, it was a propitious time for making cuts. The window for rejuvenating overgrown shrubs like my lilac is open from Feb. 1 to April 1, which gives new shoots a full growing season before winter. In addition, this is the time when trees and shrubs are best able to seal off the wounds created by pruning — a process known as compartmentalization.

Clearly, some big cuts were in order for my lilac. The Prince of Pruners wasn't kidding about the chain saw. I don't own one, but I went to see my neighbor Mark Schildkraut, who has more tools than I have seed catalogs. I not only returned with a chain saw but with a two-man saw and Mark himself. Richard was impressed.

When my husband came home from work, I enlisted him, too. I felt a little like Tom Saywer when he conned his friends into whitewashing his fence. But my lilac was no one-woman or one-man job, and besides, this was a learning experience.

So there we were. Richard at the handsaw, Mark at the chain saw, my husband carting off and piling up shorn branches and me admiring the snow falling on my witch hazel, or *Hamamelis*, as Richard corrected me, frowning at his lazy former student.

I'm only kidding, of course. I got into the act and the lilac, too. I made a few swipes with a saw myself, but I was no match for my lilac. Instead, I pulled branches back for the cutters. It was rough in the bush. When the snow wasn't getting in my eyes, I could see the puny look of the young canes that were being deprived of the sun.

By now, we were a drenched but merry band. Especially Mark, who was clearly born to wield a chain saw. It didn't matter that the chain was slipping and the saw was smoking and the snow was falling; he didn't miss a stroke.

"Give it a straight, horizontal cut," Richard directed, explaining that a sharply angled cut exposes too much of the shrub's internal tissue.

The pruning took a few hours. When it was over, the pile of cut canes was high enough to hide an elephant. And the lilac wasn't even entirely leveled. Before we started, we decided on a modified version of method 1: We pruned out about two-thirds of the Goliath, leaving the back portion intact to screen us from a neighbor's yard. We'll attack the back side of the lilac in the future.

In July we'll have to deal with the water sprouts that should be growing out of the pruned shrub. "You'll get about 30 shoots to compensate for what we've taken off," Richard said, examining the remains of the day. He advised that I keep six of the most vigorous shoots and remove the others.

I must have looked a little worried when we finished, because Richard tried to reassure me that far from having perpetrated a chain-saw massacre, I had made the kindest cuts. "It was a brave thing you did today," he said afterward as we sipped tea and reflected on the nature of dead wood and new life. He called what I had done tough love. I had sacrificed some of this season's blooms for a healthier, happy lilac that should start looking up in about three years.

"Don't worry," Richard said. "You won't regret it. Your lilac will thank you. It'll come back like gangbusters."

I won't demand thanks. I'll be satisfied with a bouquet.

Pruning Primer

Give your old, overgrown shrubs a new lease on life. The best time to rejuvenate them in between Feb. 1 and April 1. Good candidates include deciduous shrubs like lilacs, mock oranges and deutzias as well as broad-leafed evergreens like andromedas, hollies and rhododendrons. Choose one of the following methods and remember to prune back to an outward-facing bud. In midsummer, remove at least half of the newly sprouted canes, staggering the heights.

Method 1:
For tough love, hack back the entire bush to within 6-10 inches of the ground.

Method 2:
If you want to show a little mercy, just remove half of the oldest, innermost branches at the base of the plant.

Method 3:
If you're a real softie, go slow and do your pruning over a period of three years, taking out one-third of the oldest stems each year.

SOURCE: Cornell Cooperative Extension

In his Malverne garden, Ed Rezek recreated what he saw as a young marine in China.

Living Out

Many years ago in China, a young marine from Queens wandered about the royal enclave in a city that was then called Peking. The gates of the Forbidden City had just been lifted for outsiders, and Ed Rezek, a staff sergeant who had survived the battle of Okinawa, strolled happily through gardens of serene beauty. He wondered at miniature plants he had never seen before and gazed at the artfulness of their arrangement and the strangeness of their shapes and sizes.

In the years that followed, the vision clung to the corners of his mind — burnished by time as such visions often are. We are all prone to such memories, wispy cameos that become the stuff of dreams. But unlike most of us, Ed Rezek found a way back.

"I carried a picture of the Forbidden City in my mind," Ed says. "Then years later, a friend got me hooked on dwarf and unusual conifers — plants that in those days you couldn't find on Long Island. We'd travel all over — Pennsylvania, Virginia, Washington, Oregon, Canada — looking for specimens. It was like the picture in my mind was coming to life."

Ed Rezek is a 74-year-old retired mail carrier who has been married to his wife, Maureen, for more than half a century. Who has three children and six grandchildren and remembers when he dug up the rosebushes in the front yard and replaced them with dwarf evergreens and knew "that was it." Who only has to walk outside the Cape Cod home in Malverne that he and Maureen bought 48 years ago to truly understand the scale of things.

The gardens that surround Ed Rezek's house are firmly planted in memory as well as in the earth. More than 1,000 evergreens thrive on his 70-by-100-foot property. And in the nooks and crannies of his yard he's tucked away another 1,500 in containers — youngsters he propagated in winter in a greenhouse where he keeps his plant babies happy with country

a Forbidden Fantasy

music. In the process, Ed has grown into an internationally known collector and propagator of dwarf conifers — a gardener who thinks small in a big way.

The gardens he saw in the Forbidden City were examples of penjing, the Chinese art of miniature landscaping that is believed to predate bonsai and that depends to a large extent on dwarf conifers. Essentially, a dwarf plant is one that matures at a smaller size than normal for the species. It can be one-half or one-twentieth the usual size. Some dwarfs result from chance mutant seeds. Others are propagated by cuttings taken from abnormal, congested growths called witches' brooms that form on branches.

Ed does it all. He propagates and plants and prunes and creates bonsai. And he keeps his garden of small wonders in shape with espaliering and topiary. "It's not that I don't like larger-growing plants," he says. "But why plant something that's going to swallow you up in 10 or 20 years?"

A good question for those of us with picture windows and daily lives dimmed by giant evergreens whose size we never counted on. Instead of the great walls of privet and arborvitae and rhododendron that crowd the foundations of many split-levels and high ranches, Ed has dwarf evergreens and selectively pruned and cleverly grafted plants, from cedar to cypress. A weeping Atlas blue cedar has been trained to drip from the roof like a set of stalactites. And for color and contrast a dwarf golden Hinoki cypress has been grafted to the base of a mini Japanese umbrella plant that is more than 20 years old and just one foot high. "It's not nice to fool Mother Nature," says Ed, a master grafter, "but I do it all the time."

His backyard is a living testament to the palace gardens that soothed a young marine's soul. It is serene and beautiful year-round, even when snow fringes the green. Stand next to the pool and fountain Ed built and you can almost hear the temple bells ringing and imagine the emperor himself strolling by with his royal retinue. The yard holds the whole spectrum of green from yellowish to near-blue. And everywhere you wander, small wonders abound. Evergreens from a few inches to a few feet tall grow slowly — very slowly — around the lawn.

A white pine the size of Ed's fist is almost 10 years old. The most venerable plant in his yard has existed for a century and stands just 3 feet high and 5 feet across. It was given to him by the late Jon Spann, a famous horticulturist in the state of Washington who had brought it from Sweden in 1892. As with most of his plants, Ed doesn't bother with common names. He rattles off the Latin in his Long Island accent. *Chamaecyparis pisifer* Compressa. Some of his plants have botanical names that are longer than the plant is high. *Picea abies* Nidiformis. *Cedrus deodara* Pygmy. *Tsuga canadensis* Hussii. "Here's a miniature *Abies lasiocarpa* Duflon," Ed says. "It's very rare." The *lasiocarpa* grows about a sixteenth of an inch a year. The specimen in Ed's yard is 4 inches tall.

Ed raises most of his plants from seeds and cuttings and is in touch with collectors from New Zealand to the Czech Republic. And he spreads the word near as well as far. "You can go up and down this street," he says, "and see dwarf conifers all over the place."

He's even made a convert of Maureen. "I have a different perspective now that the kids are grown," his wife says. "I used to resent the garden. I was busy with three kids, and Ed was busy with his dwarf conifers. Now that we've grown old together, I love the garden. I thank God I have such a beautiful view." When Ed had a quadruple bypass a few years ago, Maureen learned to trim in the gardens for him. "But only under the eyes of the expert."

Ed smiles at his wife and at his little plants and the Forbidden City doesn't seem that far away.

> *It's not nice to fool Mother Nature, but I do it all the time.*

Hearts And Flowers

It makes sense that if two people care for a garden, they should care about each other. To share life and beauty, to plant and nurture together is a definition of love in bloom. The couple who garden together grow together. It is that way with Mary and Harry Van Allen. In July, when the clematis and the coral bells are out, Mary and Harry will celebrate their 55th wedding anniversary. They'll say most of it with flowers, because for 50 of those years they've been gardening together. Through all the days of children and careers and sorrows and joys and rain and sunshine, their marriage and their garden have flourished.

It makes sense to write about them in the month when we mark that celebration of hearts and flowers called Valentine's Day. The way they smile at each other is proof that they've mastered the art of marriage. And if they ever needed evidence that they're expert in the art of gardening, it came awhile back when they were chosen by the Cornell Cooperative Extension of Nassau County as the master gardeners of the year. They were the first couple to receive the award in the history of the Nassau program, which has graduated 400 master gardeners — all of whom took an intensive, 22-week horticulture course.

They were chosen by their peers in a write-in ballot. "Everyone was coming in to say we can't choose between Harry and Mary," says Donna Moramarco, the program's coordinator. "They're always together. You have to put them on the ballot as a couple." When their names were announced at a master gardeners' luncheon, only Harry and Mary were surprised. Mary cried. Harry was practically speechless.

"Gardeners are honest, salt-of-the-earth people," says Donna. "Harry and Mary are just that. Harry is a big teddy bear, Mary has a way of putting things in perspective."

Which is just what Mary did on a February day as she sat in the den of her East Williston home and talked about the plaques on display in a sunny bay window along with African violets and a venerable gardenia plant and the *Anthurium* that was a birthday present from a friend.

"This award meant so much, because it came from other master gardeners," Mary said. "We don't feel like we've mastered gardening. We're still learning. You're dead if you stop learning."

The Van Allens' story has two beginnings — one in love and the other in the garden.

Love took root in the summer of '39, when 15-year-old Harry commuted from Queens to Brooklyn for summer school. That first day he noticed a tall, dark-haired girl on the subway. He saw her again in his Latin class. And she saw him. Harry was taken by her long pageboy and her quick smile. Mary was smitten by his green eyes and blond hair. They were married five years later, just before Harry was shipped overseas during World War II.

It took five more years for them to get into the garden together. That didn't happen until the spring of 1949, after Harry had graduated from Lehigh University and they were living with Mary's mother in Queens Village. They planted sweet peas and *Gladiolus* in a horseshoe-shaped plot in a sunny backyard, and there was no turning back. "Once you start, you're hooked," Harry says, "and then you're a goner."

They were already far gone the next spring when they moved into a home of their own in a Mineola development without a tree or a speck of topsoil in sight. They put in some roses and irises. A peach tree and a peony. A vegetable garden. They were raising two sons — and 750 gladioli, many of them blue-ribbon winners. "If you're going to exhibit glads, you have to be out there planting in early March. We'd burn wood in a metal garbage can to keep warm," says Harry. And they put in a strawberry patch. "The day before we moved we picked 42 quarts of strawberries," says Mary.

Thirty-three years ago they bought their two-story colonial in East Williston with a huge wild cherry tree in the back. They gave up their beloved gladioli and learned about shade gardening — about the green and gold beauty of hostas and the wispy gracefulness

of astilbes. But eventually storms and sickness claimed the cherry tree. Sun returned to the garden — until a neighbor planted a row of maple seedlings along the rear of their property. "We'd water our garden and the trees would grow a foot," says Mary.

Harry and Mary built raised beds to protect their vegetables from maple roots. Daffodils and roses run alongside the house. A perennial border in the backyard was widened from 3 feet to 12. There are rhododendrons and azaleas and a deep purple clematis that climbs a trellis on the side porch. And a blue Atlas cedar Mary gave Harry one Christmas and a river birch that was a gift from their sons.

Still, they didn't become master gardeners until they retired in 1991 — Mary from her job as admissions director for a private school and Harry as an account executive on Wall Street. "I learned about the master gardener program and life hasn't been the same since," says Harry.

"I wonder how I ever had the time to go to work," says Mary.

Harry and Mary have more than paid back the 150 hours of volunteer time required of master-gardener graduates. They stopped counting at 600 hours, but they didn't stop answering phone calls on the extension service's horticulture hotline and training other volunteers to take questions from the confused, the uncertain and the occasionally angry public.

"To me," Mary says, "gardening is part of living. It's just one of those things you do — like breathing. I can't imagine life without a garden."

Neither can Harry. It's called love.

Mary and Harry Van Allen at home in East Williston. They were the first couple to win the "Master Gardener of the Year" award.

A Year in the Garden

Afew years ago, I bought a garden journal — a 10-year-diary in a green hardcover binding. It reflected both style and substance and I thought that I would enjoy writing in it, but the demands of daily life eroded my good intentions. For a longer time than I care to specify the journal sat — imposing but unopened — on a desk in my upstairs office.

Then in 1997, I began to write in the journal. It was a precious time in my own life because I was recovering from breast cancer surgery, and each day echoed the idea of life renewing itself. And so I thought the journal of that year would be a good way to end this book because it was a time when hope blossomed in my world and life went on just as gardens do. On Feb. 2, I made my first entry. "Groundhog Day," I began. "No shadow — easy to believe it will be a short winter." I noted that the Alberta spruce by the front door had spider mites and wondered if the mazus in the nearby path would flourish.

It was winter in my life and I craved spring. I wanted a sign of tomorrow and the garden came through. On Feb. 8, there was snow — "about one inch; the cotoneaster and ornamental grasses are dusted white." But by Feb. 19, the witch hazel was in bloom, and two days later yellow crocuses were peeking out around the Bradford pear by the mailbox.

My observations meandered from the practical to the poetic. The theme of rebirth, of recovery, was a constant — preserving hope like an evergreen in winter. "Windstorm today but my garden is slowly coming to life," my entry for March 6 noted. "Buds everywhere. We'll get there."

Spring came early and I hoarded each sign of the approaching season, each sprig of color. Crocuses and *Leucojum* in March, and our tomato seedlings sprouting indoors. "A perfect Easter Sunday. Forsythia starting to show. Remember to put pansies on Dad's grave." My stepfather died of lung cancer four years ago. His life was full of grays; he wasn't much for gardening, but I figured he'd like the bright faces of the purple and yellow flowers.

April 1 was the day I tried to run away from chemotherapy, and my husband pleaded with me in the snow to come back, and my oncologist, Paula Schwartz, read our faces later and talked to me with caring. It's all there in my journal. "No April Fool's joke — we had a snowstorm. Forsythia in the snow looks a little silly. By day's end everything melted away. Despite my pre-chemo scene, I took pleasure in the sight of bulbs coming up all over — add purple hyacinths to the list."

I read my journal and wonder how I ever got by without a garden. I wonder about all the springs of my life that flashed by without flowers. I filled the pages of April with pastel pansies that seemed almost Victorian and star magnolia buds that reminded me of pussy willows, and daffodils that came in waves. "We have a sea of daffodils," I wrote on April 10. "Salome in the daylily patch, Minnow with a charming tiny two-tone face and Sundial in pure yellow by the koi pond."

"One year ago we left for Holland," I remind myself several days later. "This year it looks like Holland on our front lawn — sort of. Purple and yellow hyacinths. Ice Follies and February Gold daffodils all over the place. Tulips ready to pop. Scilla, pansies, phlox, forsythia, Bradford pears — oh wow. Do we live here?"

The splendor continued through May, but not everything was successful. A *Fritillaria michailovskyi* in a terra-cotta pot did well, but otherwise my bulbs-in-containers experiment was a failure. The Irene of years ago would have been rent with self-doubt, but my entry shows I've become a gardener. Gardeners don't give up easily. "I'll try again next year with Sally's help." On the next page, I thank my bulb expert friend Sally Ferguson for introducing me to *Iris bucharica* and *Erythronium revolutum* Pagoda. It occurs to me how many friends I've made through gardening.

May faded into June. I gave the lady's mantle and bishop's weed rave notices and, on June 14, I was looking through rose-colored glasses. "Roses, roses everywhere. Bride's Dream and a pink climber on the fence in the old vegetable garden and a red, red rose by the front walk and minis galore by the driveway. I want more."

What I didn't want as the month passed was the evidence of aphids turning Bride's Dream into a nightmare. And I was disturbed by the sight of an old adversary laying siege to the white clematis nearby. "Do I see poison ivy at its feet?" Sherlock Holmes had Professor Moriarty; I have poison ivy. Another life lesson straight from the garden — it's elementary that you always have to beware of the bad guys.

Soon it was summer, and the talk of our house was the flower and vegetable garden on our front lawn. "Today was my last chemo," I wrote on July 8, "and we started the day with morning tea in the Garden of Health and Joy. All the planting is done. Harvey and I looked at the lilies and the sunflowers and the hydrangeas and the tomato plants and the lettuce and the Swiss chard and cried."

A month later, on Aug. 13, weary from radiation treatments, I found something to smile about in the new plantings. "Irene and Harvey, Irene and Harvey — how does your garden grow? With purple asters and hollyhocks and pink cosmos all in a row. Not to mention tiny white clematis and pink cleome peeking through the picket fence and four pairs of sunflowers standing tall. All of it thanks to water, full sun, good soil and lots of compost." No wonder I love to compost. Life enriching itself. Like it says on a T-shirt our friend Dan Koshansky gave my husband: "Compost Happens."

Seasons changed in my garden journal and flowers faded with the turning earth. As I read the lined pages now, I can almost feel the days growing short. "The colors of the dahlias and asters seem even more intense in the waning light of summer," I noted on Sept. 9. "Yellow snapdragons are the color of the sun itself — the pink ones are gorgeous, too." And the entry for Sept. 22 summed up the Earth change: "The crickets are singing by 5."

October was marked by the morning glory vines around the cedar obelisk in the center of the Garden of Health and Joy. "A glorious cobalt blue. The archway and the obelisk are totally embraced." The same month, we moved a white pine tree and canned tomatoes and gave away basil by the bagful. By the beginning of November, we were busy planning the future.

Nov. 5: "Rototilled yet another bed. This one surrounds the locust trees in the front yard and skirts the stone wall. Maybe the shade garden of my dreams will bloom here instead of in the back, as I'd always imagined. Where will we transplant the star magnolia? Can we afford all this?" The following week, sunflower heads sat on the patio wall for the birds to nibble, and the garden was saying goodbye but leaving something to remember. "The river birches have lost their leaves but the peeling bark is beautiful."

Winter entered mildly, as if ashamed to be the death of autumn. "By now the only green in the garden is the leftover parsley and Swiss chard," I wrote as November ended. "We put a wreath around the mailbox and roping and red bows on the garden gate. It's sort of funny to see Christmas greenery next to the pink Fairy roses still in bloom."

The roses faded and my husband tied errant canes to the garden arbors. December came and went and so did 1997. On the first day of the new year we walked around our house. "Silver stalks of Russian sage dance in the backyard. I'm glad I never cut the hydrangeas. The dried flowers form a beautiful bouquet next to the Hinoki cypress. We sit on a bench in the Garden of Health and Joy and look at the empty beds. Just brown earth. How beautiful."

The 10-year journal now sits open on my potting bench. Inside, there is a story. A year in my garden. A chapter in my life. There are chapters to come. I wish you all Gardens of Health and Joy.

About the Author

*I*rene Virag is a Pulitzer Prize winning reporter whose journalistic background adds depth and color to her garden writing. For the past four years, she has been Newsday's garden columnist — writing twice a week about the gardens of Long Island and the people who tend them. Her columns merge the practical and the poetic. To Irene, a breast cancer survivor, gardens are a metaphor for hope and rebirth. She has won four Quill & Trowel Awards presented by the Garden Writers Association of America. She is a master gardener and nurtures her flowers and vegetables on the North Shore of Long Island with her husband, author and Newsday senior editor Harvey Aronson.

Art:
Design Director: Bob Eisner, Art Director: Joseph E. Baron, Illustrations: Robert Newman

Graphics:
Linda McKenney, with assistance from Richard Cornett and Brigitte Zimmer.

Photography:
Cover Photos: Ken Spencer
Preface: 2, Nassau County Museum/Long Island Studies Institute. 3, Tony Jerome. 4, 5, 6, Bill Davis.
March: 11,12,14,15,16,17, Ken Spencer. 19, J. Conrad Williams. 21, J. Michael Dombroski.
April: 23,24,26, Ken Spencer. 28, Courtesy National Garden Bureau. 31, 32, Ken Spencer. 35, Tony Jerome
May: 37, Newsday File Photo. 39, Ken Spencer 45, Ken Spencer. 47, Tony Jerome. 48, 49, 50, Ken Spencer. 51, David L. Pokress. 52, Phillip Davies.
June: 57, Ken Spencer. 58, 59, 60, Don Jacobsen. 62, Butterfly, Newsday file photo. 62-63, Cliff DeBear. 63, J. Michael Dombroski. 64, Ken Spencer. 66, Irene Virag. 67, Ken Spencer. 68, Dick Kraus. 70, Family picture, Julia Gaines. 70-71, Courtesy of Tallman Family.
July: 73, Irene Virag. 74, 75, 76, 77, 78, 79, 80, 81, Ken Spencer. 82, Jim Peppler. 84, Ken Spencer. 86, J. Michael Dombroski. 88, Bill Davis.
August: 91, Ken Spencer. 92, Tony Jerome. 95, K. Wiles Stabile. 96, Don Jacobsen. 98, 99, Bill Davis. 100, Ken Spencer. 102, Al Raia. 103, George Argeropolos. 104, 105, John H. Cornell. 106, 107, Irene Virag.
September: 111, 112-113, 114, Ken Spencer. 115, 116-117, Tony Jerome. 118, Julia Gaines. 119, Thomas Ferrara. 120, K. Wiles Stabile. 121, 123, Ken Spencer. 125, 126, 127, Don Jacobsen. 128, 129, Ken Spencer.
October: 131, Ken Spencer. 132, Julia Gaines. 135, Tony Jerome. 137, Michael Ach. 138, 139, 140, Ken Spencer. 142, Dick Kraus. 144, 145, Ken Spencer.
November: 147, Ken Spencer. 148, Acorns, Tony Jerome. 148, Jim Peppler. 150, 151, Ken Spencer. 152, 153, Tony Jerome 154-155, 155, Sune Woods.
December: 159, 160, 161, 162, 164, 165, Ken Spencer. 166, 167, Audrey C. Tiernan.
January: 169, Ken Spencer. 170-171, Tony Jerome. 173, Baltimore Sun photo. 174, 175, 176, Ken Spencer. 178, 179, Irene Virag.
February: 181, Jim Peppler. 182, Ken Spencer. 183, Jim Peppler. 184, Newsday file photo. 186, Jim Peppler. 188, 191, Ken Spencer.
Epilogue: 193, J. Michael Dombroski.

Prepress: Production:
Newsday Color Services   Julian Stein

Index

Index

Index